A Spring without Bees

A Spring without Bees

How Colony Collapse Disorder Has Endangered
Our Food Supply

MICHAEL SCHACKER

Foreword by Bill McKibben

THE LYONS PRESS
Guilford, Connecticut
An imprint of The Globe Pequot Press

To buy books in quantity for corporate use
or incentives, call **(800) 962–0973**
or e-mail **premiums@GlobePequot.com.**

The Lyons Press is an imprint of The Globe Pequot Press.

Text designed by Sheryl Kober

Library of Congress Cataloging-in-Publication Data is available on file.

ISBN 978-1-59921-432-0

Printed in the United States of America

10 9 8 7 6 5 4 3 2 1

TABLE OF CONTENTS

FOREWORD

Late February, 2008—an item from today's paper:

NEW YORK (CNNMoney.com)—Häagen-Dazs is warning
that a creature as small as a honey bee could become a big
problem for the premium ice cream maker's business.

At issue are the disappearing bee colonies in the United
States, a situation that continues to mystify scientists and
frighten foodmakers.

That's because, according to Häagen-Dazs, one-third of
the U.S. food supply—including a variety of fruits, vegeta-
bles and even nuts—depends on pollination from bees.

Häagen-Dazs, which is owned by General Mills, said
bees are actually responsible for 40% of its 60 flavors—
such as strawberry, toasted pecan, and banana split.

No toasted pecan? That's an emergency.

I've been paying attention to bees for years, in part because a neighbor, Kirk Webster, is one of the country's premier apiarists—a regular contributor to the bee journals, and a low-key guru of what you might call holistic beekeeping. I love watching him work—roaming the hillside meadows of our corner of Vermont with his hives—and I love listening to him talk, trying to figure out the various ways we might keep these colonies alive. I stay my distance—I'm allergic to bee stings—but it fascinates me.

Because, if you think about it, and as this powerful book makes clear, the very act of keeping a colony is a pretty amazing feat. It's not like having a pet—a bee hive is a society, which we know from our own experience is infinitely more complex than an individual. More robust in certain ways, but more delicate too. These are incredibly balanced, lovely, evolved little nations.

And so it's no real surprise that the simplistic and crude ways we've taken to using chemicals are now helping do them in. Think about the humming, unfolding, minutely timed operation of a bee colony, and then compare it with the blunt stupidity of some new agrochemical industry compound designed, well, to kill everything with six legs. Are you really surprised that they end up killing more than we want them to?

The reason for all those pesticides, of course, is that we've replaced human labor on the farm with fossil fuel and chemicals—allowed our agriculture to become huge, industrial, monocultural. It's given us cheap food—and also impoverished rural communities, poisoned water, lots of extra carbon in the atmosphere and lots of extra inches around our middles. And maybe no more bees.

And so the way out, as Michael Schacker suggests, is to stop and think again, especially about our agriculture. Not just organic farming, but a type of organic that restores the diverse patchwork of land use where bees thrive. And not just agriculture, either. Everyone can play a part in bringing the bees back. Homeowners could think more carefully about the products they are using on their lawns. Children could plant linden trees on Arbor Day, as well as flowers for "bee gardens." Professional beekeepers themselves could move away from chemical use within the hive, while encouraging the farmers they serve into going organic.

These kinds of changes are dismissed by some as impossible—they simply can't imagine an agriculture or a suburban lifestyle strikingly different from the one we currently know. But as Schacker makes clear, it is possible to imagine. And easier, in fact, than imagining how on earth we'd survive without bees. Without toasted pecan.

-Bill McKibben
February 2008

ACKNOWLEDGMENTS

Acknowledgment, first of all, must go to Rachel Carson, who predicted the vanishing of the bees back in 1962, and who began the modern environmental movement with *Silent Spring*. *Silent Spring* was my main inspiration, and I could always guide myself by asking "What would Rachel do?" Much thanks to David Hackenberg, of Hackenberg Apiaries, for his taking the lead on colony collapse disorder and providing information to the media and for this book. He is a tireless advocate for the beekeepers. Great thanks also to Chris Charles, Dale Bauer, and the seven other apiary plaintiffs for their information, their inspiration, and for their standing up for the bees against a mighty multinational corporation.

Thanks to Dr. Marc Colin of the University of Montpellier for all his work in France, plus some guidance to me for this book. Dr. James Amrine, President of the Acarology Society of America and a Medical Entomologist at West Virginia University, receives special thanks. Dr. Amrine read and reviewed the manuscript, and gave the best answer yet to one of my main questions about colony collapse disorder: Why does CCD occur in France in July, but mainly occurs over the winter in America? Dr. Amrine was helpful on many other points, too numerous to mention. Many thanks, too, to beekeeper Robert Noel of Honey-B-Healthy, for his information and particularly for his and Dr. Amrine's promising work with bees and essential oils. Although she is no longer with us, special thanks, too, to Robert's sister, Marlene Noel, who first thought of using wintergreen oil to control the varroa mite. Thanks also to David Vander Dussen of NOD Apiary Products for all his information and his good work on formic acid and mite control. Acknowledgments must also go to Henri Clement and the French beekeepers for their incredible work in saving the bees, for their information on CCD, and for their confirmation that the bees *did* return to SW France after 2005.

A big thank you is also due to attorney Aaron Colangelo and entomologist-attorney Gabriela Chavarria of the Natural Resources Defense Council in Washington, D.C., for guiding me through the intricacies of court actions against the EPA. Thanks also to Timothy LaSalle, CEO of The Rodale Institute, and the researchers there who are supporting my work, and who stand ready to help the USDA and the farmers of the world convert to organic methods, so we may someday create a sustainable future.

A big thank you is also due to literary agent Jacqueline Hackett of Literary Works in Atlanta, Georgia, for understanding the great need for this book and taking it on. Thanks to my editor, Holly Rubino, at The Lyons Press for her faith in a first-time author and thanks to everyone there who got this book out so quickly. And special, special thanks to Barbara Dean Schacker and Melissa Schacker, for putting up with me and helping out on so many physical and metaphysical levels in the writing of this book and helping with Plan Bee.

-Michael Schacker
March, 2008

One

To Bee or Not to Bee

I will arise and go now, and go to Innisfree,
And a small cabin build there, of clay and wattles made:
Nine bean-rows will I have there, a hive for the honeybee,
And live alone in the bee-loud glade.
—William Butler Yeats, "The Lake Isle of Innisfree"

Imagine you are a kindly beekeeper. For decades, you have lived with your bees, taking care of them and enjoying the honey sales and pollination fees, while doing something that you love. Once in a while you got stung, and you never made a lot of money, but you would not give up your beloved craft for anything in the world. To you, beekeeping is a way of life.

Then a horrible thing happens. A new and unknown disease strikes your hives. One week you go down to check on the bees, and find that they have all flown away! In some of your honey bee colonies, not a single bee remains, while in others just a queen and some immature brood are left. It's a terrible shock—and a great mystery. Your bees are gone—and they aren't coming back. Then you find out bees are dying all over the world. You know that the growers of ninety common food crops around the world are dependent on honey bees and cannot produce high yields without them. If all the bees die, many agricultural crops would go with them, natural ecosystems could fail—the world would take another huge economic and environmental hit, just when it needs it least.

No one, not the other beekeepers, not the scientists, not the most accomplished experts in the world, seem able to solve this great puzzle. It is not even known if the cause is natural or man-made. Colony collapse disorder, or CCD, is the greatest mystery of the day. There appears to be no hope.

The loss of the bees around the world raises all sorts of unsettling questions. Are the honey bees trying to tell us something? Are they the canary in the coal mine, warning us of a hidden danger to the planet and all of humanity? On a deeper level, are the bees telling us we are unaware of a deep systemic problem threatening our own species, are we missing the big picture here? Could our own human colony come undone, through some kind of "Civilization Collapse Disorder"?

Most important of all, is there a way to avoid this "Beepocalypse"? Can we learn what the cause is in time to implement a practical solution?

CAUGHT IN AMBER
100 MILLION YEARS AGO

All good mystery stories start at the beginning. In the case of the bees, the story began some 100 million years ago, in Southeast Asia, as we now know from a rare 2006 find made in a northern Myanmar amber mine. It was the fossil of an extinct bee, *Melittosphex burmensis*, so well preserved it still had pollen stuck to the hairs on its back legs.[1]

We have these first bees to thank for helping to create the world we enjoy today—for flowering plants co-evolved with the first pollinating bees, one of evolution's most significant planetary transformations. The first plants began their evolution 400 million years ago, reproducing by spore or by fertilized seed. Beetles helped the primitive fertilization process along, as their feeding delivered pollen, equivalent to sperm, to the female stigma of the plant, starting seed reproduction.

With the evolution of flowers about 130 million years ago, something incredible happened. The seductive secretion of sugary nectar in the middle of brightly colored and aromatic petals led a species of wasp to evolve into a tiny bee, only three millimeters long. This was *Melittosphex burmensis,* our little friend from the amber mine, destined to change the world. In effect, over the next 100 million years bees would reshape the biosphere, allowing flowering plants to dominate the planet by taking the uncertainty out of pollination and thus reproduction. Today there are 250,000 species of flowering plants and trees, providing most of the crops and ornamentals we depend on. Of those plants, 130,000 rely on insects, mostly 20,000 species of bees, to ensure reproduction. Bees are thus essential to biodiversity, a main indicator of the health of an ecosystem.

In short, the bee is not only the prime insect responsible for the creation of the world today, it is critical to maintaining the fragile balance of half the flowering plant ecosystem, as well as one-third of all agricultural plants. Although we may live today in a world that has "insectophobia," the obsession to remove all insects from our daily life, without the honey bee it is likely that advanced agriculture, and thus civilization, would have never developed.

MAPPING THE HONEY BEE

We know far more about bees today, thanks to the recently completed Honey Bee Genome Sequencing Project, a collaboration of scientists around the world, funded by the National Human

Genome Research Institute, the National Institutes of Health, and the United States Department of Agriculture (USDA). According to this new genetic map, the main honey bee species, *Apis mellifera* L., evolved some 60 million years ago. Most know the European honey bee as a small, golden, furry pollinator, and as the hardest-working animal on the planet. It is little wonder that honey bees are such successful agents of planetary change—they are seemingly designed by evolution to reshape the Earth. In just one day, a honey bee will harvest several thousand flowers, making twelve or more trips, gathering pollen from just a single species each time. Bee pollination is a system made to reproduce flowers on a massive scale.

A hive can gather pollen and nectar from up to 500 million flowers in a year, getting about seven million flight miles per gallon—of honey, that is. For the hive to produce one surplus pound of the sweet energy source, it takes about eight pounds of honey for foraging, brood rearing, and winter food. Any extra honey, of course, can be taken by beekeepers for income. Typically, bees will only fly about two to two-and-a-half miles from their hive, giving them over 12,000 acres to find nectar. If a source is farther away, however, the honey bee will sometimes fly up to ten miles at a speed of twelve to fifteen miles per hour. All of this energy spent by the worker bees, which are all female, is supported by an incredibly complex social structure. Besides the queen bee, which can lay 2,000 eggs per day and store male sperm for years, layers of different types of bees keep the colony going.

In particular, there are the caretaking or nurse bees, which intensively groom and decontaminate the returning workers, and generally care for the health of the hive. These caretaking bees are there to protect all members of the colony, removing dirt, debris, and mites, fighting pathogens, and helping to care for the young. Without them, the hive cannot survive. Besides the all-important nurse bees, there are the guard bees, the heating and cooling teams, the cleaning squads, comb-builders and honey-processors, and of course the foraging worker bees. All these bees are sisters, daughters of the same mother queen bee.

Then there are the males, the drones. They are the big, hairy, clumsy, stingless ones. A male drone just eats, does nothing its entire life—then it mates with the queen, and immediately dies when its genitals snap off. Not quite a glamorous life for male bees, you might say—in contrast to the "Pollen Jocks" portrayed in Jerry Seinfeld's *Bee Movie*.[2]

All these facts we have long known from observation. With the recent breaking of the honey bee genetic code, however, we can now finally see what a unique creature *Apis mellifera* truly is. Following the fruit fly and the mosquito, researchers in 2006 completed the genome map of *Apis*. The results are revealing, and key to understanding humanity's best friend among the insects. They include the following:

- Honey bees have a high number of genes related to learning, more than fruit flies or mosquitoes. Bees can not only learn, they have been found to be able to know what is the "same" or "different"—and they communicate in many, many ways, from sounds and motions to pheromones and more.

- They also have a very high number of olfactory genetic families, meaning bees have incredible powers of smell, explaining their ability to find far-off nectar. They actually navigate partly by smell.

- Fewer gene families are related to immunity, giving bees a lowered resistance to new pathogens. The grooming behavior of the nurse bees apparently makes up for this genetic deficiency; a big job as colonies of up to 60,000 bees live so closely together and could easily infect each other.

- The honey bee has a lower number of genes governing detoxification, making them susceptible to pesticides and other toxins. Here again the nurse bees take up the genetic slack, preventing poisons from entering the hive. Another behavior aiding in this effort is that a scout bee focuses on a single nectar and pollen source on each foraging trip, in effect acting as a food-taster for the colony. Bees that appear seriously ill are quickly ejected from the hive. When poisoned by plants or pesticides, a worker will do an alarm dance, zigzagging over the comb and buzzing loudly. This alerts the hive and the nurse bees that the nectar source of the day is poisoned.

The high number of learning genes helps to explain another behavior: the honey bee's legendary "waggle dance," the way a returning worker will excitedly tell her sister foragers where the best flowers are. Deciphered in 1967 by Karl von Frisch, in *The Dance Language and Orientation of Bees*, the complexity of this behavior is astonishing.[3] Like a person giving directions both verbally and with their hands, in order to create a miniature copy of the trip, one bee can tell all the others where a flower is and exactly how to get there and back. The scout bee will "waggle" to the left and to the right, climbing up the side of the hive to show the guiding angle of the sun and how far away the flowers are. Through a highly complex series of figure-eights, sounds, move-ments, aromas, tastes, and thirty-one different pheromones, the waggle dance lays out the exact way to the nectar. Like Map-Quest, return directions are even provided. As the time of day changes, however, and the position of the sun in the sky shifts, the flight instructions become obsolete and no longer lead back to the hive. So if a foraging bee tarries too long, she may not be able to find her way home. To add to the complexity of it all, as the seasons progress, the scouts adjust their waggle dance for the changing solar angle.

Connected to their ability to navigate and locate nectar sources is the honey bee's incredible ability to smell, and to remember smells. This is due to the number of olfactory receptor genes, far more than either fruit flies or mosquitoes. There are also a lower number of taste genes. Apparently evolution selected development of the additional olfactory genes over taste receptors. Much of the worker bee's brain is thus devoted to remembering where smells are in the region around the hive.

While honey bees have these strengths, the cracking of the genetic code reveals they also have some striking weaknesses. With fewer gene families devoted to immunity, the honey bee would theoretically have little resistance to new pathogens, something that beekeepers have reported over the decades. Other species of bees may not have this problem. In fact, the presence and behavior of the nurse bees themselves likely channeled genetic development away from immunity, where it was not needed, and toward learning, navigation, and enhancing the sense of smell. The 2006 USDA-ARS Bee Research Lab reports in "Immune pathways and defense mechanisms in honey bees":[4]

When compared to the sequenced Drosophila *(fruit fly) and* Anopheles *(mosquito) genomes, honey bees possess roughly one-third as many genes in 17 gene families implicated in insect immunity. We suggest that an implied reduction in immune flexibility in bees reflects either the strength of social barriers to disease, or a tendency for bees to be attacked by a limited set of highly coevolved pathogens.*

What this means is that *Apis* has an inherent weakness against disease; they are not able to easily fight off new viruses and pathogens. Other than the nurse bees and the ejection of sick workers from the hive, there is little defense against them. Once some take ill, the closely packed hive is soon infected. A weak immune system is something that has long been known to beekeepers and researchers.

Another major weakness revealed by the Genome Project is the poor ability of the honey bee to detoxify itself through the secretion of cleansing enzymes. Once again, the effectiveness of the nurse bees in grooming returning workers physically prevents poison from contaminating and killing the hive. The alarm dance also protects the hive from poisons. The number of detoxification gene families found in the fruit fly and mosquito were therefore simply not needed, and bee evolution focused on other challenges. This finding would suggest that honey bees are highly susceptible to man-made pesticides and other toxins. Beekeepers and researchers know this as well from their work in the field. The Research School of Biological Sciences, Australian National University, Canberra, Australia, deciphered this part of the bee genome map, discovering that honey bees have ten times fewer protein coding genes linked to insecticide resistance than either the mosquito or the fruit fly.[5]

Since recently invented insecticides have no precedence in the long history of evolution, there would be even less defense against them. Bee colonies naturally try to cope as best they can with toxins. In the worst cases of poisoning, of course, this genetic weakness is fatal and the hive dies.

The long, slow development of evolutionary time cannot match the speed and killing power of human invention in the field of chemistry, something noted forty-five years ago by Rachel Carson in *Silent Spring*. Evolution is initially at a disadvantage—

especially in the case of the genetically challenged honey bee. Although the destructive, targeted insects often adapt and gain resistance to new chemicals, the nontarget beneficial insects like the honey bee are very vulnerable.

Man's Second-Best Friend: The Honey bee in History

Up until now, humanity and the honey bee have enjoyed a long history together. Neolithic tribes loved the sweet honeycombs and honey they would happen upon, while Bronze Age peoples used fermented honey to create mead, probably the first alcoholic drink. According to Eva Crane in *The World History of Beekeeping and Honey Hunting*, honey gathering and beekeeping may have started as far back as 20,000 BCE. We know that *Apis mellifera* helped make civilization itself possible by pollinating the early agriculture of Neolithic villages and then ancient towns and cities. Beeswax has often been a treasured, even sacred item, in history, sometimes being used as a medium of exchange or collected in taxes. Medicine has made great use of honey and beeswax throughout the ages, particularly for treating burns and wounds and as an antibacterial agent. Settlers first brought the European bee to North America in the 1620s, where the insects found the temperate climate much to their liking, joining the 5,000 species of pollinators already inhabiting the continent. Colonists used the European bees rather than the natives, because they naturally formed large hives around a queen and were thus easy to transport and concentrate upon one field or orchard. But the honey bee in America did more than just pollinate crops. During the American Revolution, a young Quaker girl, Charity Crabtree, was walking down a country road, carrying her skep, or pouch, of honey bees. In her day, women of the Enlightenment were in charge of many things agricultural, including beekeeping. A wounded and dying Continental soldier suddenly came riding up, pleading with her to take his horse and warn General Washington: by Monday, the British would be upon him in a surprise attack. At that early point in the war, such an assault would have surely meant the end of the fledgling nation.

As the messenger lay dying, Charity could hear the rumble of the onrushing British Guard. She mounted his horse and rode off but was soon being pursued closely. The young Quaker, who was also a pacifist, had but one chance and she took it. Opening the skep of bees, she flung it on the ground. The stinging swarm immediately stopped the British horses in their tracks. Miss Crabtree arrived to warn the general in time—who credited her with saving the nation.[6] Alluding to the geese whose warning once saved Rome from the Gauls, George Washington is supposed to have declared: "It was the cackling geese that saved Rome, but it is the bees that saved America!"

So America, you see, owes the honey bee a return favor.

Since the European honey bee is not native to the New World, wild plants of the Americas, like ragworts and goldenrods, do not need it to reproduce, but they certainly do benefit from the improved pollination. For many agricultural crops, however, such as almonds and blueberries, the *Apis* honey bee is essential. Although other bees are more efficient in their ability to gather pollen, *Apis* is unique for being able to concentrate tens of thousands of individuals into portable small hive boxes, at virtually any time in the growing season. They can then be sealed up and trucked directly to the field needing pollination. When released, the colony is able to fly to over a million flowers in a single day. It takes two weeks, for example, for two hives to fully pollinate one acre of Maine cranberries.

Starting at the beginning of the twentieth century, beekeepers began moving their honey bees south for the winter and then around the country to service various crops for pollination fees. Today, migratory beekeeping and commercial pollination are crucial to a full third of all U.S. crops, estimated in 2000 to be worth more than $15 billion.[7] Almonds, blueberries, apples, cranberries, peaches, tomatoes, pumpkins, and many other crops all rely on *Apis* colonies. In fact, it is the honey bee that is primarily responsible for the high yields these plants and trees produce. California almond orchards use commercial pollinators the most, and in 2006 sold $1.5 billion worth of nuts.

THE VANISHING OF THE BEES

For commercial pollination, native bees in North America cannot match the European honey bee, which can be concentrated in great numbers to cover a specific field. Yet native bees are essential to pollinating 130,000 types of flowering plants, species that are critical to regional ecosystems. Unfortunately, in recent years native bees have been hit hard by mites and the unintended consequences of pesticides, with many species devastated. Other factors might have led to the native bees falling prey to the mites, but little research money ever goes to these native pollinators. This is a significant strategic error, as whole ecosystems are dependent on plants needing bees, bats, hummingbirds, and butterflies to reproduce and flourish.

One of the most important pollinators besides the honey bee is the native alkali bee, which is the best species for getting high yields of alfalfa. Without bountiful crops of alfalfa, dairy and beef prices would soar. Alfalfa flowers, however, keep their sexual parts hidden, under tension like a spring. Bees must trip the spring to get at the pollen, and in so doing, they are hit on the head—something honey bees are not particularly fond of. The alkali bees, which nest in the alkaline soils of the western U.S., however, don't mind getting hit in the noggin and will happily pollinate a field of alfalfa. Farmers learned in the 1950s how to expand populations by transplanting soil from alkali bee nests into wooden flats. U.S. alfalfa production soared thereafter, allowing the production of inexpensive dairy and beef.

Then something went terribly wrong in the 1970s. The lygus bug, a sap-sucking feeder, began to attack alfalfa crops, and farmers began using various insecticides to combat them. Although it is not certain, this might have been the start of the problem. Plus pesticides began to be used far more widely in general. Whatever the cause, alkali bee populations crashed and the critical alfalfa crop was threatened.[8] Fortunately, the Canadian leafcutter bee doesn't mind getting repeatedly smacked on the head either, so it was imported to replace the alkalis. Canada, unfortunately, now has "chalkbrood" disease among its leafcutters, a fungus that infects the larva, so these bees are threatened too. Dairy and beef price rises are thus a real possibility in the U.S. if alfalfa yields shrink.

In the 1990s, a bumblebee species, *Bombus occidentalis,* was accidentally made extinct when experimenting breeders mixed species in Europe and shipped queens back to America. The queens carried with them an exotic disease that *Bombus occidentalis* had no immunity for. This bumblebee produced an intense vibration, like a tuning fork being struck, pollen gathered from other flowers literally exploded off *Bombus*, making it able to efficiently pollinate certain plants that the honey bee cannot, such as the tomato. Tomato growers had thus come to depend on *Bombus occidentalis* to "buzz pollinate" their greenhouse plants, but now are forced to resort to less efficient species.

There has also been a dramatic decline in the number of European honey bee hives being kept in the U.S., plunging from six million colonies in 1944 to three million in 1980 (USDA). The reasons for losing half of the hives in those thirty-five years include older beekeepers retiring, urbanization, pesticide poisonings, and different kinds of mites and diseases. Then, in 1987, the worst mite of them all, *Varroa destructor,* appeared in Wisconsin honey bee colonies. *Varroa destructor* soon decimated commercial as well as wild honey bees alike. The varroa mite attaches itself to the abdomen of the bee with suckers on its feet and then feeds with its sharp fangs in a bite that transmits various diseases like acute bee paralysis, sacbrood, and deformed-wing viruses. Depending on conditions and hive health, the colony dies in anywhere from a few months to a few years. Remember that *Apis,* the honey bee, has a known weakness in the number of gene families controlling immunity. The viruses transmitted by the new mites thus met little natural defense and increased in strength when delivered by the mite's bite.

The beekeepers fought back with miticides, which were initially successful, while organic beekeepers used physical innovations like mite screens to battle *Varroa destructor.* Without human assistance, however, were the native bees, as well as the *Apis* honey bees (the Euros) which had escaped domestication over the centuries and were living in the wild. They were now on their own against *Varroa destructor.* As the genome research on immunity would predict, by 1994, 98% of the wild honey bee population was wiped out by the mites and all the viruses and other pathogens they carry.[9] The number of kept hives meanwhile continued to gradually decline. Then the mites began to grow resistant to the miticides and doses had to be raised. By 2006, there were only 2.4 million honey bee colonies left in the U.S., and it was getting harder and harder to be a beekeeper.

The honey bee was thus already on the ropes when the knockout punch came.

Two

Colony Collapse Disorder

*Then a strange blight crept over the area and everything changed.
. . . It was a spring without voices. On the mornings that had once
throbbed with the dawn chorus of robins, catbirds, doves, jays,
wrens, and scores of other bird voices, there was now no sound;
only silence lay over the fields and woods and marsh. . . . The
apple trees bloomed but no bees droned among the blossoms,
so there was no pollination and there would be no fruit. . . . No
witchcraft, no enemy action had silenced the rebirth of new life in
this stricken world. The people had done it themselves. . . .*
—Rachel Carson,
Silent Spring

THE HEADLINES READ LIKE THE BEGINNING OF A STEPHEN
KING NOVEL: "Where Have All the Bees Gone?" *(New Scientist)*,
"Honey bees Vanish, Leaving Keepers in Peril" *(The New York
Times)*, "Collapsing Bee Colonies Puzzle Beekeepers, Scientists"
(The Patriot Ledger), "Beekeepers: Half of Hives Lost" *(Cape May
County Herald)*, "Mysterious Disappearance of U.S. Bees Creat-
ing a Buzz" *(Agence France Presse)*, and "As Bees Vanish, Crops
Endangered" *(The Telegraph)*. It all sounded very much like what
Rachel Carson had predicted in 1962.

The new crisis hit with barely any warning. In the fall of 2004, and again in the fall of 2005, what were then called bee "die-offs" were reported in the Midwest and noted in Florida as well. This was merely the harbinger of what was to come. In November 2006, colony collapse disorder (or CCD) was first officially reported in the U.S—just south of Tampa, Florida. The beekeeper was David Hackenberg, a former president of the American Beekeeping Federation. In a March 2007 letter to growers, Hackenberg writes: "In October I brought several loads of bees to Florida from Pennsylvania and New York and they appeared to be strong healthy hives when I unloaded them, but by mid-November several of my larger yards had less than 10% of the hives still alive."[1]

Hackenberg was reporting something new, a disease he had never seen before. With mites and viruses, the end of the hive is slow and painful, and with pesticide poisoning, the dead bee bodies would pile up on the ground directly under the entrance to the hive. Hackenberg's bees had simply flown off and never returned, leaving the queen, some immature workers, and a doomed brood of larvae and pupae. The colony had collapsed.

It was soon called colony collapse disorder, or CCD. The symptoms of CCD were very odd. In the collapsed colonies, the beekeepers found:

- No adult bees in the hives and surprisingly few or no dead bodies in the hive or on the ground in front of the entrance.

- There was still unhatched brood in the affected hives.

- Honey and pollen were left by the hive, which is very unusual, and then that honey was not stolen by other bees.

- Weeks would pass before predators like wax moths and hive beetles moved in to eat the abandoned honey and pollen, indicating they could sense something wrong.

In cases where the hive was in the process of collapse, keepers discovered:

- Not enough worker bees to sustain the brood.

- The worker bees were primarily young adult bees and not good foragers.

- The queen had not yet flown off and was still in the hive.

- The remaining hive members would not feed, even when artificial syrup and protein supplement was provided.

This set of symptoms was very unusual, especially the symptom of pests like the hive beetle and wax moth waiting weeks before moving into the dead hive. Nor did other bees steal the honey and bee pollen as they normally would from a dead colony. Something was repelling the bees and the pests, something they could sense. Moreover, while the hive was collapsing, the remaining cluster of bees would not feed on their usual syrup and protein. And the female worker bees just flew off, abandoning their hive, a behavior contrary to every ingrained instinct to build and defend the colony for the queen. All of these behaviors were unique to CCD and very puzzling to the professionals.

The beekeeper is helpless when CCD strikes. Hackenberg Apiaries ended up losing over 2,000 out of 2,950 hives. It was devastating. Hackenberg said he had to spend more than $450,000 in order to start rebuilding his lost colonies. With no idea of the cause, he took the dead bees to Penn State, to the team that became the "CCD Working Group." Susan Milius reported in the July 2007 issue of *Science News:*[2]

> *To start tracking down the cause of Hackenberg's troubles, state apiarist Dennis van Engelsdorp, based at Penn State, and his colleagues undertook detailed case studies of affected beehives.*
>
> *In mid-December of last year, van Engelsdorp's team released its first results. From interviews with seven beekeepers in four states, the researchers learned of substantial losses. One beekeeper expected to lose all but 9 of his 1,200 colonies. A hive can empty and collapse in as little as a week, the beekeepers said.*

Reports from other states started pouring in, often from the biggest commercial pollinators. By the time the American beekeepers met in mid-January 2007 at their annual convention in Austin, CCD had been reported in twenty-two states. Some apiaries lost up to 95% of their hives to CCD. Hackenberg solemnly wrote in his March 2007 letter to growers:

> *I have had reports of disaster in California where over one million hives are now pollinating the almonds. Beehives that were full of what appeared to be healthy bees in early January are now empty boxes with a few sick and dying bees left in them. A Texas beekeeper with a 10,000 hive outfit has less then 1,000 hives left. A package bee and a queen bee producer in Georgia that supplies beekeepers in the north in the spring with replacements, cancelled all his orders this past Monday. There is speculation that maybe 150,000 or more hives may have already died nationwide,*

but this is only a guess since numbers are impossible to estimate while hives are still collapsing.

The Apiary Inspectors of America now estimate that about 30% of all hives in the country were lost due to die-off.[3] Since 17% to 20% is normal, the rest of the die-off is because of colony collapse disorder. Hackenberg desperately asks the growers in his letter:

Beekeepers that have been most affected so far have been close to corn, cotton, soybeans, canola, sunflowers, apples, vine crops and pumpkins. So what is it about these crops that are killing the bees?? In the last three years, what changed about the growing practices that would have this effect?

Poland, Greece, Italy, Portugal, Spain, and then also Switzerland, Germany, and Croatia also soon reported CCD. The theories were many as to the cause. Everything from environmental stress to pathogens, mites, pesticides, genetically modified crops, and even cell phone radiation were suggested as the reason. There is also the "Bee Rapture" theory, in which a radio talk show listener called in to say that the bees, summoned by God, were flying off to Heaven.[4]

Whatever the cause, if colony collapse disorder is not solved soon, 100 million years of evolution perfecting the honey bee and other pollinators could be irrevocably lost. Colony collapses were actually reported intermittently as early as 1896, and in the past several decades the syndrome has been given many different names, including "disappearing disease," "spring dwindle," "May disease," "autumn collapse," and "fall dwindle disease." Yet all these instances were very intermittent and isolated compared to the modern disaster, where some keepers nationwide reported losses of over 80% of their hives. Without a doubt, the CCD of 2006–07 was the worst sudden bee die-off in history.

However, as this book goes to press, by January 2008, a *second wave* of CCD struck the U.S. and Canada. Only this time the impact appears to be heavier than before, soaring to 36% of all U.S. hives dead, from 30% in 2007.[5] Dr. Jeff Pettis of the USDA told Hackenberg that CCD is now not a crisis, but a catastrophe. Some large commercial beekeepers, on the brink of financial ruin before, now could be headed for bankruptcy. At the beekeeper conference in mid-January 2008, Dave Hackenberg reports keepers coming up to him in tears. Banks were beginning to cut off their credit.

Fortunately, by hiring every available hive for the almond orchards, and because of the best weather in memory, a good yield is expected. Despite the number of hives dying in 2008, the migratory pollinators are saying there should now be enough bees for the rest of the crops. The start of the "Beepocalypse" was just avoided by a whisker.

WHICH STATES HAVE CCD AND WHICH ONES DON'T

As of March 2008, CCD was officially reported in thirty-five states.[6] Reports at first did not include Arizona, but it turns out that the state had no data-collection apparatus at all—so there was no office to report bee problems to. Arizona does indeed have CCD. In 2007, Arp's Mountain Top Honey Company in Arizona saw their production slashed in half. Meanwhile, Delmar McCann, a beekeeper in Laveen, Arizona, also reported CCD.[7] Arizona thus makes thirty-six states. See Appendix 5 for a chart showing the states compiled from phoning each state or from the Apiary Inspectors of America report.

As far as the CCD-free regions go, there do appear to be some explanations. Some southern areas of the U.S. are not reporting CCD. This might correlate with the spread of the Africanized bee, the so-called "killer bee," into honey bee populations in those places. African honey bees so far seem to be immune to colony collapse disorder, at least according to anecdotal reports in small-town newspapers.

States that have inexplicably reported no CCD include Vermont, Maine, West Virginia, Delaware, Rhode Island, and Maryland. It should be noted that all the major beekeeping states do have CCD, including California (20% of all bees), Florida (10%), the Dakotas (7%), Texas (5%), Montana (5%), and then Minnesota, Idaho, Michigan, Washington, Wisconsin, Oregon, Pennsylvania, and New York making up another 20%. Why do these states have it, and others like Nebraska and Kansas, surrounded by CCD states, do not? The CCD-free states, however, present a true mystery, although some appear to be areas where there is less large-scale agriculture, such as New Mexico and Nevada. As for Vermont and West Virginia, they too have less agriculture than most places.

KILLER BEES AND ORGANIC BEES NOT AFFECTED?

The African honey bee is known to be hardier in hotter climes. In fact, that is why it was originally imported from Africa to South America, to breed with Euro honey bees and make them more resistant to disease and the lack of seasonal cooling in the tropics. The African strain in the southern U.S. might be immune to whatever is causing CCD among the Euro honey bees. For instance, according to small-town newspapers, El Paso, Texas is one area with no reported CCD, as are the bees that feed on tupelo trees in Wewahitchka, Florida.[8] Some beekeepers have been able to keep the African invaders out of their hives, yet it is becoming increasingly difficult to prevent colonies from mixing. Others have given up and now raise the Africans.

Also unaffected by CCD seem to be the *Apis* Euros kept by organic beekeepers. Organic keepers usually have their bees gather wildflower nectar, placing their hives far from civilization and possible chemical use. It is the only way to keep the honey organic, as bees will fly only a few to several miles to collect nectar. In June 2007, the *Sierra Vista Herald* in Arizona reported that Dee Lusby, who has 900 organic colonies, is not having any problems at all. She keeps her bees far from all chemicals outside the hive, and inside as well. "Why? Because healthy, happy bees don't need any additives," she said. "You want a natural, sustainable beekeeping system. To me, the disappearing disease is a last stress factor that causes our bee colonies in this country and other places in the world to collapse due to increased dependency on many artificial management ways today that simply don't work." Lusby made a smaller comb size, creating a smaller, more natural-sized bee—which seems to be far less susceptible to the mites.

No significant CCD being reported among the organic beekeepers is thus another possible clue to the problem. Although the Organic Consumers Association reports that 1,000 organic keepers have no CCD, it would not be surprising to see some, but these organic operations claim to have none at all. If so, what is keeping the organic bees safe from harm?

Not Enough Honey bees by 2010

The large migratory beekeeping operations have been hit the hardest by CCD, especially in California. One theory is that trucking the bees all over the country puts so much environmental stress on them that their immune system and general health are compromised and they fall prey to CCD. The almond orchards in California have been expanding dramatically—so quickly that between CCD and the rise in almond acres, by 2010 there may not be enough bees to pollinate the almond crop alone. Of course, the bees that are moved seasonally can be focused on single crops and then go on to the next one, so one hive will pollinate several different crops in a year—but even so, the numbers here obviously do not add up to there being enough bees after 2008 or 2009.

Then the bird-lovers sounded another alarm. Birds are also pollinators. In analyzing the annual Christmas bird counts by the Audubon Society of the last four decades, along with the summer breeding surveys organized by the U.S. Geological Survey, it was discovered that all twenty species of common birds lost at least 50% of their numbers by 2007.[9] Something was killing the birds as well.

Then, around the same time CCD struck the bees, the largest documented die-off of bats was reported for 2007. In New York State, 8,000 to 11,000 bats died of white nose fungus in caves and mines. Bat researcher Craig Stihler of the West Virginia Department of Natural Resources says the problem is not the fungus itself. "Pathologists that have examined the carcasses recovered from the New York sites do not believe the fungus is the main culprit. One guess at this time is that the fungus invades after the bats are stressed by some other factor."[10]

To sum up, not only are the honey bees suffering recent die-offs, so are the birds and the bats. Could all this be related?

Back at the Penn State CCD Working Group, a preliminary report was given to David Hackenberg, saying that mites and disease had been found but that the cause of his CCD was unknown. For all the science thrown at it, colony collapse disorder was still a mystery.

Three

The Potential Impact of Colony Collapse Disorder

There's a lot of beekeepers quitting or the bank's selling them out.
If we get another winter and spring like the last one, there's going
to be a whole lot more of them going out of business.
—David Hackenberg, Former President, American
Beekeeping Federation, 2007

Your grocery list for the day includes honey—but when you arrive at the store, you find none for sale. Next on your list are apples, but there aren't any of those either. Nor do you see any nuts, cucumbers, peaches, cherries, or blueberries. Going down your list, they are all out of avocados, oranges, soybeans (good-bye tofu), asparagus, broccoli, celery, squash, and grapefruit. You can't even find a cantaloupe. What happened?

This could be the future if colony collapse disorder is not reversed. What would be the impact of CCD on agriculture, beekeeping, and the economy in general? Will it be a major disaster or merely a minor, ongoing problem? And what of the loss of native bees and the effect of declining pollinators in the wild? Can our ecosystems adapt?

Beekeepers around the country and the world are worried about going broke due to CCD and problems like the mites. It simply doesn't pay to be in the bee business when CCD raises your annual die-off rate from 10% up to 40–50% and more. For instance, California beekeeper David Bradshaw went to inspect his hives in January 2007. Instead of the 100 million bees he expected to see, he suddenly had only half that. As quoted in an article that appeared the next month in *The New York Times*, "'I have never seen anything like it,' Mr. Bradshaw, fifty, said from an almond orchard here beginning to bloom. 'Box after box after box are just empty. There's nobody home.'"[1] For a beekeeper, this is the ultimate heartbreak.

To stay in business, Montana keeper Lance Sundberg reportedly had to spend $150,000 for fourteen million bees to replenish his 7,600 colonies—and was worried that they too would eventually succumb to the strange disease.[2] The price of queens has meanwhile risen from $10 to $15 each, and the cost of controlling mites has also gone up. Tanker truckloads of corn syrup have to be fed to the bees while they are pollinating—at a rate of $12,000 a truck. Even though prices have risen from $45 per hive (one per acre) to $150 per hive, the margin for pollinators remains too small. Some make as little as $11 annual profit per hive, and that's before CCD. Keeper Bradshaw says from 4,200 hives he now produces a net income of only $30,000 a year. Commercial pollinators like Bradshaw and Sundberg are clearly not in it for the money.

The beekeepers mostly do it because they love their craft. It is hard to love something so much, however, that you willingly go on losing substantial amounts of money every year. In addition, many beekeepers are older and nearing retirement. After all the struggles with mites, CCD is just the thing to push them into early retirement from the bee business. On top of all this, is the simple fact that CCD is killing so many colonies, there soon won't be enough honey bees to do the job.

SHORTAGES OF FRUITS, VEGETABLES, NUTS, AND EVEN BEEF AND DAIRY

If too many beekeepers go bankrupt or retire, certain sectors of agriculture will be in real trouble. Honey bees today pollinate more than ninety flowering crops in the U.S., with most of those crops totally dependent on *Apis* for vegetable, nut, and fruit formation. Take away commercial pollinators, and prices for these crops could soar, putting them out of reach for many families. In April 2007, U.S. Agriculture Secretary Mike Johanns warned, "This crisis threatens to wipe out production of crops dependent on bees for pollination."[3]

But losing all those food crops is not the end of it. Leafcutter bees, you see, are needed to pollinate alfalfa, and they are threatened by chalkbrood disease. Without inexpensive alfalfa to feed their beef herds, meat prices will first soar and then many ranchers will be squeezed out financially. Now you're talking no steak. No ribs. No hamburger in your grocery store either. Plus dairy prices have already skyrocketed without cheap alfalfa feed. Kevin Hackett, the USDA's national leader for the bee and pollination program, says if CCD gets any worse the U.S. could be "stuck with grains and water."[4]

In testimony before Congress, Dr. May Berenbaum, head of entomology at the University of Illinois Urbana-Champaign and chairwoman of the National Academy of Sciences pollinator decline committee, was deeply concerned for the future.

Even before CCD came to light, our committee estimated that if honeybee numbers continue to decline at the rates documented from 1989 to 1996, managed honeybees will cease to exist by 2035. Even the complete disappearance of honeybees would not fundamentally jeopardize food supplies in terms of calories because grains—the world's

primary source of dietary energy—do not depend on ani-
mal pollinators. However, supplies of animal-pollinated
foods—most fruit, vegetable and nut crops, which provide
the bulk of vitamins and other necessary nutrients in our
diets—may well be dramatically affected.

Food prices would at first rise on many different products, but then shortages would appear that would become longer and longer. Malnutrition, especially among poor children, could become a great problem.

Could CCD Help Cause a Depression?

Calling the fragile honey bee the "workhorse" of our agricultural system, and thus our civilization, the Pulitzer Prize–winning entomologist E. O. Wilson warned, "We have hung our future upon a thread." The number of large-scale commercial pollination operations in the U.S. can be numbered in the dozens. This is a slender thread indeed, as we depend on these top operators to stay in business and pollinate much of the fruit, nut, and vegetable crops. With little in the way of proper funding for bee research or any kind of planning, the U.S. and the world are suddenly vulnerable to economic catastrophe.

Middle-class families would suffer a knockout blow—food bills that suddenly triple and quadruple would be the straw that broke the camel's back. After years of inflation, huge mortgage bills, high oil prices, big electric bills, and the ever-rising cost of healthcare, taxes, and housing, many could go under. Every family would have to tighten its belt. And as family nutritional needs are not met, healthcare costs would presumably rise even further. It would be the "perfect storm" for the middle class.

People would be forced to bring a bag lunch to work and to

eat in. Restaurants, delis, and food stores of all kinds would then see a marked drop in their business. Large parts of the leisure sector would also go under. Stocks based on cheap food, tourism, and conspicuous consumerism would plunge in value.

The giant consumer locomotive that is the United States would then not only slow down, but likely slip into reverse, causing a global economic pileup of shrinking markets and ruinous overcapacity of stores and inventory. U.S. exports, based on cheap food product, would meanwhile plunge (excepting grains), creating a much bigger trade deficit than the horrendous one we have today. The U.S., for example, supplies 80% of the world's almonds.[5] There wouldn't be enough almonds in this future to ship hardly any of them overseas. Many almond orchards would go bankrupt. All the while, food production is falling, as the human population in an already hungry, sometimes even starving world is exploding.

At the same time, drought and extreme weather from global warming might affect the bees, farmers, and the economy even further. Drought will make colony collapse disorder worse, by weakening the bees and empowering the varroa mites. Bees need enough rain in their local region so there are abundant flowers to feed upon, and drought is already affecting bee populations in France and Australia.

As in the 1930s Dust Bowl, the collapse of this much agriculture could help lead to a world depression. This would leave less and less money to address impending needs such as the climate crisis, global poverty, healthcare, infrastructure, and education. It is not a pretty picture. Economically, after the sub-prime meltdown and a looming recession, the loss of the bees is the last thing the world needs right now.

The global economy, and thus our modern civilization, has an Achilles' heel: the loss of the simple honey bee could cause it all to unravel. For in the final analysis, the strength of a civilization depends upon its ability to produce enough food for its population.[6]

Environmental Catastrophe?

There's more. The further depopulation of bees would have a huge impact on the environment, which is reliant on insects for pollination. There are other pollinators, such as bats, hummingbirds, and butterflies, but these species have been disappearing as well. We have already seen that 98% of the wild *Apis* colonies in the U.S. were wiped out by 1994, from mites, pesticides, and habitat loss, and that 130,000 flowering wild plants need bees or other pollinators to reproduce.[7]

As most pollinator species disappear, entire ecosystems could themselves collapse, like a set of dominoes. Break a link in the chain of the ecosystem, and whole bioregions will degrade. Loss of native plants would lead to wide-scale spread of noxious alien weeds, further degenerating our environment. Add drought again to the picture, and some regions could become like deserts.

Before these unwelcome future scenarios come to pass, we need to find out—what is killing the bees? If it is a new disease, there may be little humanity can do to save our little friends. If it is a man-made cause, however, society can change, solve the problem, and we can perhaps avoid the "Beepocalypse." As soon as humanly possible, before it gets any worse, we must know—why do the bees die?

Four

It's Not the Cell Phones . . .

I don't think anyone really has a clue as to what's going on, but if it turns out to be cell phones, it's the greatest metaphor in the history of metaphors. Starving the planet in pursuit of one more text message with your broker seems the very epitome of going out with a whimper, not a bang.
—Bill McKibben, author of *The End of Nature and Deep Economy*[1]

IF YOU ASK THE AVERAGE PERSON WHAT THEY THINK IS KILLING THE BEES, they will likely answer, "Isn't it the cell phones?" By early 2007, colony collapse disorder was beginning to cause a form of mild hysteria in the world media.

Then an intrepid reporter at *The Independent* in London discovered an experiment conducted by researchers at Germany's Landau University, a newly converted teacher's college. The German scientists had been able to disrupt the normal behavior of bees by placing a cordless phone base inside the hive, although later reports called it a cell phone by mistake. Nonthermal EM radiation from the cordless phone base was found to have disturbed the bees, even preventing them in some cases from returning to the hive, which seemed to fit the reports of CCD. *The Independent* ran the original story, titled "Are Mobile Phones

Wiping Out Our Bees?".[2] The article caught the world's attention by announcing that "some scientists suggest that our love of the mobile phone could cause massive food shortages" and "the theory is that radiation from mobile phones interferes with bees' navigation systems."

After this report appeared in *The Independent* in late April 2007, the story reverberated around the globe, giving the impression that a solid scientific study had found the answer to colony collapse disorder. Yet Stefan Kimmel, the graduate student who co-authored the study with his physics professor, was upset that the story implied a cause had been found for CCD: "Ever since *The Independent* wrote their article, for which they never called or wrote to us, none of us have been able to do any of our work because all our time has been spent in phone calls and e-mails trying to set things straight. This is a horror story for every researcher to have your study reduced to this. Now we are trying to force things back to normal."[3]

The physics professor who co-authored the now famous paper, Dr. Jochen Kuhn of the physics department at Koblenz-Landau, was very clear that he was not claiming that EM radiation causes CCD. "We cannot explain the CCD-phenomenon itself and want to keep from speculation in this case. Our studies cannot indicate that electromagnetic radiation is a cause of CCD."

THE EXPERIMENT ITSELF

What exactly was the experiment conducted and why do the researchers themselves say it cannot point to cell phones being the cause?

The name of the paper was: "Can Electromagnetic Exposure Cause a Change in Behaviour?"[4] The experiment was looking for nonthermal effects of electromagnetic radiation on the behavior of bees, which were known to be sensitive to EMF waves. This experiment sought to discover whether the learning ability of a bee could be disrupted by EMF waves.

A cordless phone base was placed in four of the eight hives and calls were made to the handset. It was found that the EM radiation lowered the ability or desire of the bees to return to the hive. Honeycomb weight was also reduced from 2,500 grams in the four control hives to 2,050 grams in the four test hives. The main difference between the control and test hives was in the return rate of bees leaving the hive. As reported by Dr. Mae-Wan Ho, Institute of Science in Society in London, "For two control hives, 16 out of 25 bees returned in 45 minutes. For the two microwave-exposed hives, however, no bees at all returned to one hive, and only six returned to the other."[5]

Some of the colonies under study "broke down," but that included a control hive that had no phone base embedded in it. This fact, of course, invalidates any claim that this study shows EMF waves to be the cause of colony collapse disorder. Both exposed and nonexposed hives failed. The dead colonies could have been caused by a bad case of mites, which can sometimes kill a hive after just a couple of months, or a number of other reasons. Then a basic mistake in experiment design was made in calculating the average honeycomb weight. The control hives only had one colony break down, while the exposed hives had three out of four die. But the honeycomb weights of all four control and all four exposed hives were averaged. This skewed the average—as one is comparing three healthy hives with one healthy hive. In fact, the authors of the cell phone study exhibited little knowledge of basic bee behavior, as shown by their methods and by their interpretations of what they were finding. No entomologists or beekeepers were involved in the Landau research, and the papers were submitted and reviewed by the "International

Institute for Advanced Studies in Systems Research and Cybernetics," an information science institute. Another problem arises from the claim that the bees would not return to the hive.

Bees were trapped as they left the hive, sedated with CO_2, tagged, and then released 500 meters from the colony. They were no doubt trapping bees that were leaving to go off on long foraging trips and were still hungry for nectar. The researchers did not realize these bees would not care to return, at least for an hour or two. In addition, the bees could have gotten confused by first getting their exacting waggle dance flight instructions, then suddenly waking up 500 meters from where they were supposed to take wing. This change in starting points might have easily confused the worker bees, especially those on their first flight. Without knowing which bees were still hungry or which were the first-timers, the experiment's measure of "return time" is meaningless.

What Do Bee Scientists Think of the "Cell Phone" Theory?

When asked about the cell phone theory, Dr. Jeff Pettis from the USDA dismissed it: "The authors of that story were from Germany. It wasn't even a cell phone. It was an old cordless phone [it was actually the base of a cordless phone]. They tested it in small hives and saw some very minor effects. We work with bees in a lot of areas where you can't even get a cell phone signal. The amount of energy is very, very remote. Even the authors themselves now say that was a big stretch."[6]

Common sense would seem to agree. Cell phone towers have been around for a while, yet CCD is new. And, as Pettis points out, cell coverage does not reach many rural areas and the energy is extremely low, nothing like the EM waves produced by putting the phone base directly into the hive. There simply isn't enough power to affect the bees.

So why did the story get so much coverage? People are intensely looking for the answer to the mystery of the bees—but there is something more. It is, of course, the irony of it all that fascinates us. The idea that cell phones could be killing the bees and bringing about the end of civilization as we know it is just too good a conversation starter to pass up. Pamela McCorduck, the futurist who wrote *Machines Who Think*, was disappointed cell phones had been ruled out: "We now know it isn't cell phones, alas, alas. I so longed to shut such people up with a sanctimonious 'You're killing the bees, you clod!'"[7]

Yet the science is simply not there to back up such a theory.

In the end, the cell phone episode shows not only how sloppy modern journalism has become, but also how science itself can sometimes design experiments that appear to say much, but in fact have no solid data and so signify little. Journalists need to slow down and do the actual legwork of understanding the issues and possible critiques of the experiment's design and conclusions. Unfortunately, there has been far more media coverage spreading the idea than there has been debunking it. Even today, several months after it was disproved, most people still think cell phone tower radiation is confusing the bees and making them lose their way home.

Stefan Kimmel, the graduate student who co-authored the Landau study, said: "If the Americans are looking for an explanation for colony collapse disorder, perhaps they should look at herbicides, pesticides, and they should especially think about genetically modified crops."[8]

So if it's not the cell phones—or the cordless phones—what is causing colony collapse disorder? What about what Kimmel suggests, herbicides and other possible reasons? Or is it the mites? New viruses? Previously unknown parasites? Genetically engineered crops? Global warming? Maybe it's modern bee-management practices, where colonies spend half their time being trucked up and down the interstate. Or could it be something else?

To find out why the bees die, is the U.S. government acting posthaste to pull together resources in a pollinator research version of the Manhattan Project? Or has the Bush Administration dropped the ball, Katrina-style? What do we know so far? What is the *real* research telling us about colony collapse disorder? It's time to start answering these questions.

Five

It's Not the Mites
or a Virus . . .

I thought we had a problem with mites but compared to this,
they're nice little fellers.
—Beekeeper Delmar McCann,
Laveen, Arizona[1]

MITES HAVE BEEN A PROBLEM FOR DECADES FOR U.S. HONEY BEES. In 1984, tracheal mites were found in Florida bee colonies. Three years later, the *Varroa destructor* mite appeared in the Wisconsin colony and eventually spread to most states. Before CCD ever arrived in the U.S., the varroa mite had long been killing and weakening bees. As we saw, the varroa mite attaches itself to the abdomen of the bee and with its bite transmits different diseases like acute bee paralysis and deformed-wing virus. A badly infected hive can die after four years, sometimes in just a couple of months.

Varroa destructor made beekeeping a true pain, as one had to use either a powerful miticide within the hive, or learn a whole new way and switch to organic beekeeping, which works fine but is more labor-intensive. Most beekeepers turned to chemicals to save their hives, using a "fluvalinate" on an impregnated plastic strip called Apistan. Fluvalinate is the common name of a pyrethroid pesticide that in the right dose is effective against mites, but does not affect honey bees. Bees would crawl over Apistan strips attached to the walls of the brood nest, with the miticide coating every bee within just a few hours. At the same time, beekeepers were also misusing antibiotics on their colonies, by mixing Terramycin into "extender" grease patties which soon led to resistant strains of foulbrood disease, a bad bacterial infection. The fatal flaw of the extender patties was that the antibiotic was constantly present in the hive at sublethal doses to the bacteria, a certain recipe for development of resistance. Thus, an antibiotic that had been effective for decades suddenly became useless. Whatever chemical or drug beekeepers defended their hives with, when left in the hive for considerable periods at sublethal doses, it does not take long before the target organism becomes immune to it—sometimes within just two years.

During the 1990s, varroa, too, became resistant. Evolution had adapted to the chemical attack. At the time, ARS environmental toxicologist Patti J. Elzen admitted that widespread use of Apistan "inadvertently contributed to the rise of mites resistant to this chemical." Working out of the ARS Beneficial Insects Research Unit at Weslaco, Texas, Elzen and other researchers discovered fluvalinate resistance in varroa mites from the far-flung states of California, Wisconsin, Arkansas, and Florida.

Far stronger doses of miticide were now needed, and beekeepers had to be careful not to hurt their bees or themselves with the caustic chemical. They were also warned to follow strict procedures so as not to contaminate the honey and beeswax being made by those same fluvalinate-covered bees. With the rapid development and spread of so much mite resistance to Apistan, however, an alternative organophosphate chemical named coumaphos was then approved by the EPA with Section

18s, through an "emergency authorization". (See Appendix 4 – FIFRA Section 18).

Perhaps you have never heard how the EPA regularly approves barely tested toxic chemicals through the loophole of a "temporary emergency authorization." While the environmentalists fume, stew, and often sue over these maneuvers, a state merely has to write a simple request letter, outline its specific emergency and use plan, and the EPA will likely grant it another two years. The emergency status allows the chemical company to forgo the usual rigorous environmental testing that must be done before a toxin can be permanently approved for a new purpose. In this way, the EPA and the chemical industry have regularly bypassed the safety tests for the environment and human health tests that were written into federal law decades ago.

To environmentalists, this is high-risk behavior. In a letter on Section 18s to the EPA dated November 2, 2004, the Natural Resources Defense Council, World Wildlife Fund, American Bird Conservancy, Center for Biological Diversity, Washington Toxics Coalition, Beyond Pesticides, and others, stated that the EPA has its priorities reversed:

EPA seems to have the precautionary principle backwards: the Agency hurries to get Section 18 pesticide uses approved on the basis of minimal information, but requires mountains of evidence and years (or decades) of review to impose restrictions on currently approved pesticides.

Hundreds of chemicals get these one or two-year extensions annually. The universities, which receive huge research grants and donations from chemical companies, in turn gladly offer to teach how to use the new toxin safely. Here is the 2002 letter sent by the New York State DEC to the EPA for temporary use of the new bee miticide using coumaphos, marketed by Bayer in the product CheckMite+:

This is the fourth year that we are requesting coumaphos (CheckMite+ Strips) for emergency use to control the varroa mite and small hive beetle in bee hives in all counties of New York State. The anticipated total use is 84,328 strips (118,059 grams active ingredient) Statewide.

As discussed in the submission, the varroa mite is developing resistance to Apistan Strips and is only suppressed by the Formic acid gel pacs that are the registered alternative. Of year-round colonies, 12% are estimated to be infested with Apistan-resistant mites. Of migratory colonies, 90% are estimated to have some degree of resistance to Apistan. For small hive beetle, no other pesticide has been identified that will control this pest without also killing bees. For control of varroa mite, twice-a-year treatments of coumaphos are being requested. Effective control of varroa mites may be achieved by treating hives in the spring before the honey flow and in the fall after the last honey flow. Strips are to be left in the hive for at least 42 days (six weeks), but not more than 45 days. For control of small hive beetle, a maximum of four treatments, lasting at least 42 days (six weeks), but no more than 45 days, are being requested.

Bayer Corporation, the manufacturer of CheckMite+ Strips, fully supports our efforts to obtain an emergency exemption for the use of CheckMite+ in bee hives in New York State. . . Cornell University is committed to training beekeepers in the proper use of coumaphos strips. Through a combination of a nine-hour IPM course, talks with local beekeeper groups and programs at the state honey producers meeting, many of the states' applicators have had

an opportunity to learn of resistance and residues in bee
products if these strips are applied improperly.

So powerful chemicals were authorized for emergency use in beehives to fight varroa, essentially an ad hoc experiment in the field using beekeepers, the bees, and the public as guinea pigs, but that appears to be standard operating procedure for the EPA.

Unfortunately, little thought was given by the EPA that further use of chemicals might lead to more adaptation by the mites, that they would "inadvertently" once again evolve and become resistant to coumaphos as they had to fluvalinate. It did not take long. By 2001, *Varroa destructor* was showing resistance to all the "approved" pesticides.[2]

Does this mean that the varroa mites or perhaps the miticides are the cause of colony collapse disorder? The answer seems to be no. Researchers have not been able to correlate CCD with varroa and/or miticide use, as there are other cases where CCD has occurred but mites and thus miticides were not present. Plus, the hive death from varroa is quite different from colony collapse. With CCD the worker bees fly off within a few days, leaving the hive to starve. One must also keep in mind that varroa and some of the miticides have been around for over a decade and a half and yet there was no CCD in the U.S. during all that time.

Mites may be a symptom of a hive weakened by CCD, and certainly using powerful chemicals within a weakened hive could lead to further problems, but varroa mites do not appear to be the cause of CCD. There might be an indirect connection, however, in that fluvalinate and coumaphos could be synergizing with other toxins in the bee's environment and making CCD worse. According to the general thrust of the CCD Working Group, synergies between chemicals is another likely cause, so that concept would seem to deserve further research. Mites therefore do not appear to be the primary cause of CCD, although they could be a means, weakening the hive so that some other means can knock the colony flat.

Is It Bacteria or Parasites?

What about pathogens, perhaps a new bee bacteria or parasite? Have researchers found something in the CCD colonies indicating a new disease? One problem in doing research is that the bees fly off and so there are only the bodies of the bees that remained behind to starve. This makes it more difficult to find the cause. Remember, the bee genome research showed bees have a weakness beyond certain specific older pathogens. Although researchers have found new viruses and parasites affecting some bee populations, once again these are not consistent with global colony collapse disorder, nor does CCD fit the pathology. Death from these diseases comes in other ways, primarily evidenced by piles of dead bees in front of the hive. The cause behind CCD must be consistent; it must correlate with the places where CCD occurs. Mites, viruses, parasites, and bacterial infection have simply not been found in all the CCD hives, nor do they fit the symptoms of CCD.

There have been other theories as well. MacArthur Foundation "Genius Grant" winner and biochemist Joe DeRisi, who played a key role in the discovery of the SARS virus in 2003, has conducted his own genetic research to solve the mystery of the bees. Using a "microarray," which allows the rapid comparison of genetic codes of different organisms, DeRisi found a genetic marker for a single-celled, spore-producing parasite called *Nosema ceranae*. Meanwhile, Mariano Higes, from an apiculture center in Guadalajara, Spain, had published a paper in *The Journal of Invertebrate Pathology* claiming that *Nosema* could wipe out a bee hive in eight days.[3] Higes concludes that CCD is caused by the parasite. Now two researchers were pointing to *Nosema* being linked to CCD.

Most bee researchers, however, such as Dr. Jeff Pettis of the USDA, dismiss the parasite as being responsible for colony collapse disorder. Infected colonies have *Nosema*, and healthy hives have it as well, as Pettis has repeatedly explained: "while the parasite *Nosema ceranae* may be a factor, it cannot be the sole cause. The fungus has been seen before, sometimes in colonies that were healthy." He added, "Mostly we think of *Nosema* as a stress disorder of honey bees." DeRisi himself did not believe the genetic find was definitive proof of CCD being caused by *Nosema*; "We don't want to give anybody the impression that this thing has been solved."

Nosema ceranae was first described in 1999 in Taiwan where it had jumped species from the Eastern honey bee, *Apis cerana*, to the Western honey bee, *Apis mellifera*. Unlike the ubiquitous *Nosema apis* that had been infecting *Apis mellifera* since it evolved, *Nosema ceranae* is virulent and is new to North America, appearing here shortly after showing up in Europe in 2006. The parasite, however, is not known to cause symptoms like those of CCD.

The *Nosema* parasite invades the mid-gut cells, taking over the cells' function (procuring nutrients), by making several hundred copies of itself, killing the cell which then ruptures, releasing the parasite into the gut "lumen," the internal mucous surface of the stomach, and from there into the "mid-gut cells." Large numbers of dying mid-gut cells then weaken the bee (nutrition becomes impossible), giving it diarrhea or "dysentery," thus spreading the parasites as other bees lap up the feces accidentally expelled in the hive instead of the normal release outdoors. Only adult bees are affected. This parasite is far more virulent than *Nosema apis* which usually appears only during winter stress and then clears up when bees can fly freely in warm weather in the spring. In contrast, *Nosema cerana,* can kill a hive after just eight days and occurs year-round. Slow spring buildup of the colony, disjointed wings, distended and bloated abdomen, and dwindling populations are all symptoms, as well as yellow streaks outside the hive. These are very distinct features that are not seen in all CCD hives. Unless *Nosema* suddenly evolved into a new beast capable of producing CCD (not likely), it does not appear to be the cause—although it could very well be a symptom of a colony weakened by something else.

Maybe Genes, Stress, or Nutrition?

If it's not mites, bacteria, or parasites, perhaps the culprit is the loss of genetic integrity? Less than 500 breeder queens produce the millions of queen bees—and so all the commercial honey bees—bought in the U.S. This "genetic bottleneck" is being investigated as a possible cause of CCD as well. The honey bee is, for all practical purposes, a monoculture, a single species; and monocultures are highly susceptible to new diseases or pests. Might not the genetic bottleneck of the breeder queens explain CCD? This question could unfortunately take untold years of research to answer. Once again, however, the low level of breeder queens is not a likely answer, as hives bred from queens from elsewhere can also suffer from CCD.

What about bee management? Could the way modern commercial pollinators treat their bees be getting them all stressed out, weakening the hive to such an extent that CCD strikes? The massive commercial pollination of today requires loading thousands of hives onto eighteen-wheel flatbed trucks and transporting them from coast to coast. Large pollinating operations generally move from the West in the spring (especially for the almond crop in February) to the North, Midwest, and East in the summer (including blueberries in New Jersey and many other crops). When the worker bees arrive at their migrant jobs, they are released to mingle with bees from many other hives, allowing the easy spread of mites and viruses. This constant movement and the intermingling of different hives no doubt helps explain why the varroa infestation and the *Nosema* parasite are more of a problem in the U.S. than overseas. Beekeepers outside the U.S. don't move their hives nearly as much.

In another theory, the Penn State CCD Working Group found that before the hives collapse there is a period of "extraordinary stress," typically brought about by poor nutrition or drought. In fact, the Working Group reports that this stress is the single factor that is common to 100% of the reported CCD cases. Since CCD happens in the winter when keepers feed their bees artificially, this has led some researchers to blame the practice of using high-fructose corn syrup (HFCS) to bolster winter stores, which does not fully meet the nutritional needs of the colony. As a result, companies are creating new, more nutritious formulations to feed the bees. Here again, however, many hives killed by colony collapse disorder were never fed high-fructose corn syrup. So the syrup itself does not appear to be the cause.

IT CAN'T BE GENETIC ENGINEERING . . .

What about genetically modified organisms, or GMOs, plants that are altered in many ways, often to produce their own insecticides? The spread of genetically engineered crops is recent enough. Could there not be a gene that inadvertently crosses over from the GM plant to the honey bee, causing a reaction among the worker bees that makes them fly off and never return? The random crossing over of genes to other species is perhaps the main hazard in GMOs. Could this be causing the calamity? The planting of GM crops is skyrocketing in the six countries they are allowed in, now covering 200 million acres. This is a fifty-fold increase in just ten years. Bt corn is the main crop planted, so-called because genetic engineering causes the plant to produce its own Bt insecticidal protein, a gene borrowed from the *Bacillus thuringiensus* bacteria. Farmers can thus grow a crop with less need for insecticide because the plant is making its own. This lowers expenses per acre, making Bt corn wildly popular with growers.

One study in Germany looked at the effect of Bt corn on honey bees. Conducted at the University of Jena from 2001 to 2004, researchers found that Bt corn pollen did not seem to affect bee colonies, concluding there was no "toxic effect of Bt corn on healthy honey bee populations." The study then deliberately contaminated fructose bee feed with ten times the amount of Bt toxin found in the field Bt corn pollen. Hives fed this Bt-laced corn syrup, which coincidentally then got infested with *Nosema* did suffer a "significantly stronger decline in the number of bees" compared to control hives that were not fed the contaminated syrup.

In the final analysis, however, the Jena research on GMOs and bees did not show a link between GM plants and colony collapse disorder. Most important, genetically modified plants are not allowed in all countries and thus do not correlate with the wider reach of CCD. GMOs are basically not permitted in Europe, for example, yet CCD has appeared there. Colony collapse disorder is therefore *not* caused by genetic engineering.

ORGANIC BEES DO NOT HAVE CCD

Going down the list of possible causes of CCD, it is helpful to take a look at organic beekeeping. The simple fact is that the organic beekeepers are not suffering greatly from colony collapse disorder.[4] Why? Naturally, organic keepers have their own opinion of CCD and what causes it, or rather they have many opinions.

One is that some organic beekeepers are using smaller-sized brood cells. The claim is that larger bees are more susceptible to mites and disease, as there is simply more bee for the parasites to grow in or on. Organic beekeepers also note that the larger cells discourage drone production, which could compromise genetic integrity by reducing the amount of male diversity available to the queen for mating. Over time, queens could become less fertile. This is another instance, says the organic side, of "The Law of Unintended Consequences," the concept of which is to keep things as close as possible to the way nature intended, so as to introduce far fewer variables and hazards, hazards which will almost always create unintended and unwanted consequences.

Organic keepers also do not substitute artificial feeds like soy protein for pollen and high-fructose corn syrup for honey. Compared to their organic counterparts, commercial keepers take much more honey to sell and then give artificial feed to tide the colonies over for the winter and during the times they are traveling and working. The corn syrup and soy, however, cannot match raw honey and pollen as the perfect bee feed, with all the enzymes and protein that the hive must have to survive. Commercial keepers do leave honey in the hive, but their organic counterparts simply leave more of it so they don't need the artificial feed.

Another big difference between conventional and organic beekeeping is the use of chemicals. Large commercial beekeepers, and most smaller-scale beekeepers, use powerful antibiotics, miticides (which are insecticides), and other toxic chemicals seasonally during the year. Most are knowledgeable and careful to avoid misapplications and thus contamination of honey during times of "honey flow."

Organic keepers use none of these chemicals. All are apparently being replaced effectively by the use of essential oils to fight mites and other pathogens, or through hive design, and in the sharing of natural methods and techniques. A small minority of organic keepers also use a new small-cell "top-bar" hive, a hive without the foundation which the honeycomb usually sits in. This allows air circulation at the bottom of the hive, a design, they say, which helps to control varroa.

The effectiveness of these methods must be real, or the organic keepers would not be in business. Some of these organic approaches are labor-intensive and would require many workers if thousands of hives were being managed, as the commercial pollinators have, and therefore would lead to cost increases for them. Most organic beekeepers run small operations.

But there's more. To make organic honey, a keeper must spirit the hives far away from civilization and the fields where insecticides and herbicides are applied. Most organic product is wild honey, produced from wildflowers, from forests and meadows where no spraying occurs. Since bees only fly a few miles from the hive, this can be easily accomplished by keeping the colonies in the most rural and wild of areas. So not only are there no miticides in the hive, the organic bees are not bringing back residues of herbicide and insecticide from their foraging trips. In contrast, bees kept in commercial farm areas return with many toxic compounds.

Even though organic practices seem to be unaffected by CCD, commercial beekeeping had been around for decades with little or no sign of colony collapse disorder. Pesticides and miticides have been around for decades as well. What is new that is affecting the bees so badly this time around? It must be something that was not present just a few years ago.

A New Virus Theory

On September 6, 2007, a team of bee researchers from the USDA, Columbia, and Penn State put forth a new theory in the journal

Science. They claimed that a new disease, called Israeli acute paralysis virus, or IAPV, appears to have a connection to CCD-affected hives, although they immediately cautioned that the virus is not likely to be the single cause of colony collapse disorder. IAPV, so-called because it was first identified in Israel in 2004, coincides with the early reports of CCD, for Australian bees with IAPV were imported into the U.S. in 2005. Seizing upon the coinciding time-frame, the researchers began looking for links between CCD and IAPV. Using genetic sequencing of bee bodies, IAPV was found in twenty-five out of thirty CCD hives. In contrast, only one out of twenty-one non-CCD hives was affected by the disease. The researchers believe that the paralysis caused by IAPV might be a factor in why the worker bees are not returning to the hive. Dr. W. Ian Lipkin, however, who led the gene sequencing project, said, "What we have at present is a marker. We do not think IAPV alone is causing this disease."

USDA entomologist Jeff Pettis warned: "I hope no one goes away with the idea that we've actually solved the problem. We still have a great deal of research to do to resolve why bees are dying." Although the symptoms of IAPV are different from CCD—the dead bee bodies pile up in front of the hive instead of there being no bodies—the study theorizes that perhaps, in combination with varroa mites, the result might be CCD.

Bees infected with IAPV first suffer from shivering wings, easily differentiated from wings at rest when the bee is crawling about. The disease then leads to paralysis and death just outside the hive. Since only one out of twenty-one non-CCD hives had IAPV, the researchers said that meant a colony with IAPV was sixty-five times more likely to be hit with CCD than a hive without IAPV. The authors, however, admit that IAPV is found in Australia, where there has been no CCD, and that healthy and unhealthy bee colonies alike are infected with IAPV.

Reminiscent of the cell phone story, the media once again pounced on the news and reported the study as the possible answer to CCD, even while the authors were urging caution. The IAPV hypothesis was quickly challenged on several grounds, some obvious, others quite technical. The researchers state that only four beekeeping operations suffering from CCD were sampled and only thirty total CCD colonies were looked at. Healthy colonies were also a small sample, with just twenty-one hives being studied, and some of those bees came from Hawaii, an isolated environment. Thus only fifty-one colonies out of 600,000 lost were examined. Major contradictions within the IAPV theory are brought up in the paper itself:

- There's IAPV in Australian colonies but no CCD.

- IAPV appears in both non-CCD hives and CCD hives.

- The symptoms of IAPV differ from CCD, as the bees dead from IAPV pile up in front of the hive.

Bees carry many microbes and viruses, so the correlation found between IAPV and CCD is perhaps not significant, especially when one remembers that CCD causes most of the bees to go missing, so we don't have those bodies to dissect. To look at it another way, just because a high percentage of human cancer patients have the antibodies to Influenza A, it doesn't mean that Influenza A causes cancer. *All* human populations have a level of flu antibodies. IAPV being found in higher numbers in the remaining CCD bodies may therefore not tell us much. In addition, whatever is causing colony collapse disorder also appears to be weakening the immunity of the bee, which we already know to be genetically weak. This would theoretically let viruses like IAPV have a greater impact.

The main IAPV theory claim was disproved on November 19, 2007, when a key finding was released by USDA entomologists working for the Agricultural Research Service. After a detailed genetic screening of several hundred bees collected from hives in Maryland, Pennsylvania, California, and Israel, they found that IAPV first came to the United States in 2002, not 2005 as previously thought by the IAPV group. Unless the virus somehow mutated between 2002 and 2005 and suddenly began causing CCD in America, the hypothesis that it is responsible is not tenable. The IAPV argument is based on the virus coming in 2005 from Australian imports, the same time that CCD appeared. Outside of a dramatic mutation, the new data now made that connection in time impossible.[5] If IAPV is the cause or major factor, why was CCD not reported in the U.S. from 2002 to 2006?

Dr. Judy Chen of the USDA said, "Our study shows that, without question, IAPV has been in this country since at least 2002. This work challenges the idea that IAPV is a recent introduction from Australia." Dr. Jay Evans of ARS, and a co-author of the study, maintained that IAPV research would still go on, that the earlier date "in no way rules IAPV out as a factor in CCD." Evans predicted several years of further study: "Research by several groups will now focus on understanding differences in virulence across strains of IAPV and on interactions with other stress factors."

What do the Australian scientists think about the IAPV story, since their nation's bees are being tagged as the prime suspect behind CCD? Dr. Dennis Anderson, an Australian entomologist with the Commonwealth Scientific and Industrial Research Organisation, conducted his own research and found no connection that IAPV caused CCD, or was even a factor. He disputed the veracity of the IAPV study claims. "This paper only adds further to the confusion surrounding CCD." In the Australian press, it was repeatedly noted that IAPV should not be considered a prime suspect, that the USDA itself found that the disease had been in the

U.S. since 2002, three years before Australian bees were imported to America, a fact that has never appeared in the U.S. press. *The Australian* reported that Australia's federal Agriculture Minister, Peter McGauran, complained, "Someone owes Australian bee-keepers a big apology, but we won't hold our breath waiting for it." The same article said, "Max Whitten, former head of CSIRO Entomology, added that there was never any evidence that IAPV caused CCD, let alone that it was spread by Australian bees."[6]

There are three different ways to transmit IAPV: bee to bee via mouth-to-mouth and physical contact (like the flu in humans), transmittal by blood-sucking varroa, and transmission when nurse bees clean up virus-laden varroa feces from cells. When the virus is transmitted only via bee-to-bee contact, the disease is mild and unremarkable. But when it goes through the varroa mite, the severity greatly increases. Australian bee yards, which are free of varroa therefore show very few or no symptoms despite the presence of the virus. Bring the same bees to the U.S., add varroa, even in small numbers, and voilà; you get collapsing colonies. These collapsed colonies, however, exhibit the symptoms of acute bee paralysis, with the bees piled in front of the hive. With colony collapse disorder, the hive is depopulated and there are no bees in front. Plus hive beetles and wax moths stay away from the dead CCD hive for weeks, another odd symptom that cannot be explained away with IAPV.

Many American beekeepers, meanwhile, believe IAPV is more likely to be an indirect *symptom* of CCD and not the direct *cause*, or maybe not even a factor. It should be noted that most of the top beekeepers in the U.S., informed in a conference call on September 6, 2007 about the IAPV theory, were skeptical. They believe that other factors, especially insecticides, are responsible for colony collapse disorder. Jim Doan, a western New York beekeeper, told *The Washington Post* that the study was underestimating pesticides, a point even echoed by one of the study's authors, Diana Cox-Foster at Penn State.[7]

The IAPV theorists themselves are planning an experiment to infect hives with varroa and IAPV and see if CCD appears. This, they say, will prove or disprove the IAPV suspicion. However, given that the symptoms of both IAPV and varroa infestation produce problems nothing like CCD, and given that both the virus and the mites take months to develop—whereas CCD can depopulate a hive in a few days—this line of inquiry does not appear promising. To the beekeepers, the virus cannot be the problem; the symptoms simply don't match CCD. And they say they can't wait five years for studies to prove or disprove this theory.

Here's what we've learned so far. It's not the cell phones causing CCD. It does not appear to be the mites, nor the *Nosema* parasite. It's not the high-fructose corn syrup. It's probably not the stress from being trucked coast to coast—although that certainly doesn't help. It can't be the GMOs, and it doesn't seem to be the breeder queens or the larger bee sizes. And the recent virus theory, IAPV, appears unlikely to prove out for the many reasons mentioned above.

If it's none of these, then what is it? And why have some regions escaped CCD altogether? For that matter, why are the organic bees *not* experiencing colony collapse disorder? Both seem to be major clues that need further investigating. The beekeepers are meanwhile dismissing the latest virus theory as a waste of time. How could the entomologists get that far off track if IAPV seems so unlikely a culprit? Is there a single cause behind CCD, or a combination of factors? And if we finally do discover the cause, *how can we bring the bees back?*

Six

The French Say
They Know Why

Even bees, the little almsmen of spring bowers, know there is
richest juice in poison-flowers.
—John Keats

In July 1994, beekeepers in France began noticing something they had never seen before. Over the course of a few days, just after the sunflowers bloomed, a substantial number of their hives would collapse, as the worker bees flew off and never returned, leaving the queen and some immature bees to die. And where the usual beetles and mites would ordinarily move in and take over a dead hive, here the scavengers would leave the affected hive boxes alone—for weeks. Something unusual was repelling them.

Why did some hives collapse and others not? Winter die-off was typically up to 30% or even 50%, but these were strange collapses of the colony in the late spring and early summer where the bees simply flew away. Cold weather ordinarily left dead bees in front of the hive, as did lethal pesticide poisoning. The last thing a female worker bee wants to do is abandon the hive and the brood she is feeding. It is like a human mother abandoning her baby.

It was CCD, colony collapse disorder—only this was 1994, not 2006.

The usual list of suspects was considered, except for the cell phone theory. The French beekeepers, however, soon believed they knew the reason. They quickly realized that a brand-new insecticide called GAUCHO had just been authorized and was being applied to sunflowers for the first time. The insecticide was known to be highly toxic to bees, and it was now being used on flowering food crops.

The suspect ingredient in GAUCHO is imidacloprid (IMD), a chlorinated nicotine-based insecticide or "neonicotinoid." IMD is actually similar to DDT, another chlorinated hydrocarbon, except it is designed to affect insects and be relatively safe for humans and mammals. If you were to look at their respective molecular diagrams, you would see that they are relatively simple compounds. Both are neurotoxins, with properties similar to nerve gas. The goal of these chemicals is to block vital parts of the insect nervous system and keep them from functioning, causing a rapid death. IMD and all neonicotinoids work by inhibiting the acetylcholine receptors in the nervous system, which stops the transmission of signals across the synapses between neurons. In plain English, a lethal dose of IMD would disrupt the very way the nervous system of an insect works and kill it quite quickly, much as nerve gas kills a human being. Thanks to the mapping of the bee genome, we know that the nicotinic acetylcholine receptor in the honey bee's nervous system has eleven subunit members, more than either the fruit fly or mosquito.[1] This means the honey bee has more of the particular type of receptor blocked by IMD than other insects, theoretically making it extremely susceptible to IMD and other neurotoxins.

IMD is either painted on seeds to poison seed-devouring maggots and larvae, aphids, or other sucking insects, or it is poured around a plant in a "soil drench" that lasts up to a year and—as we now know—much, much longer. Monsanto's U.S. Patent #6,660,690 protects the painting of genetically modified seeds with pesticides, including IMD. In Europe, genetically modified plants are banned, but the seed paintings are not, so IMD seed-paintings are common in Europe. IMD is also sometimes sprayed on some cereal crops in France, as well as rapeseed.

THE FRENCH BEEKEEPERS DEMAND THAT IMD BE PROVED SAFE FOR BEES

In autumn 1994, the French beekeepers asked the German agro-chemical giant Bayer for a study on how sublethal doses of IMD might affect honey bees. The bees were not dying from a lethal dose, but perhaps sublethal doses were affecting behavior. Was IMD somehow making them lose their way home after foraging on tainted sunflowers?

It is interesting to note that the label on Bayer CropScience's product PREMISE 75—which is 75% IMD, 25% inert, and sold for termite control—boldly states, "PREMISE causes a range of effects in termites, *they stop feeding and are unable to maintain their colony* [italics mine]. A second effect, exclusive to PREMISE, is called PREMISE plus Nature. *This product makes termites susceptible to infection by naturally occurring organisms.* Either way, the termites die and your home is protected."

The honey bees, like termites, appear to be suffering from these exact same problems, especially when one considers the recent surge in honey bee mites and pathogens. That second effect, "PREMISE plus Nature," is very telling. IMD is clearly designed to lower insect resistance to all predatory organisms and viruses, opening the way for the hive to be attacked by pests—just like a colony of IMD-treated termites. If true, it would certainly help explain the overwhelming number of new and uncontrollable diseases afflicting the honey bee in the U.S. and around the world

There's Parts per Billion, and There's Parts per Billion

Bayer CropScience, which created IMD in 1985, did comply with trials in 1995 and 1997 in central France and in 1996 in Germany. When the chemical was first submitted for authorization, Bayer's original test documents had said that only the plant's roots would absorb IMD—that it would never reach the flower and the nectar. They further declared that 5 parts per million (or 5,000 parts per billion) was the lethal level for bees. These claims were not quite accurate. The company's revised conclusion in the new studies of the mid-90s was that the lethal bee dose was in reality in the range of 50–100 parts per billion (not 5,000 PPB). Bayer declared GAUCHO safe for bees, since the nectar sipped by bees would never reach 50 PPB.

Beekeepers, however, claimed there were flaws in Bayer's research, that the company data could not definitively prove IMD was safe in tiny, *sublethal* doses. In these mid-'90s tests, Bayer had primarily studied down to the 50 PPB lethal dose range. Moreover, the Bayer CropScience studies were in the lab and not in the field, where the availability of IMD from several different sources, such as the flower, pollen, and the leaves, adds up to an even more potent dose.

Honey production was meanwhile plunging in France, and the desperate keepers now believed it was certain—it was IMD affecting their hives. Production of 110,000 metric tons of sunflower honey in 1996 fell to just 50,000 tons in 1999, more than a 50% decline in honey production. It was a disaster. So the beekeepers appealed to the government.

The French Agriculture Ministry, in the meantime, had always had close ties to the agrochemical industry, especially the department dealing with pesticides. On December 11, 1997, the Commission Des Toxiques met on the IMD suspension and, noting the contradictions between the beekeepers' claims and Bayer's declaration of safety, they decided that six million francs would be spent to conduct immediate studies to resolve the "conflict." They turned down, however, the request for an immediate suspension of IMD on sunflowers.

The following year, 1998, thus became a time of intense CCD/IMD research in France. The semicontrolled field trials and laboratory tests, carried out by feeding hives various levels of IMD-contaminated syrup, used expensive gas spectrographs to confirm residues less than one part per billion. Results told a safety story quite different than the one given by the manufacturer, who had only studied down to about 50 PPB.

Intoxication from a Flower?

The French researchers got all the way down to less than one part per billion with their detector, and found that as little as a *few parts per billion in the nectar or feed syrup* could make the honey bee groggy, impairing the bee's short-term memory in smell and theoretically blocking normal foraging. IMD is, after all, designed to block an insect's nervous system from operating properly. The French study (Colin, 1998) said it was doing its job all too well, even diluted down to a few parts per billion. It wouldn't kill the bees, but it would disrupt their ability and desire to feed and forage.

In short, the French research claimed that all those female worker bees were getting intoxicated. If so, we could think of IMD-tainted nectar as "bee whiskey." This would certainly be a good explanation of how something could cause the otherwise mysterious CCD. Imagine spiking all the coffee urns in a large corporation with whiskey. Pretty soon all those workers wouldn't be working anymore and making money for the company—they would be smashed on Irish coffee and doing God knows what. Now imagine that the coffee urn get spiked with whiskey day after day. What would happen? The business would stop making money pretty soon, wouldn't it? So the French research says that honey production appears to suffer greatly with sublethal doses of IMD, as foraging ceases and the hive goes into a rapid decline.

From the Genome Project, we know that honey bees have fewer detoxification genes and are more vulnerable to pesticides than other insects. The genome map also told us about the additional learning and memory capability of the honey bee. Could IMD be causing CCD at such a low level, due to the honey bee's genetic weakness to pesticides, diminishing the bee's genetic strength in learning, foraging, and organization?

It all seems to fit—a far more viable theory than viruses, bacteria, or cell phones.

French beekeepers further charged that the use of IMD, and the areas where it was heavily applied, coincided with CCD outbreaks. Every July, when the sunflowers bloomed, the bees started ingesting the contaminated nectar. Colony collapse disorder would appear like clockwork within three or four days.[2] The onset of CCD, said the beekeepers, was now predictable and tied to the flow of nectar in the sunflowers. It was the same thing, year after year. In 1998, when the bloom was two weeks late due to bad weather, the onset of CCD was also two weeks later. The French beekeeper's Web site, from the UNAF, tells of their own experience in the field:

Since 1994 for some, from 1995 or '96 for others, depending on the region, they have witnessed exploitation problems concerning the bees on the sunflower nectar flow: problems of acute hive depopulation and of aberrant behaviour patterns, being accentuated year on year. For them, there is no longer any doubt that these phenomena are linked to the crop flowering period. It requires only 3 or 4 days from the start of the sunflower flowering period to initiate the problems—this taking place at the beginning of July or 15 days later in the case of 1998.

It is the same and unique itinerary every year—and only when the hives are in the areas of crops treated with GAUCHO. Those hives moved beforehand to other areas for such nectar flows produced by sweet chestnut trees, lavender, pine and wild blossom escape totally the forementioned phenomena. The year that GAUCHO is introduced into an area the troubles appear for the first time. The phenomena: Destabilizing the bee colony to the point that it becomes impossible to undertake all normal activities associated with the honey flow.

Was "The Case of the Missing Bees" solved? The more accurate and exacting French research concludes that as little as six parts per billion of IMD was enough to disrupt feeding. A foraging bee in the field, feeding on multiple flowers all day, and also getting the toxin from other sources, could theoretically get the needed sublethal dose. Dr. Colin et al's research showed that the foraging of the hive was then profoundly altered, and that bees on video displayed clear signs of intoxication and grogginess from IMD-tainted crops.

Certainly IMD use would now be suspended—or so the beekeepers and researchers thought. Even with this new data, however, instead of suspending GAUCHO use on sunflowers, the Commission des Toxiques decided it could not resolve the "apparent contradiction" between their own scientists' research and Bayer's claim of safety. So the commission decided to punt—to simply continue trials in 1999. More study was needed, said the commissioners. The French beekeepers were stunned. Despite the data that showed as little as six parts per billion could disrupt foraging, the commission still refused to suspend GAU-CHO. Beekeepers had only one course of action left to them.

TAKIN' IT TO THE STREETS

France is famous for its farmer protests, oftentimes with milk or worse being spilled upon the Parisian roadways. With that model in hand, the beekeepers now organized the first protest parade of their own. Their last chance for an IMD suspension was the Minister of Agriculture himself, Marc Galvany, who had the power to overrule the Commission des Toxiques. So the day before the minister was to decide, 700 members of the beekeeper federation, the UNAF, gathered at the Eiffel Tower. They were supported by large agricultural organizations, including the Con-federation Paysanne and the FNSEA (the Fédération Nationale des Syndicats d'Exploitants Agricoles). "Stop GAUCHO" and "Stop Poisoning Our Bees" read some of the protesters' signs. UNAF President Henri Clément urged the minister in a fiery speech to suspend the use of IMD on sunflowers.

The protest worked. On January 22, 1999, Minister Galvany directed that IMD be suspended for use on sunflowers until further tests could be made, citing the "Principle of Precaution." Prudence dictated that IMD be suspended from use on sunflow-ers until research proved it safe. It was the first time the Prin-ciple of Precaution had been used in an environmental decision to remove a product from market. In this case, the Minister was indeed being wary of the unwritten "Law of Unintended

Consequences," the environmental side-effects sometimes caused by high-impact technologies like powerful agro-chemicals. The ruling said IMD use was still allowed for corn, cereals, and beets, but that it should be temporarily suspended on sunflowers to help "'limit the risks of exposing bees to the potentially detrimental effects of GAUCHO."

Bayer vigorously defended itself. It had spent $150 million developing IMD, and according to annual reports it was selling several hundreds of million of dollars' worth of IMD every year. Its tests showed that IMD was safe. Arguing before the State Council, Bayer sued to have an inquest cancel the decision. Joined by three agricultural unions, the council voted in December 1999 against the giant chemical company, letting Galvany's IMD suspension stand.

Bayer also lost in August 1999 when The Netherlands, following a scientific paper, found that (1) IMD persisted in the soil for too long, thereby violating environmental standards; that (2) small birds eating IMD-painted seeds got a lethal dose; and that (3) honey bee toxicity did not meet the "Uniform Principles," safety policies established in Dutch environmental law.[3] The company then fought to keep its product on the market there too, inundating the Dutch government with a mountain of paper and opinions from university professors on the safety of IMD, claiming "new scientific data." Bayer eventually won the day in the Netherlands through this effort, and imidacloprid is used there to this day.

Further Discoveries about IMD
At the same time, further French research in 1999 and 2000 dug deeper in an attempt to confirm the beekeeper's claim that IMD was the sole cause of CCD behaviors. The studies found that when the seed was painted with IMD, sunflower nectar by itself

could have an unsafe level at only 5 PPB. GAUCHO, moreover, degraded into very persistent IMD "metabolites," and these were even more toxic than the chemical itself. Dr. Marc Colin, of the Institut National de la Recherche Agronomique (INRA): "For Imidacloprid, the effects are always present at 6 PPB. At 3 PPB, the effects are present under certain conditions. The toxicity of the Olefin metabolite is clear at 1.5 PPB: they are still present at 0.75 PPB, but less regular." In another experiment, from October 2000, Dr. M. H. Pham-Delègue of the INRA reported that "prolonged ingestion of syrups contaminated with Imidacloprid induces a significant reduction in olfactory learning performances at levels equal to or above 12 PPB."[4]

Beyond IMD itself, beyond the metabolites, the French turned their attention to a new area: "bioavailability." Due to the trace amounts of IMD in the environment all around them, the little honey bee was getting hit with a multiple whammy. Corn syrup, used by beekeepers around the world as a feed, was now often contaminated with traces of IMD from the painting of seed corn and residues in the soil. Beyond nectar, bees also collect tainted pollen on their legs and bring it back to the hive. Sunflower pollen contained up to 5 PPB IMD by one count. At the same time, as they alight on the sprayed leaves and flowers, any foliar applications of IMD can rub off on the body of the bee and quickly enter the nervous system. Bees also drink IMD-contaminated water in the fields. Then there is the stored honey and pollen itself. In the winter, the hive must eat their stores, and the residues of IMD are found there as well.

During the growing period of sunflowers treated with GAUCHO, the levels of imidacloprid decrease. From the start of the flower head formation, this level shows an important and rapid increase. Depending on the plant variety, the average value in the flower head at the beginning of the flowering period varies from 5 to 6 PPB. Equally in maize (corn), imidacloprid is found throughout the plant, notably in the tassel (average: 4 PPB) and in the ear (average: 10 PPB). Sunflower and corn both create significant bioavailability during the flowering period. In the environment wherever sunflowers are treated with GAUCHO and also whenever it was so for corn, the pollen from traps commonly contained around 5 PPB imidacloprid.

Other French scientists showed that IMD concentrations were very large when a plant is young and growing, with 10 to 20 PPB in upper leaves, 100 to 200 PPB in other leaves, less than 1.5 PPB in nectar, and 2 to 3 PPB in pollen. Bayer had originally said the toxin would only be absorbed by the plant's roots, but the government research showed that the sap circulated IMD all the way up to the flower and nectar. "A Survey of Pesticide Residues in Pollen Loads" made by the Agence Française de Sécurité Sanitaire des Aliments, studied pollen samples from 125 hives in 5 sites around France. IMD or its metabolites were found in 69% of the pollen, with concentrations from 1.1 PPB to 5.7 PPB.[5] The French beekeepers found what they felt to be the best evidence in the research by Dr. Colin et al., who compared videos of conventional bees drunk on IMD and unaffected organic bees. The UNAF summed up the difference: "foraging by bees on sunflowers treated or contaminated with GAUCHO takes place with less efficiency and with behavior very different from bees foraging among sunflowers growing in Organic conditions, on soils that have never received any GAUCHO treatment."

STUDIES FROM BAYER CROPSCIENCE

Bayer CropScience, of course, conducted its own subsequent studies. In 2001, a Bayer CropScience study was led by Dr. Richard Schmuck, who co-authored with Drs. Schoning, Stork, and

Schramel. Their paper was called "Risk posed to honey bees (*Apis mellifera* L, Hymenoptera) by an imidacloprid seed dressing of sunflowers."[6] The experiment, however, a thirty-nine-day feeding experiment in the lab, seems to have little usefulness in confirming or disproving the effects of imidacloprid, which is available from many different sources in the field. The company study concluded that there was no observed effect even at 20 PPB IMD.

Thirty-nine days, however, is a short period and the researchers did not appear to take into account bioavailability in the field, or the increased potency of IMD on a hot summer's day in France, or whether their bees were then eating their honey. Honey increases the potency of IMD, as much of the water from the nectar is evaporated, concentrating the neurotoxin. Their own measurements found no observed effect at 20 PPB, contradicting the French research which repeatedly found intoxication at 3 to 5 PPB.

The Schmuck et al. paper did mention the Kirchner study in 2000, which had found something very interesting, something that may help explain the seeming contradiction between the French and the Bayer CropScience experiments. Kirchner, said the "Risk" paper, found that "At concentrations of 20 PPB, hive bees perceived the contaminant and responded by rejection of that food." Just as hive beetles and wax moths can sense something wrong with hives emptied out by CCD, and do not scavenge them for weeks, bees can smell IMD at levels of 20 PPB and above and then stop eating that food source.

This discovery is very important, for it means that the "Risk" study and previous Bayer CropScience studies may be compromised by the simple fact that the bees sensed the high levels of IMD, then did not eat it vigorously and so did not display any observable effects. You can't get drunk if you spit out the whiskey and never drink it. This could explain why the French bees got intoxicated on smaller sublethal doses, while the

Bayer-study bees remained sober even though offered a more potent brew in the lab. They appear to be able to smell the IMD above 20 PPB and then reject it, which would clearly skew results for that level or higher. Drs. Colin's and Bonmatin's bees, sensing nothing at a few parts per billion, drank heartily—and their ability to forage was diminished or deactivated. What this means is that, when this phenomenon is taken into account, there may actually not be any contradiction between the Bayer studies and the French research. Bayer CropScience tried to settle the matter by researching higher-level doses, but it's likely those unwittingly tipped the bees off that the feed source was contaminated, and that would have thus tended to show there was little or no effect. Since this rejection factor was not taken into account by the Bayer scientists, along with other important considerations, said Dr. Colin in an e-mail for this book, their results do not necessarily contradict his own—but they do not prove IMD's safety to bees.

The "Risk" study was nevertheless touted by Bayer as providing evidence against the French research, and used by the company to argue against new restrictions on the toxin. The study, however, used technical grounds to dismiss the earlier French research that found disorientation and the disruption of foraging activity. It should be noted that the "Risk" paper in 2003 was published several months before the extensive Comité Scientifique et Technique report, which showed that IMD was available in great enough quantities to disrupt foraging.

Although Bayer CropScience managed to overturn the threat of a Dutch ban, the French minister continued the suspension of GAUCHO in 2000. Gerard Eyries, the marketing manager for Bayer's agricultural division in France, complained. Disputing that IMD was dangerous to bees, he did admit that a small residue was in the nectar and pollen. "It is impossible to have zero residue. What is important is to know whether the very tiny quantities which have been found have a negative effect on bees." Eyries then stated there had been no side effects reported in the seventy nations IMD was sold in.

THIS STUFF JUST DOESN'T GO AWAY

Another issue arose around persistence of IMD in the soil. Even on a field where IMD was no longer being used, the chemical and its metabolites apparently persist for several years. And picogram for picogram, the metabolites were even more potent than the original chemical (a picogram is a billionth of a gram). From the French beekeeper Web site on the experiments of Dr. J. M. Bonmatin of the Centre National de la Recherche Scientifique: "Even in the case of only one 'GAUCHO' treatment two years previous imidacloprid is still detectable in the soil. He . . . concludes that sunflowers are capable of absorbing and expressing the presence of residual imidacloprid from crops treated two years previously with GAUCHO."

Bayer's own studies actually do not disagree on this point.

Bayer's soil retention research by Dr. Hans-Jorg Vogel of the Centre of Environmental Research at Halle-Leipzig found that IMD was far more persistent than advertised, that 56% of the compound was still in the soil at day 412. That meant that large quantities of IMD would be absorbed by subsequent crops planted in that field. In fact, Bayer emphasizes that crops should be rotated so that successive plantings using IMD-painted seeds or soil drenches not follow one another. The flowers of any crop that grow the following year could express tiny amounts of IMD in their pollen and nectar, as the neurotoxin is systemic and tends to travel from the soil to the roots and up through all the cells of the plant. The industry group on insect resistance, in fact, urges growers to use integrated pest management, chemical rotation, and limit their use of IMD to prevent rapid pest resistance.[7]

IMD is used nearly everywhere. It is sold for sod insects in lawns and golf courses, for termite control, for field crops, for fruit trees, for termites, for ornamental and forest trees, for ant control in lawns, for flea control in animals. We have no idea of the number of pathways still undiscovered in France and Europe for residues of imidacloprid and its metabolites that might yet threaten the honey bees and other organisms in the environment. The fact that the chemical is so persistent compounds the problem for each succeeding year.

In short, this stuff just doesn't go away. It could stay in the soil for years, and thus in plants. Sunflowers and corn, in particular, absorb the old IMD from the soil and then their pollen and nectar can become contaminated. According to the French research, one could stop using IMD, and the residual amounts would be enough to affect bee behavior for the next couple of years or so, depending on soil, sun, and weather. If you spray or drench the soil season after season, IMD can actually accumulate in the ground, especially in times of drought.

When one takes into account all the different ways the bees are ingesting or coming into contact with the neurotoxin, the French researchers say IMD was clearly present at high enough levels to cause memory loss in the bees and disrupt foraging behavior.

"WE ARE ON AN EARTH SHIP OF FOOLS"

Despite all the new research of 1999 and 2000 linking IMD with colony collapse-type behavior, and the conclusions of Drs. Colin and Bonmatin, the Commission des Toxiques still did not appear ready to suspend IMD use on sunflowers. The beekeepers were incensed. Honey production was now worse than ever. Older beekeepers were retiring in large numbers, and the UNAF worried that the whole industry would collapse, leaving much of French agriculture to whatever native bees remained. The profession they loved was on the line. So the beekeepers went back to Paris en masse for the December 2000 meeting of the commission.

They were not about to take "No" for an answer.

On December 18, 2000, three thousand angry beekeepers swarmed into the French capital, noisily marching to the meeting of the Commission des Toxiques. Some of the signs read "The Death of Bee-Keeping!" "Idiots!!" and "We Are on an Earth Ship of Fools." Henri Clément gave his usual fiery and eloquent speech. Once again, however, the commission, with close ties to the chemical industry, refused to act. The Agriculture Minister Galvany, who depended on the goodwill of the farmer unions, voted with the beekeepers, extending the suspension on IMD on sunflowers for three years.

With some victories under their belt, the French beekeepers were suddenly starting to feel better and better about the future. But would the restriction on IMD work? Would the bees come back?

Seven

The Return of the Bees!

The poisoning of the bees, the abnormal behavior and the collapse of the honey harvests that we saw between 1996 and 2004 have been reversed this summer. . . .
—Henri Clément, President of the National Union of French Apiculture, October 2005

After IMD use was suspended on sunflowers for a couple of years, did the bees immediately come back in France in 2003 and 2004? No. Colony collapse disorder continued and even worsened in the first years of the new millennium. Bayer CropScience began touting the still-missing French bees as proof that IMD could not possibly be the culprit. Yet the beekeepers countered that another insecticide, Regent—containing fipronil—had replaced IMD for sunflower and corn treatment. They also shot back that IMD itself stayed in the soil and was still being applied to many other crops besides sunflowers, including corn.

What is fipronil? Made primarily of carbon, nitrogen, and chlorine, fipronil is another chlorinated hydrocarbon that blocks part of an insect's nervous system, in this case disrupting the passage of chloride ions through the GABA receptor and the glutamate receptor. These receptors normally inhibit the nervous system, keeping it in balance, so when they are disrupted the nerves fire haphazardly. Fipronil thus causes "hyperexcitation," leading to trembling, motor problems, and death. In sublethal doses, however, it apparently intoxicates the bees even more effectively than IMD. The beekeepers charged that while the bees may no longer have been getting inebriated on sublethal doses of IMD, they were now getting drunk on sublethal doses of fipronil. If true, it would be like giving up whiskey for gin.

Fipronil is the active ingredient in Regent, sold by BASF. Like IMD, it can be used on field corn, as a soil drench, sprayed on leaves—or it can be painted on seeds. In May 2003, the French Agriculture Ministry reported a case of bee mortality due to fipronil use in southern France. It appeared that toxic dust was generated from defective seed treatments—so the beekeepers now demanded that fipronil be suspended for corn and sunflowers as well.

IMD Is a "Significant Risk" at Just a Few Parts per Billion

On September 18, 2003, a long-awaited 108-page report detailing the effects of IMD on honey bees was finally released by the Comité Scientifique et Technique (CST). Conducting the research were the Universities of Caen and Metz, as well as the Institut Pasteur. This is the extensive research which the beekeepers and some scientists say links IMD to what would become known as colony collapse disorder, confirming the earlier behavior findings that implicated the neurotoxin imidacloprid.

The summary of the report on the issue of sunflowers was clear: "The treatment of seeds by GAUCHO is a significant risk to bees in several stages of life." Since the bees had not returned after the suspension on sunflowers in 1999, the beekeepers had asked that the scientists also study the effects of IMD from corn pollen gathered by the colony. Here again, the evidence showed that IMD-painted corn seeds were just as dangerous as sunflowers: "Concerning the treatment of maize-seeds by GAUCHO, the results are as alarming as with sunflowers. The consumption of contaminated pollen can lead to an increased mortality of caretaking-bees, which can explain the persisting bee-deaths even after the ban of the treatment on sunflowers."[1]

As we saw before, the caretaking or nurse bees are essential to the health of the hive; without them the colony quickly succumbs to various infestations and pathogens. They are like bee doctors and nurses, and—as the bee genome data showed—they make up for the honey bee's genetic weaknesses in immunity and detoxification. Not enough nurse bees, and hive immunity to mites, viruses, and bacteria is compromised. With this new Comité Scientifique et Technique report in hand, the 50,000 beekeepers of the UNAF immediately demanded a complete suspension of the toxin.

THE BEES STILL GO MISSING

All through 2003 the missing bees did not come back. Maurice Mary, a spokesman for UNAF, explained that despite the suspension for the chemical on sunflowers, the bees have not returned due to the prolonged retention of IMD by the French soil. "Since the first application of GAUCHO (IMD) we have had great losses in the harvest of sunflower-honey. Since the agent is staying in the soil up to three years, even untreated plants can contain a concentration which is lethal for bees." The drought France was experiencing at the time no doubt increased the persistence of IMD and its metabolites in the soil, for it is rain that eventually leaches the chemical away, and helps the sun and soil degrade the toxin.

Then there was the fipronil in Regent, which now appeared

to have the similar neurological effects as IMD. Desperate bee-keepers posted this plea on their Web site: "The suspension of 'GAUCHO' on sunflowers during the last two years has allowed a more recent molecule to establish itself into the market: 'Fipronil.' . . . Beekeepers have observed that where sunflowers are treated with 'Regent,' bees become ill once the sunflowers start to flower and produce nectar."

In 2004, it was once again up to France's Minister of Agriculture. On February 23, 2004, Hervé Gaymard, the new head of the ministry, reluctantly extended the suspension on GAUCHO, expanding it to corn—and he also suspended use of fipronil. Finally, it appeared to the beekeepers that they might have a chance to fend off Bayer CropScience and BASF, the makers of fipronil.

Then it happened.

A Local Magistrate Investigates Bayer and BASF for "Loss of Livestock"

The controversy broke in the March 4, 2004 *Le Monde* with the headline: "Insecticide Ban as Billions of Bees Die." *Le Monde* stated that Agriculture Minister Gaymard had suspended several fipronil products beyond Regent, although farmers and whole-salers were allowed to use up current stock.

Le Monde further explained that Bayer and BASF were being investigated by a magistrate in southwest France over fipronil and GAUCHO—that the chemicals actually lacked the proper authorization for such widespread use. An investigating magistrate in France is similar to a grand jury investigation in the United States. Serial "Temporary Sales Authorizations" had been given by the Commission des Toxiques, said the judge of Saint-Gauden, regulatory loopholes which did not require the rigorous tests of a "Marketing Authorization." The chemical companies and the state bureaucracy had used a temporary emergency authorization tactic that we shall see again in the U.S., the U.K., and elsewhere. Bayer and BASF had taken advantage of a gray area in the regulatory process, which they claimed was perfectly legal, yet that the magistrate found improper. So on February 23, 2004, the judge in Saint-Gaudens decided to investigate Bayer and BASF for "the sale of a toxic product harmful to the health of human beings and animals," "complicity in the destruction of livestock," and "the marketing of a product without authorisation."

Le Monde reported the argument of Jean-François Narbonne, a professor at Bordeaux University and an expert on food safety: "until 2003 the product had benefited from an official classification that did not reflect its true level of toxicity. . . . It would seem that since coming on to the market in 1996 the product has received a series of renewed temporary sales authorisations, rather than a marketing authorisation that requires a more rigorous procedure." Bayer and BASF were thus spared the usual safety tests required for such toxic chemicals, and livestock—in this case the bees—were claimed to have been destroyed as a result. The documents taken by the investigating magistrate from the offices of Bayer, BASF, and the Commission des Toxiques clearly showed how the agency had given the chemical companies the temporary authorizations instead of the full marketing approval.

The judge of little Saint-Gaudens felt he had the giant multinationals dead to rights. Bayer's lawyers retaliated, however, with a request to investigate the magistrate himself on the grounds of "legitimate suspicion," which helped to delay the court case. Then a lawyer's strike caused further delays. Evidence was finally turned over to the prosecutors in December 2007, with a trial scheduled probably in early spring of 2008.

BAYER CROPSCIENCE LOSES
A COURT BATTLE

In April 2004, Bayer CropScience lost in court when the company sued Henri Clément, the president of the French beekeepers, in a personal court action—charging he had defamed their products. Bayer CropScience claimed that Clément personally was disparaging a good product and costing them revenue. Citing the 2003 Comité Scientifique et Technique report that linked low doses of IMD to the disorientation and the disruption of foraging, and objecting that he was being sued as an individual in an attempt to intimidate him, Clément defended himself against the substantial legal team of the giant multinational.

In a crowded courtroom, Clément thundered that Bayer's IMD did indeed harm the bees, through intoxication and the poisoning of the hive. Repeating the government research that concluded that IMD was a significant risk even in trace amounts of just a few parts per billion, he charged that Bayer CropScience was responsible for the decline of French beekeeping. Incensed Bayer would sue him as a person, Clément threatened to bring in the powerful Fédération Nationale des Syndicats d'Exploitants Agricoles or FNSEA, the French Farmers' Union. The court quickly threw out the defamation case against Clément, and Bayer was forced to pay his attorney fees of 5,000 francs, as well as 5,000 francs each to cover the costs for the UNAF and the French farmer's association, which had supported Clément.[2]

AN EXACTING FRENCH STUDY: BEES, IMD,
AND FIPRONIL

While all this controversy was going on, six French scientists, Dr. Marc Colin of the University of Montpellier, Drs. Bonmatin and Moineau of the University of Orléans, and Drs. C. Gaimon, S.

73

Brun and J. P. Vermandere of the Institut National de la Recherche Agronomique at the University of Avignon, conducted an experiment with bees, fipronil and IMD. The title of the study was "A Method to Quantify and Analyze the Foraging Activity of Honey Bees: Relevance to the Sublethal Effects Induced by Systematic Insecticides" and was published in the *Archives of Environmental Contamination and Toxicology* in September 2004. Placing small bee colonies in screened-in "tunnels" that were 8 meters wide and 10 meters long, the researchers observed two behaviors: bee attendance at a feeder and bee inactivity, where the workers arrive at the feeder but do not sip the syrup.

While the control colonies did not show any abnormal behavior, two out of three colonies fed 6 PPB IMD attended the feeder, but many by day four were not taking the syrup. Meanwhile, colonies fed fipronil at just 2 PPB had collapsed feeder attendance, and then almost no attendance by the fifth day. Such a result appears to correlate with the advertised effects of IMD and fipronil, that both insecticides are designed to reduce the desire to eat. In addition, the bees in the test colonies displayed clear signs of intoxication while the control bees exhibited none. The entire experiment was videotaped.

What the researchers were trying to prove was that the study of risk to bees needs to expand beyond the large lethal doses, and focus on the equally significant risk from tiny, sub-lethal doses. On the first two days of feeding, both the control hives and the IMD hives fed at about the same equal rate. IMD nucleus A then collapsed from an average of about 60–75 bees per observation being active at the feeder down to 40 bees per observation by the fifth day. IMD nucleus B collapsed from a high of approximately 110 to a low of 60, with the range falling from over 100 to just under 80 by the fifth day. IMD nucleus C, however, showed only a slight decline. The control hives meanwhile had a regular slight decline over the five days, just several bees per observation lower on the fifth day.

The conclusion was that, over five days, a sub-lethal dose of just 6 PPB IMD or 2 PPB fipronil was enough to disrupt feeding. "The quantitative effects of imidacloprid and fipronil were linked to a global disturbance in the main task of the colony, i.e., feeding activity. Investigation of toxic effects is not limited to counting dead adult bees but instead deals with sublethal effects on feeding and, consequently, on the food supply of the colony, both of which affect its long-term survival. Such sublethal effects induced by systemic insecticides should be considered in risk assessment schemes when considering beneficial insects such as honey bees."[3]

THE STRUGGLE WITH BAYER CROPSCIENCE AND BASF IN OTHER NATIONS

The battle over the bees now turned to other countries. Back in December 2003, a group in Germany, named the Coalition Against Bayer-Dangers, cited the French Comité Scientifique et Technique report on IMD, calling for a complete ban on GAUCHO in Germany and throughout Europe. The organization pointed out "The report on bee-deaths, published by the French Comité Scientifique et Technique (CST), shows that the use of the pesticide GAUCHO (IMD) is jointly responsible for the death of hundreds of thousands colonies of bees. Environmental and beekeeper unions are calling for a ban on the agricultural toxin."

The Coalition Against Bayer-Dangers went on to accuse Bayer and the top bee institutes—and the scientists it hires to look at CCD—of using mites as a smoke screen, to avoid researching IMD's safety further. To this day, the Coalition Against Bayer-Dangers believes the industry supporters are using the mite theory as an "excuse," as they state in this December 2003 press release: "The thesis, as stated by bee institutes, that infestation by varroa mites would be responsible of the bee-deaths, appears to be an excuse according to Fridolin Brandt of the Coalition against Bayer-Dangers: 'We are concerned with varroa-mites since 1977, and for decades they haven't been a danger. It is the extensive use of pesticides and the accompanying weakening of the bees which is leading to the bee-deaths.' Brandt has been a full-time beekeeper for more than 30 years."

In the summer of 2004, beekeepers and environmental organizations began to demand that IMD be totally banned by Germany. A new press release accused Bayer of thinking only of its profit and ignoring evidence that IMD affects the bees. "German apiarists and environmental groups have demanded an interim prohibition of the pesticide GAUCHO as well as further remedies containing the active agent imidacloprid in Germany. Imidacloprid is under serious suspicion of being responsible for the death of bee-populations in vast parts of Europe. The Association of German Professional Apiarists (DBIB), the Naturschutzbund (NABU) and the Coalition against Bayer-Dangers appealed to the Federal minister for consumers Kuenast to withdraw the pesticide's permission unless all actual data can be fully verified."

Despite the plea from environmentalists and beekeepers, as well as the French research on IMD, Germany turned down the request for the IMD ban, voting for the company studies showing safety over the French studies showing a hazard. It was beginning to look like IMD use would not be suspended in the rest of Europe.

THE BIG QUESTION: WOULD THE FRENCH BEES RETURN IN 2005?

Meanwhile, back in France, farmers were being allowed to use up the stocks of fipronil they had already purchased, up until June

2004. The chemical was therefore still used in France in 2004 on many, many fields.

The big question then confronted one and all. IMD in the form of the GAUCHO product had been suspended for sunflowers and corn, and would have leached away to a large degree by the winter of 2004–05, leaving far less residue than before. And the last of the fipronil was used on those crops in June 2004. Bayer had repeatedly claimed that IMD could not be responsible for the missing bees, as IMD had been suspended since 1999—yet the honey bees never returned. If Bayer was right, the colonies would continue to collapse, for IMD and fipronil were in their eyes innocent. Bayer had always maintained that the cause was not man-made and recommended research for some kind of new bacteria or virus to explain CCD.

It was the critical point for both beekeepers and the agrochemical industry. Now that both IMD and fipronil were finally suspended for sunflowers and corn, would the bees come back in spring 2005? Would hive collapse reports drop dramatically and hives appear healthy again? Or would the colony deaths continue unabated, thereby suggesting that a different cause might be at work?

"BEE-COLONIES HAVE REGAINED THE VIGOR THEY ENJOYED"

On October 7 and 8, 2005, the long-awaited beekeepers' conference in the "Test Year of 2005" finally arrived and President Henri Clément addressed the UNAF:

2005 is a crucial year for beekeepers. For the first time, the two disputed insecticides have been banned for use on fields of maize, oilseed rape, and sunflowers. Their use has been progressively suspended as a result of victories won by beekeepers during a long legal battle. A govern-

*ment moratorium forbade the use of 'GAUCHO' on sun-
flower seeds from 1999 and from 2004 on maize. The use
of 'Regent' has been suspended on all crops since 2004.*[4]

Then the big news—the bees were coming back! To the
beekeepers, this was the ultimate proof positive that IMD and
fipronil were the cause of what would later be known as colony
collapse disorder. The reports from the field seemed unequivocal.
The decrease in the bee population was "reversed this summer."

It should be noted that although some regions did not return
in 2005, this was due, said the UNAF, to the extra persistence
of IMD and fipronil in drought conditions. But UNAF President
Clément was optimistic: "For the first time in a dozen years, the
honey-harvest has improved in certain regions of France."

Despite some areas not having yet bounced back, Henri Clément proclaimed that the "reward" of the struggle to ban GAU-
CHO and Regent was the "net improvement of the stocks of
bees." Not only were the bees coming back, said the beekeeper
president, they were coming back strong. Clément spoke of
"strong and vigorous colonies" and he confirmed that southwest
France enjoyed a very good honey harvest indeed. He proudly
revealed the good news: "Since the ban, we have found that bee-
colonies have regained the vigor they enjoyed before imidacloprid and fipronil were allowed." As for the areas where CCD still
continues, the IMD update notes: "The long-term persistence of
imidacloprid and fipronil in soils where the pesticides were used
freely over a number of years, is the cause of continuing bee-
losses even after the ban, according to beekeepers. In addition,
'GAUCHO' is still allowed for use on cereal crops such as wheat,
barley and oats."

In 2006, French keepers in the southwest reported that the
massive depopulation of their colonies had ceased. The bees had

truly returned in those areas, showing that 2005 was not a fluke. In other regions, drought and the continued persistence of IMD and fipronil metabolites naturally kept hives at low production, said the UNAF. With extremely dry conditions, there are far fewer flowers to feed on, and bees themselves need water. France, and much of Europe, was at the time in the grip of a historic drought accompanied by record summer heat.

Despite the drought and residual toxins, Loïc Leray, a bee-keeper and president of the UNAF in the Loire-Atlantic region, was happy to note in UNAF's *2006 Media Kit* that bee behavior was starting to return to normal in 2005 and he was able to get some honey from the hive: "In spite of the drought, I have nevertheless made 50 kg with the hive, which corresponds to a half of normal harvest and it is already satisfactory! But what it is important to note . . . is the clear improvement of the behavior of the bees: usually, during the summer, they prevented the individuals who appeared ill to enter the hive. This behavior was not seen much this summer."[5]

Due to a series of record multiyear droughts, continued use of IMD on cereal crops, and many amateur beekeepers either giving up or retiring despite the comeback of the bee, French honey production fell and then leveled out, and the country was forced to import 20,000 tons in 2006 to meet the market demand. The heat was so bad in 2003 that 35,000 people died in Europe that year from heat stroke. Then the drought got worse. From 2004 to 2006, the dryness simply increased, and the crops in the affected regions withered. In July 2006, forty people in France died directly from the heat, the second warmest month on record after the deadly August of 2003. The problem continued into 2007, with water rationing in seven out of ninety-six departments (the French word for counties). If people were dying from the heat, along with whole regions of crops, one can understand why the bees still were having a tough time in most of France during those years. Honey production slipped from 20,000 metric tons in 2005 and 2006 to 18,000 tons in 2007 (UNAF press release).

The evidence pointing to IMD as the prime suspect behind CCD continued to accumulate. In 2006, the Agriculture Ministry assured the UNAF that no new insecticides would be approved for the coming year. And following the completion of the bee genome in October 2006, a researcher at the INRA in France, Bernard Vaissiere, said the genetic map revealed why IMD might be so potent for the honey bee. "The honey bee has less genes for detoxification than other species of insects. [This] explains and confirms their sensitivity to pesticides." Vaissiere also noted that by feeding exclusively on nectar and pollen, which are rarely toxic in nature, bee digestion never had to evolve defenses against poisons. To sum up, the French researchers Drs. Colin and Bonmatin et al. say that under the right conditions, tiny, sublethal doses of IMD will cause colony collapse—type behaviors, disrupting foraging and causing intoxication. And in 2005, after suspension of IMD and fipronil on corn and sunflowers, the French bees did indeed begin their comeback, demonstrating that until IMD and fipronil are proved safe, suspending their use is the prudent thing to do. For the most part, the UNAF says that 2006 and 2007 have since enjoyed normal bee populations in areas that are not in extreme drought, showing that the resurgence of the French honey bee was not an aberration.

Today, the French beekeepers continue the fight, as Bayer attempts to introduce new systemic insecticides to replace IMD, including "PONCHO" and thiamethoxam, and IMD itself as it continues to be used in some crops. When this book went to press, the magistrate of Saint-Gauden had just turned his evidence over to the prosecutors, and the trial against Bayer, BASF, and their CEOs was, after four long years, due to begin.

BAYER, BASF, AND THE EU COMMISSIONS
IGNORE THE COMEBACK OF THE BEES

The battle over IMD, however, does not end here. Despite the fact that the French bees came back strong, and in the year they were expected to—Bayer and BASF did not relent. The striking comeback in France was simply not accepted, and pro-Bayer data was allowed to dominate German and EU appeals over IMD. Other European nations, which had never banned IMD or fipronil, then started to suffer their own losses from colony collapse disorder. Spain, Italy, Germany, and the Netherlands all reported colony collapse disorder in the last few years—and all had allowed heavy use of IMD and/or fipronil on numerous crops. Beekeepers, consumers, and environmentalists thus joined together in an even wider coalition to beseech the European Union to suspend the use of imidacloprid, fipronil, and other similar chemicals such as thiamethoxam and clothianidin, pending detailed studies.

The coalition charged that these chemicals violated the EU directive for bees, specifically the Hazard Quotient for bees. A November 2006 letter, sent to Markos Krypianou, the EU Commissioner of Health and Consumer Protection, was signed by the beekeeper associations of Great Britain, Italy, Belgium, Germany, Luxembourg, Spain, Hungary, and of course France (see Appendix 2 Beekeeper Letter to EU Commissioner for the entire letter).

The IMD theory as to why the bees die is thus quite well known in Europe, and a ban on IMD, fipronil, thiamethoxam, and clothianidin is at this time still being requested of the European Union. How could the chemical companies possibly stop the beekeepers and environmentalists from succeeding in a ban of their products after all the French history? The IMD opponents claim there has been a "disinformation" campaign. Just as

Big Oil funds scientists and lobbyists to advance questionable theories about whether fossil fuel is responsible for global warming to create uncertainty, the agrochemical industry is charged by beekeepers as having done the same with CCD. Beekeepers and environmentalists accuse Bayer, BASF, and numerous scientists from universities worldwide of trying to confuse the issue by first ignoring or disqualifying the damning evidence on insecticides, then introducing other "theories" on mites or viruses, so that more study is needed.

The October 2005 update from the UNAF states that "The industry denies any link between their products and the damage suffered by bees." It quotes Jean-Marc Petat, director of the environment department at BASF, as saying, "The theory that there is a sole explanation does not hold. . . . We would like an independent expert opinion, scientists need to resolve the matter."[6] "Scientists need to resolve the matter" is just a talking point, say the beekeepers and environmentalists. To them, it is the only way for the industry to stall the process, as they say the actual data from a properly designed experiment is showing IMD to be the prime suspect behind colony collapse disorder.

The IMD opponents believed that all the other theories are simply made to muddy the waters, so that no ban is ever enacted, allowing Bayer and BASF to continue receiving their huge income streams. "The industry puts forward other hypotheses: the weather, lack of available food to the bees due to crop-monoculture, bee-diseases, bad practice on the part of the bee-keeper." To the beekeepers, entomologists and toxicologists at many universities were acting to protect the corporate donors, who provide many of the research grants and laboratories they depend on. European beekeepers, nevertheless, welcomed the challenge for more research and, with consumer and environmental organizations, asked for more tests from the European Union.

COLONY COLLAPSE DISORDER IN ENGLAND?

It has been reported—although there is no full survey—that CCD has destroyed about 12% of hives in the U.K. The government, however, still denies that there is CCD in England, yet some beekeepers there are reporting 50% to 75% losses to CCD, with a third of all members of the London Beekeepers Association losing 100% of their hives. In 2007, the *Guardian* reported: "Government bee inspectors met yesterday, but Mike Brown, head of the national bee unit based in York, reported no signs of CCD in Britain. 'There is no evidence in the U.K. right now of colony collapse disorder,' he said in a statement. 'The majority of inspectors said that they can put the current mortalities in honey bee populations around the U.K. down to varroa or varroasis.'"

If there is CCD in the U.K., is there also a link to IMD? It appears so. In 2004, IMD seed dressings were used in the U.K. on 114,948 hectares of sugar beets, while IMD mixtures were applied to 341,157 hectares of oilseed rape, 25,099 hectares of linseed, and 242,999 hectares of cereals.[7] That's more than 1.5 million acres. If IMD is the culprit, that would appear to be enough IMD-applied acres to cause widespread colony collapse disorder in England, especially when ornamental, lawn, and golf course use is added in.

CANADA DENIES IT HAS COLONY COLLAPSE DISORDER AS WELL

Meanwhile, in Canada, government officials have consistently denied there is colony collapse disorder, yet British Columbia beekeeper Jean Marc Le Dorze believes IMD caused some CCD in his 1,200 hives. His colonies were doing fine, with only a 5% to 7% winter die-off rate when suddenly, after pollinating blueberries in the Fraser Valley, he suffered the loss of thirty hives. They had what appeared to be all the symptoms of colony collapse disorder. Le Dorze said, "The adults weren't there. Kind of like that CCD thing—large, broad, sudden, unexplained die-off of adults. That's a telltale sign of CCD."[8]

Also in British Columbia, Planet Bee owner Ed Nowek lost 70% to 75% of his colonies since the summer of 2006, from 12 million bees down to 1 million. "It was unusual. The bees were just gone." He, too, pollinated blueberries in the Fraser Valley. His pattern of loss clearly fits CCD. Nowek nevertheless claims that varroa mites and drought were to blame. He is also the president of the Canadian Honey Council, an organization that says there is no colony collapse disorder in Canada. So many bees have died in Canada recently, however, that the provinces of Ontario and Manitoba have instituted a program to bail out the beekeepers, paying them around $100 for every lost hive. This has allowed the apiaries to stay in business. In the face of apparent CCD losses by the English and Canadian beekeepers, why would these governments risk their credibility by flat-out denying that colony collapse disorder exists in their countries? Are they so close to the chemical companies that they cannot even admit the problem has entered their shores? Is it trade issues? Politics? Do they deny the reports? Do they deny the science? Perhaps there is something deeper going on here.

WE SHOULD HAVE LISTENED
TO RACHEL CARSON

In 1962, Rachel Carson faced great opposition from the chemical industry when *Silent Spring* declared that the insecticide DDT was killing not only the songbirds, but people as well. She was derided as a hysterical woman by industry spokespersons. Carson's sanity was actually questioned, and her argument spun out of all proportion. "If man were to faithfully follow the teachings of Miss Carson," said one American Cyanimid executive at the time, "we would return to the Dark Ages, and the insects and diseases and vermin would once again inherit the earth."

The amazing thing is that forty-five years later, little has changed—and in some ways it's worse. We still don't know how to avoid such disasters. Or perhaps we do—but the current Establishment and power structure are too close to the chemical industry, and generally do its bidding. According to environmental groups like the Sierra Club and the Natural Resources Defense Council, there was never enough scrutiny and testing after DDT was banned, and they charge that the industry has recently been given a relatively free ride by regulators, allowing temporary sales authorizations without the usual rigorous safety tests. The neurotoxicity testing insisted on by Rachel Carson, for example, was only recently instituted after court action.

Being an environmentalist and heeding the Law of Unintended Consequences, Carson also argued that pesticides be replaced wherever possible with biological controls, using predatory insects designed by Mother Nature to feed on or destroy specific insect pests naturally. The chemical companies' revenue base, however, is threatened if too much of the marketplace turns from insecticides to organic methods. Environmental organizations say any information generated by chemical companies or their allies must therefore be taken with a grain of salt and examined carefully due to this basic conflict of interest. Most ecologists call for the reexamination of pesticides in general and believe that there should be a wholesale move to organic farming and turf management. There is a mountain of evidence showing that organic methods, including biological controls, are successful in controlling insect pests, as seen by burgeoning organic food production.

And that brings up the mysterious cases of Australia and New Zealand.

AUSTRALIA AND NEW ZEALAND HAVE NO CCD—WHY?

Australia and New Zealand do not have any reports of colony collapse disorder, and the beekeepers in those countries confirm this. Logic would say that this is an important clue. Although IMD is registered in those nations, there are some telling differences in how it is handled. A strict biosecurity program has, first of all, attempted to keep out known crop pests like aphids, as well as pathogens and organisms that would threaten hives Down Under. So there are fewer pests, especially aphids, than there are in the U.S., Canada, and Europe. Plus rather than conventional "spray in the early spring" management, Agriculture Ministries in both Australia and New Zealand stress Integrated Pest Management (IPM), a mixed form of farming that relies on biological controls and applies pesticide only when bug or weed counts demand it.

Lacewing flies, whose larvae are nicknamed the "aphid lion," are used to control the aphids. The Lands Down Under are blessed in that two species of lacewings are native and widespread, with one being a warm weather lover and the other liking things a little bit colder. Large IPM programs using lacewings have been underway for several years and are being implemented by some of the largest growers of lettuce and soybeans.[9] In addition, Australia has the largest organic soybean farms in the world, and they never did use insecticides like IMD. In fact, they must nurture or buy their lacewings to control aphids, so they must be *adding to the lacewing population*.

Besides having fewer aphids, plentiful lacewings, IPM programs, and therefore less use of IMD, Australia and New Zealand have instituted a very careful terms-of-use legal system with their farmers. Like all other insecticides, IMD is alternated with not only biological controls like the lacewings, but also the use of other toxins. This is done so the pests don't develop a resistance as quickly as they might when the same insecticide is used in many consecutive applications.

On top of that, the Australian and New Zealand governments test food products for IMD residues, and these show very low levels, if any. There is thus far more caution in using IMD, and other pesticides as well. If IMD truly is the prime suspect, Australia and New Zealand would serve as models to immediately follow.

WHAT DOES ALL THIS REALLY TELL US?

The story of IMD and the bees, and the French beekeepers' fight against Bayer and BASF, reveals far more than a lesson in apiculture and proper insecticide use; it means that there is an industry in dire need of reform. Stepping back and looking at the big picture, it seems to expose the deeper nature of the issue, for it shows how far the agrochemical industry will go to protect itself and its paradigm. It seems similar to the global warming debate, where Big Oil has gone all-out to defend the argument that says global warming is not man-made, but rather is caused by increased solar radiation, natural cyclic warming, or is not occurring at all.

The fight over IMD does not seem to be about "new scientific data" that "scientists need to resolve this matter." It appears the agrochemists are defending not just a product but their entire worldview. The beekeepers say the science already appears resolved with the duplicated studies by the French and that the scientific data in the Comité Scientifique et Technique report confirms what the beekeepers were charging. There is even video of the bees intoxicated on IMD. The fight by Bayer and BASF, and the establishment supporting them, rather seems to be about protecting a paradigm that is being challenged by environmentalists and beekeepers alike. Beyond the hundreds of millions of dollars that were invested in IMD and fipronil, and the millions these companies make in annual revenue, what matters in the end seems to be a defense of the rationale for the pesticide industry to even exist.

Thomas Kuhn, who wrote *The Structure of Scientific Revolutions*, and made popular the term "paradigm shift," said these revolutions in thought are actually ideological struggles rather than reasoned scientific debates. Any person naturally defends the paradigm he or she was taught, the worldview in which they feel most invested. In fact, people are typically not even aware of their paradigm, any more than a fish is aware of the ocean around it. A paradigm, like the ocean to a fish, simply is—there can be no thought of it not existing, of it not being the universe in which you live and think. The limitations of the scientific model therefore become the unconscious boundaries of how people in an era think. Exposing the old paradigm as false can thus come as a true shock to its believers and may be resisted very strongly.

If IMD is proven to cause CCD, the whole notion that chemicals are safe to spread everywhere is directly challenged in a highly visible manner. Scientists and professors supporting agrochemistry have invested their entire lives and their educational careers in using toxic insecticides to combat agricultural pests, and could subconsciously or consciously feel all of that threatened. This vested interest quickly turns the debate over pesticides and the bees into an ideological battle, rather than a rational discussion over scientific data.

Kuhn shows how paradigm shifts are really more like religious struggles with opposing doctrines than reasoned theorizing based on scientific evidence. Evidence and data have little to do with it, said Kuhn. People are defending lives devoted to a set of beliefs, scientific dogma they will take with them to the grave. Kuhn cites a Catholic theologian who, when asked by Galileo to view the moons of Jupiter through a telescope, refused on the grounds it could be an optical trick. Yet that was simply a poor excuse, to avoid seeing with his own eyes the proof positive: that smaller bodies circled larger ones, meaning the Earth revolved around the sun, rather than the other way around.

Could this "paradigm reluctance" be at play today in the controversy over IMD? Bayer CropScience researchers, along with most agrochemists in the governments and universities, are seeing the world through the eyes of the old paradigm, as it was before the new worldview of ecology came along. In this view, the Earth itself is an inanimate object, rather than the fragile, living ecosystem that modern ecologists know. The unintended consequences that chemicals unleash upon the interconnected biosphere are for the most part ignored, instead of being accepted as an inconvenient truth. That's why the Principle of Precaution seems unecessary to many entomologists and toxicologists. It's outside the limits of the old thinking. Rachel Carson said the "myopic vision" of many entomologists and toxicologists justifies the increasing use of highly poisonous chemicals.

As Kuhn would no doubt point out, if he were here to interject, agrochemists of the older worldview don't want to think about what ecology and the fragile nature of the environment really signify, because it means their underlying scientific model is not entirely correct. And that in turn means the old paradigm is a clear hazard to the future, an idea whose time has gone. According to Kuhn, the struggle between environmentalists and agrochemists would quickly degenerate into an ideological battle, with the old school attempting to avoid reality and distort the scientific debate by belittling the opposition.

So today, many of the top university entomologists seem to shy away from the problems created by the accumulation of IMD in the soil, or multiple bioavailable sources, or possible synergism of IMD and its metabolites with fungicides, herbicides, and miticides. Looking from the outside in at how bee research has developed, it seems the one thing the agrochemical establishment feels it must fight against—at all costs—is the public getting the idea that IMD is the new DDT.

IMD and the other new insecticides were a godsend for the industry, replacing older, more dangerous, and less profitable chemicals. If IMD is seen as the new DDT, public scrutiny on any future chemicals could be a real obstacle going forward. Regulation and outright bans could threaten the entire agrochemical industry at that point, ending the free ride of recent deregulation. The whole pesticide paradigm could then be on its way out, replaced by organic methods and biological controls. This paradigm shift is the real struggle within the controversy surrounding the little honey bee.

Meanwhile, Back in the U.S.

Today, the TV news in the United States rarely takes a hard look at its corporate sponsors and owners. For example, the contribution of SUVs to additional carbon emissions is rarely reported. SUV advertising by car companies is such a large proportion of ad revenue, that news channels are naturally reluctant to bite the hand that feeds them.

Moreover, as Al Gore points out in his most recent book, *The Assault Against Reason,* special investigations of both companies and government agencies by the press have mostly been replaced by sensationalist reporting. Whole weeks, months, and years of coverage have been devoted to breathless stories about O. J. Simpson, Chandra Levy, Shark Attacks, Gary Condit, Britney Spears, Lindsey Lohan, Robert Blake, Anna Nicole Smith, the Runaway Bride, The Crazed Jilted Astronaut, the Child Predator on the lam in Thailand, the Missing White Girl in Aruba, fake anthrax attacks, and of course numerous terror alerts. This move to sensationalism has led to a "media paralysis"—a recipe for disaster, leaving little broadcast time or newspaper space to protect the public from the profit motive of corporations and potential crony capitalism.

The job of the press, after all, is "to keep them honest." The problem today is, who's keeping the media honest? Because Americans simply have not been told what is really happening, from the bees to global warming and many other issues. The consequences of losing an investigative press now have the potential to become nothing less than a true catastrophe. As of January 2008, the U.S. press had yet to write anything about the honey bees clawing their way back in southwest France, and during 2007 it reported very little about the fight between Bayer CropScience, BASF, and the French beekeepers. One paragraph on France was buried in an April *New York Times* article, while *The Washington Post* gave it one brief paragraph in June. Then, on the same night of October 28, 2007, *Nature* on PBS talked about France and IMD for a couple of minutes and dismissed it quickly as the prime suspect, while *60 Minutes* ended with the testimony of the USDA that the evidence against IMD was "inconclusive."

America was in the dark.

Eight

America in the Dark

*The United States invariably does the right thing, after having
exhausted every other alternative.*
—WINSTON CHURCHILL

IN A SYRUPY TONE OF VOICE USUALLY RESERVED FOR THE
BIRTH OF BABY PANDAS, CNN newswoman Frederica Whit-
field exclaimed, "Where have all the honey bees gone?" "No one
knows" was the answer given in her report.[1] In light of having
just studied the history of the French IMD/honey bee controversy, watching the broadcast was a surreal moment. Nowhere
had the media reported the true history of the insecticide battle
in France, especially omitting the fact that the French bees came
back in 2005. Colony collapse disorder is typically presented as a
mystery in the U.S., a puzzle that no one on Earth can definitively
give the answer to.

The official EPA response on the honey bee calamity states
that colony collapse disorder is a mystery:

> *EPA is coordinating with the U.S. Department of Agri-
> culture, academia, professional organizations, and bee-
> keepers to identify the cause of Colony Collapse Disorder,
> or CCD, a massive die-off of adult bees in established
> honeybee colonies. Though agricultural records indicate*

*that sudden honeybee colony collapse is not a new phe-
nomenon, it is imperative that we learn the cause and do
what we can to prevent it. The current scientific consensus is that the cause of CCD is unknown. EPA and USDA
have met with insect scientists and beekeeping professionals to discuss leading theories. A report of the results of
that meeting is being prepared by USDA, and scientists
around the nation and the globe are moving forward with
research to test the various theories. EPA is committed to
protecting human health and the environment and will
continue to work with USDA and others to assess this
potential threat. If there are actions identified that EPA
can take to prevent CCD, EPA stands ready to take the
appropriate steps.*

Rather than giving CCD the serious investigation that it deserves, the U.S. media sometimes has even presented the ongoing catastrophe as a joke or as an oddball type of story. U.S. Secretary of Agriculture Mike Johanns, however, was frank in April of 2007: "The crisis threatens to wipe out production of crops dependent on bees for pollination." Explaining that the honey bee is crucial for many crops, entomologist E.O. Wilson warned, "we took it for granted."

The AIA estimates that colony collapse disorder wiped out at least 10% out of a total of 2.4 million hives in the U.S in late 2006 and early 2007. Thirty-five states were affected, along with British Columbia (although Canada officially denies there is CCD in that country). Most of the top twenty U.S. beekeepers, who do a large portion of this country's commercial pollination, were meanwhile hit with a huge bill to replace their lost hives, bringing the majority to the end of their financial rope. A food production crisis now looms with likely decreases in fruits, nuts, and vegetables for 2009 and especially 2010 and beyond, according to the pollinators. There simply won't be enough of those top twenty apiaries still in business to fulfill all the needed pollination. As mentioned earlier, just the increase to 680,000 acres of almonds by 2010 would use up all the commercial bees that have survived the CCD of 2006–07, never mind the second round of losses of 36% that began in December 2007.

The American public assumes that the government is acting responsibly and has begun an effective crash research program to solve this mystery within a short period of time. They think, "Certainly scientists are about to find the answer and reverse the great loss of honey bees." The assumption is also that agriculture is a fairly stable system, that little could go wrong in a really major way—that the food supply will always be there.

A little bit of research, however, shows none of this to be true.

How the Bush EPA Loosened Pesticide Regulations

Instead of the government acting responsibly, it appears the current EPA may itself have a lot to answer for in the honey bee crisis. To a large extent, the EPA in the last several years seems to have acted quite irresponsibly when it comes to pesticide regulations in general and with IMD in particular. If IMD truly is the cause of colony collapse disorder, history will show that lax regulation by the Bush Administration had catastrophic results. Poor enforcement of the laws on chemicals predates the current administration, but in the Bush era pesticides were basically deregulated in many key ways, including arbitrarily raising the "tolerance level" for many different chemicals. A dramatic increase in the amount of pesticides sprayed on the nation's food was the end result.

IMD was one of those chemicals. The huge increase in pesticide applications started in 2004, when the country and the media were distracted by the Iraq War and the presidential election. An unsuspecting public was never told about these new tolerance levels by the media. Nor were the beekeepers. IMD began to accumulate in the soil and in the nectar in the same way it had in France, building up to the sublethal dose which the Comité Scientifique et Technique report showed caused disorientation. We saw that Dr. Marc Colin had found in his research in France that the use of GAUCHO, an IMD product, would have a profound effect upon the bees, disorienting them within a few days of nectar flow.

THE AMERICAN BEEKEEPERS GET SUSPICIOUS

By 2004 and 2005, there were the first reported die-offs among U.S. commercial beeyards, and then came the calamity of 2006–07, when 30% of the hives in the U.S. disappeared. Was it truly the IMD use, increased in 2004? As we saw in his letter to growers, beekeeper David Hackenberg was certainly wondering what was new about certain crops that was killing the bees.

American beekeepers soon arrived at the same suspicion as their French counterparts. They reasoned that CCD was so dramatic and so rapid, that some kind of new chemical *must* be the main cause of colony collapse disorder. Natural viruses and the varroa mite have different symptoms and typically attack the hive more slowly and in a very visible manner. The strange behavior of hive beetles and wax moths, who would wait weeks before scavenging a dead CCD hive, also prompted suspicions that a chemical, and not a disease, was to blame.

The EPA dutifully noted that IMD, fipronil, and neonicotinoids like thiacloprid were "highly toxic to honey bees" and that caution should be taken not to spray when fields were being pollinated. Yet that is much easier said than done. In eleven years, from 1994 to 2005, the Pesticide Action Network notes there was a thirty-five-fold increase in crops sprayed with IMD in California—from some 20,000 acres to 787,444 acres. In California alone, IMD use per year leapt from 5,178 to 163,618 pounds of neurotoxin. California's wine country sees 106,591 acres of grapes being treated every year with IMD. The largest appliers of IMD in California are the almond growers—and almonds specifically have been one of the crops hardest hit by rising prices for hives by commercial pollinators.

Hearing little from the government that helped him, Dave Hackenberg, a former president of the American Beekeeping Federation, soon found out about IMD from other sources. In his letter to growers in March 2007, he said in talking to "farmers, growers, and seed and spray company representatives, we have learned that there has been a big change in pesticides used to treat these crops." He realized that spraying in general had increased enormously. Then he heard the word "neonicotinoid," the term for chlorinated nicotines like IMD. Consulting the Internet, he soon found the French research on IMD and began to understand how trace amounts were claimed to cause sublethal effects, such as the worker bees becoming disoriented and not foraging. Hackenberg complained, "We are simple beekeepers, not entomologists, chemists, or biologists, but we are now taking a crash course in insect and pesticide interactions. Before November I knew very little about neonicotinoids. In the past three months, I have come to know more than I want to know about this newer type of pesticide. From what I have learned so far, I am convinced that neonicotinoids may play a role in CCD." Other beekeepers agreed with Hackenberg, declaring that EPA now stands for

"Environmental Polluting Agency." Beekeeper Bob Bennett of Greenville, Wisconsin, stands with Hackenberg that pesticides are responsible: "There is no doubt in my mind, and just wait until after June 15 when the pesticide applications start, they are getting pollen that is killing the bees."

Except for one fifteen-minute segment of *60 Minutes*, however, the U.S. never heard the American or the French beekeepers' complaint that IMD is their prime suspect. The media, even the PBS show *Nature* in October 2007, simply did not cover the beekeepers' side and never interviewed the concerned U.S. citizens quoted above. Only the mystery angle was reported, giving broadcast time instead to the USDA and university scientists who proposed nonchemical causes or expressed doubt about CCD being the result of a single factor. *Nature* did mention France but then said the bees there never returned, implying that pesticides could not be the cause. This is the argument Bayer had always brought up for years. Even now in 2008, the absence of French bees is still being reported, although the honey bee returned in 2005 to southwest France and has been going strong since. There needs to be a deeper investigation by the press into these matters.

Why is most of the media, including PBS, not reporting the true history, or the CCD research from France, which is widely known and easily accessible on the Internet? And the main questions remain: Is IMD powerful enough in trace sublethal doses to disorient or inactivate the foraging honey bee? Is IMD the main cause of CCD-type behaviors?

BEEKEEPERS IN NORTH DAKOTA SUE BAYER OVER IMD KILLING THEIR BEES

In 1998, beekeeper Chris Charles of Charles Apiaries went to check his hives in North Dakota and found something he had never seen before. In many of the hives, the bees had flown away, leaving empty boxes or the Queen and some brood. Charles soon suspected IMD was causing the problem, and telephoned Bayer CropScience in Germany. Nearby sunflowers had recently been treated with GAUCHO and the effect was immediate. Other apiaries in the region had the same problem.

After getting what they felt was resistance from Bayer, a total of nine beekeepers ended up suing the company in 2002 for the loss of their hives and income. Independent labs were hired to test pollen and beeswax samples for IMD, and a legal team assembled. The judge is said to soon be ready to start Bauer, et al. v. Bayer Corporation, et al., Case No. 4:CV-03-1687, in U.S. District Court for the Middle District of Pennsylvania. The world will now be watching, as Charles says their tests show IMD is present in the pollen and wax. Besides compensation, the beekeepers are demanding an apology and that the manufacturers remove the neonicotinoids from the market.

WHY DOES CCD OCCUR AT DIFFERENT TIMES IN FRANCE AND AMERICA

A big question arises. Why does CCD occur in July in France but happen much later in the United States, in November, December, and January? When that question was posed to medical entomologist Dr. James Amrine, he had an immediate possible answer.

"There are several subspecies of bees, and they are all different in behavior and timing for brood development. *Apis mellifera mellifera* [the German or Northern honey bee] may be the subspecies of honey bee most used in France. The German bee builds up slowly in spring and summer, reaching maximum size in August. Many of the plants, especially heather, bloom at that time in northern Europe and that nectar flow fits in with their building up of the colony. Since the bees are still feeding brood (and each other) in June and July, that, to me, helps to explain the sudden appearance of CCD from imidacloprid from sunflower and corn pollen at that time of year.

"In contrast, our honey bees here in the U.S., *Apis mellifera ligustica* [Italians] and *Apis mellifera carnica* [Carniolans], reach maximum size at about the third week of May. The bees then spend the next several weeks bringing in a honey harvest and storing pollen. This is called the honey flow, where the honey is not consumed, but stored. In Maryland and West Virginia, the heavy flow ends and 'dearth' then usually appears in mid-to-late-July until early September, when nectar and pollen are not available. Then, later in September to January, this food is consumed. This would explain our delay in New Jersey, Maryland, Pennsylvania, and West Virginia in showing CCD while that in France is more instantaneous."

So the North American subspecies, *Apis mellifera ligustica*, also known as the "Italian" bee, stops producing brood in late May, while the European *Apis mellifera mellifera*, the "German" bee, does not do so until September. *The U.S. bees thus are not feeding heavily in June and July when the heaviest pesticide applications are made, while the French bees are.* The French bees therefore get intoxicated immediately and stop foraging, while the American bees get inebriated several months later when they dig into their contaminated honey and pollen stores in cold weather. There are still further complexities when other subspecies and brood cycles are considered, but this realization of the three different major species by Dr. Amrine helps to start to establish the mechanics behind this otherwise puzzling difference.

THE MOTHER OF ALL FIELD EXPERIMENTS

Another huge question: Why does CCD appear in some U.S. states but not in others? Iowa has CCD, for example, but Nebraska does not (See Appendix 5 for a chart on Colony Collapse Disorder in the United States). If Sherlock Holmes were here and knew how to use Google, he might at this point try to find out where IMD has been approved for use and whether there's a correlation with the states reporting CCD. It's elementary!

Sherlock is not here, so let's do the comparison ourselves, shall we? As we saw, IMD was approved through a much abused loophole in the pesticide law called Section 18.

From 1997 to 2001, there were forty-eight IMD section 18s, but that more than doubled to 115 Section 18 requests from 2002 to 2007. These old section 18s are an important clue because IMD can accumulate in the soil. From 1994 to September 2007, IMD was then given permanent approval on food and feed crops (see Appendix 4). The Web provides access to the EPA's own Section 18 database, so anyone can look and see when IMD first started heavy accumulation in each state. First up, the mysterious state of Vermont, with no reported cases of colony collapse disorder, according to the survey for this book, even though it is surrounded by the CCD states of New York, New Hampshire, and Massachusetts. The Section 18 database for Vermont says: No issued IMD approvals. Next is Maine, another state not reporting CCD. The Section 18 database for Maine says: No issued IMD approvals. How about New Mexico, a third gap state? The Section 18 database for New Mexico says: No issued IMD approvals. Nebraska: No issued IMD approvals. Nevada—no IMD. Louisiana—no IMD. Alabama—no IMD. Kansas—no IMD. Alaska—no IMD.

Then there's the case of tiny Rhode Island, situated next to Massachusetts, a known CCD state. Surely if it was a disease causing colony collapse disorder, it would have spread to little Rhode Island from Massachusetts. Yet there is no CCD in Rhode Island. The Section 18 database for Rhode Island? There are no issued IMD approvals. So far, that's ten out of ten gap states not having any issued IMD Section 18 approvals. Arizona was thought a gap state but, as we saw from *The Arizona Republic* article, it actually does have CCD, there just was no agency to report cases to. So has Arizona been issued any Section 18 approvals for IMD? The Section 18 database for Arizona says: five issued IMD approvals.

As for the rest of the states, Hawaii does use some IMD for watermelons and some greenhouse vegetables but still has no CCD, while West Virginia has permanent approvals for IMD use on fruit, nectarines, and peaches, and it has no reported CCD. West Virginia and Maryland have a very small fruit-growing corridor in the eastern panhandle, and many of those orchards have now sold their land for subdivisions or have been using integrated pest management, and are now using less IMD. The rest of West Virginia is mostly forested mountains, with little large-scale agriculture—so the state does not appear to be a big user of IMD. Most of the rest of the CCD states have had issued approvals (although a couple, including Ohio, have none), but these states seem to have so many other toxins approved they look like chemical stews on the Section 18 Web database. And the State Apiary Inspector of Ohio continues to claim there is no CCD in that state, that all their bee-kills are winter die-offs from an unusually cold winter, so this bears further investigation. Other neonicotinoid neurotoxins, recent permanent IMD approvals, and migratory beekeeping probably account for most of the other CCD states.

Since West Virginia and Hawaii seem to have used little of the IMD they were approved for, the lack of IMD approvals among the U.S. states appears to strongly correlate with the states not reporting CCD. If IMD is the prime suspect, it should come as no surprise that California is the state hardest hit by colony collapse disorder, and in fact California does have the most Section 18 temporary authorizations for imidacloprid.

When you think about it, what the government did was conduct a multi-year, nationwide "controlled" experiment, with the states that did not have heavy IMD use (the Section 18s) as the controls. Comparative analysis must still be done, but the result of this "mother-of-all field experiments" seems to show that IMD and the other neonics appear to be a significant risk to the honey bee.

IS SCIENCE DIFFERENT IN FRANCE?

The French scientists like Colin and Bonmatin, the French bee-keepers, and some American beekeepers all believe the same thing: that IMD in tiny amounts can disrupt foraging and therefore must be considered a prime suspect for CCD. Why then do most scientists in the U.S. declare CCD a mystery? It's hard to accept that U.S. scientists are so completely unaware of the massive French studies, which were funded by the Agriculture Ministry from 1998 to 2003, especially the Colin et al. study published in 2004 that showed IMD disrupted feeding at just 6 PPB. Perhaps the difference lies in the fact that the French government still fully funds secondary education and the university system, while in the U.S. corporate donors, including the chemical companies, have filled the financial void at state universities created by conservative tax cuts. Is there a hidden agenda to protect the chemical companies as a result? Because based on the data, reason would say that the Principle of Precaution and the Law of Unintended Consequences should take over here, that Bayer should have to prove IMD is safe for bees before any more is used on food crops in America.

On September 7, 2007, it was reported by U.S. researchers in the journal *Science* that a new suspect in the bee die-offs was a recently discovered virus, called Israeli acute paralysis virus, or IAPV. Although it was presented mostly as a dramatic break-through by the researchers, there were soon many holes in the theory, as we've seen earlier. The IAPV study itself noted that CCD is not prevalent in Australia, where the virus is common, nor does it fit the symptoms of CCD, in that the bodies of the paralyzed bees from IAPV are found dead outside the hive. In colony collapse disorder, the bees fly off and don't return.

Beekeepers like Hackenberg and Doan charge that a lot of time and effort went into the new virus study but almost nothing has been done to conduct real research on IMD. Hackenberg says that fifteen commercial U.S. beekeepers, who were informed of the IAPV study in a conference call by the scientists, were not mollified by the virus theory. In fact, several claimed immedi-ately afterwards that IMD was the real problem.[2]

By the end of the September 6 conference call on IAPV, the top beekeepers now had their worst fears confirmed, for this new virus once again had different symptoms than CCD and was there-fore an unlikely candidate as the cause. In Europe, the beekeepers had charged that the virus and mite theories were nothing more than a diversion, a red herring to throw researchers and journal-ists off the IMD trail. Was this now happening in the U.S.?

Dr. Pettis of the USDA told the BBC that if the IAPV theory was correct, "We're unlikely to come up with a treatment for viruses in bees, and so beekeepers are likely just going to have to keep the other things that might affect CCD, such as mites, under control." The beekeepers would thus have to learn how to cope with ever-increasing use of IMD, while the government-industry line would be "it's a virus, there's nothing we can do."

In short, like the denials on global warming, the cause is not man-made, but natural. Just as Big Oil is innocent on global warming, Big Chemical has clean hands on colony collapse disor-der—CCD has natural causes, not man-made ones, the argument seems to be. Dr. Pettis and the CCD Working Group certainly seem to be sincere in their desire to solve the catastrophe that is unfolding. The similarities, however, between global warming "uncertainty" and the "inconclusive" argument over IMD causing CCD, are striking.

The recent discovery of how Big Oil entered into a strategy to stir up doubt about global warming illuminates a previously dark area. To try and manipulate public opinion, it now appears the oil industry deliberately injected doubts about global warming being man-made, by following an industry plan to fund papers that refuted the scientific data. On December 10, 2007 it was revealed by the House Committee on Government Oversight and Reform that Big Oil had a hidden plan to create unwarranted uncertainty in the minds of the public by presenting facts about global warming in a false light. The American Petroleum Institute in 1998 had created a "Communications Action Plan" which said: "Victory will be achieved when . . . average citizens 'understand' uncertainties in climate science . . . [and] recognition of uncertainties becomes part of the 'conventional wisdom.'" The uncertainty over global warming was thus more public relations than science.

In a similar way, could some in the entomology and toxicology communities be attempting to create false uncertainty when they declare that tests on IMD are not "conclusive," that IMD cannot be considered the prime suspect? Is this like the global warming deniers trying to protect the coal and oil industries, when their Communications Action Plan declared that "Victory will be achieved when . . . average citizens 'understand' uncertainties in climate science"? Is there a sustained industry attempt to steer research in any direction except the study of IMD—all to avoid the realization that the cause of CCD might be a man-made chemical?

Besides claiming uncertainty where there seems to be little or none, and not quickly undertaking an IMD/honey bee study, another problem is the length of proposed U.S. research. Most of the USDA bee projects are slated to take five long years, although a few are slated for two years. One must wonder, why not just use the French research which has already been done, and suspend IMD? The bees need action now, not five years from now. There won't be many large commercial beekeepers left if something doesn't change soon. Why are the USDA and some university researchers so slow?

THE ONGOING PRIVATIZATION OF HIGHER EDUCATION

It seems that universities today are often for sale to the highest bidder, aggressively seeking donations from large corporations. These donations are sometimes paid for outright. For example, an endowed faculty chair goes for $2,000,000 at Penn State Lehigh, and a professorship for $1,000,000—it's even advertised on their Web site.[3] The disturbing privatization of U.S. (and Canadian) schools is revealed in two books, *Leasing the Ivory Tower: The Corporate Takeover of Academia*, by Lawrence Soley (1999), and *Campus Inc.: Corporate Power in the Ivory Tower*, by Geoffry White. Soley states that the liberal university model is being replaced by a corporatized discourse, turning the school labs and classrooms into the research-and-development arms of the biggest companies, not to mention providing lots of public relations support for various industry stands. Intellectual freedom still reigns many places, but the threat of outright corporatization is widespread and growing.

Cal Bradford, from the University of Minnesota's Humphrey Institute, strongly criticized the "donations" to U.S. schools by corporations, saying endowed chairs and professorships enforce "what universities will teach and research, what direction the university will take. If universities would decide they need an endowed chair in English, and then try to raise the money for it, it would be one thing. But that's not what happens. Corporate donors decide to fund chairs in areas they want research done. Their decisions determine which are topics universities explore and which aren't."[4] Bradford's contract with the University of Minnesota was not renewed after this criticism.

Chemical companies, genetic engineering companies (like Monsanto), and agribusiness all give millions of dollars to U.S. and Canadian universities for research labs, equipment, specific grants, and gifts. College professors are hired at handsome prices to be consultants and speakers. Corporations even receive tax deductions for many donations. As mentioned, the endowed chairs allow corporations to donate heavily. Among many other chairs, there is the Reliance Corporation Professor of Free Enterprise at the University of Pennsylvania, the Carlson Travel Tour and Hospitality Chair at the University of Minnesota, and the Bell South Professor of Education Through Telecommunication at the University of South Carolina.

The result of all these "generous" corporate donations is that some researchers might be influenced by a fundamental conflict of interest. It's hard to bite the corporate hand that feeds you. Corporate donors to Penn State, for example, and many other universities, today help fund agricultural and toxicology programs that have been cut in recent decades by conservative state legislatures and governors.

Bayer, whose U.S. headquarters are in Pittsburgh, has very close ties to Penn State, having given $2.4 million to the university and an additional $1.3 million in research grants. The Bayer Foundation also recently gave a $300,000 scholarship grant for Penn State students in material science. Bayer MaterialScience works hand-in-hand with Penn State's Industrial Research Office, and employs 185 alumni from the school. Bayer CropScience meanwhile integrates itself with the agricultural school, especially the Turfgrass Center and the Pesticide Research Lab, which was renamed the Chemical Ecology Lab in 2004. Penn State also holds "Field Days" where new pesticides are demonstrated and training given in their use. At the June 30, 2006 "Agronomy-Industry Field Day," for example, the participating chemical companies were AMVAC, BASF, Bayer CropScience, Dow AgroSciences, Dupont, Monsanto, and Syngenta. Bayer Crop-Science and others also fund additional programs such as Penn State's 2004 Agronomic Education Conference.

All this time, there has been no funded study by the Penn State CCD Working Group to see if IMD causes disorientation. Pollen, nectar, and honey have been measured for IMD residues, but no field or semi-field research with actual bees has been conducted. Granted, it takes funding and gearing up, but where is there a serious effort to have a quick true field test? The IAPV theory meanwhile is gearing up to start quickly. Why not the test for the man-made cause, for the insecticide? Dr. Colin has already conducted a five-day test. This same experiment could be run to see if its results can be duplicated.

Are studies and interpretations of data on IMD by Penn State being influenced by a reluctance to go up against Bayer, one of the university's main corporate donors? Penn State's CCD Working Group would no doubt respond "absolutely not," and they would point to their work on pesticides, which has led the nation (which is not saying much). Then why is the critical Comité Scientifique et Technique report on IMD not linked to directly on the Penn State CCDWG Web site? The site does mention some of the French findings on sublethal doses in a PDF file, but the extensive French reports are not linked to in the main Web page that the public and press has swarmed over. If a conflict of interest is the reason for this omission by the CCDWG, it leaves the public blocked from the free flow of information, leading to potential safety and health problems dealing with pesticides. When these same U.S. scientists testified before Congress, the Comité Scientifique et Technique report was never brought up—France itself was not even mentioned. That task was left to Jim Doan, a New York beekeeper, who did speak of IMD, France, and the need to ban IMD in his March testimony to a House Agriculture subcommittee.[5] It is unknown if Doan's charges against IMD had any impact.

Maryanne Frazier of the CCD Working Group summed up the state of current research for the Congress and the public: "At this point, it is more cloudy than it is clear. We are finding a number of things, but we don't know how connected they are yet to the CCD situation."

In France, where corporate influence is far weaker, government and university scientists instead conducted a straightforward series of duplicated experiments in the lab and the field to prove or disprove the beekeepers' claim that a new chemical was killing their bees. Governments and top entomologists elsewhere, however, have focused on researching many other theories, from viruses to bee management, stress, and nutrition.

USDA's Jeff Pettis says that colony collapse disorder cannot be connected to pesticides, that the science is inconclusive. When asked by *Washington Post* reporter Joel Garreau in June 2007 about the French claim of insecticides causing "mad bee disease," Pettis replied: "They were using that [term] because they thought some of their losses over the past 10 years were connected to low-level pesticides. It's one myth. But we can't make the connection to disorientation." Pettis, in charge of finding out the cause of CCD, prefers to think it's how the bees are being managed and does not believe it harbingers doom: "I don't personally believe that the bees are the canary in the coal mine. You don't have to bring in larger human destruction of the environment. I can see things going on in the ways bees are managed that explain it." Pettis says, "there may not be a simple answer" to colony collapse disorder, that it could be a combination of factors, from bee management to stress and pathogens. Talking to the BBC, Dennis van Engelsdorp, the acting Pennsylvania State Apiarist, beekeeper, and a leading researcher at Penn State, also insists insecticides cannot be tagged as the culprit. "We have no evidence to think that that theory is more right than any other. . . . "

WHAT WOULD RACHEL SAY?

In the early 1960s, Rachel Carson warned that overuse of pesticides could be the death knell for the pollinating insects, including the bees. She began *Silent Spring* by telling a "Fable of Tomorrow," about a typical small town wasted by a blight resulting from pesticides, and actually predicts the disappearance of the bees:

> *. . . The apple trees bloomed but no bees droned among the blossoms, so there was no pollination and there would be no fruit . . .*

She explains that a chemical designed to kill any insect it encounters will of course affect both destructive and beneficial creatures. Indeed, in Chapter 2, *Silent Spring* warns that such powerful pesticides literally destroy the ecosystem itself, from birds to fish to critical insects like the bees. Carson declares that insecticides should instead be called "biocides," that they attack the entire biosphere. Humanity will, in the end, suffer the unintended consequences of this high-impact technology.

Carson, who fought back a vicious counterattack from the chemical industry over her call to ban DDT, wrote in *Silent Spring* that the industry cannot fight the truth—that there is no possible defense. So the company PR programs resort to muddying the waters, to funding research that promises spurious findings. The industry, she countered, falls back on half truths that skirt the real issue:

> *When the public protests, confronted with some obvious evidence of damaging results of pesticide applications, it is fed little tranquilizing pills of half-truth. We urgently need an end to these false assurances, to the sugar coating of unpalatable facts.*

Today, over four decades after Carson's book was published, the government and the chemical industry are far more powerful in their control of the media, and in their ability to ignore the pleas and lawsuits of environmentalists. Nearly the entire community of research facilities and compliant university labs defends the rising use of pesticides and continues to ignore or belittle attempts to develop safer, natural alternatives. The government, originally discovering the insecticidal properties of substances like DDT through chemical warfare research in World War II, decided to make peaceful use of research originally conducted to kill enemy soldiers. When some of the deadly gases were discovered to be effective insecticides, they were quickly approved by the bureaucracy for widespread use with little or no testing.

Our agrochemical establishment is, however, defending more than the use of IMD, or even pesticides in general, or that original decision to use nerve gas discoveries to make insecticides. The government, universities, and industry are defending their deep underlying paradigm, their view of the universe. It is, in the final analysis, a War of the Worldviews. There are the ecologists, like Carson, who see the biosphere as a living thing—a fragile being that could get sick and perish. Then there are the chemists, toxicologists, and bureaucrats, whose science views the Earth as an inanimate rock, a dead thing that can be manipulated in endless ways without concern for the future. So, the Law of Unintended Consequences and the Principle of Precaution are dismissed or ignored in hundreds of cases of new chemicals or technologies being introduced to the market.

Ecologists think with a biological model of the universe rather than the old machine model, as noted by such writers as Fritjof Capra in *The Turning Point* and Thom Hartmann in *The Last Hours of Ancient Sunlight*. The natural inclination of the "mechanists" is to deny or ignore research that undermines the machine model, or the anthropocentric worldview. Man-made causes of global disasters are especially taboo, for they are anomalies flying in the face of the whole human-centered concept of nature. Biological fragility is challenged and denied at almost every possible turn by the mechanists. In contrast, ecologists step back and see the reality of the interconnected big picture, that humanity is just part of the larger living biosphere, a delicate balance of species and resources that could come undone.

History shows that the government will typically support the machine model and the chemical industry over the objections of the ecologists. Despite Carson's *Silent Spring*, for example, it took a decade to ban DDT, while many chemicals like Carbaryl (Sevin), an insecticide, or atrazine, an herbicide, are still allowed by the EPA even after studies show they are decimating the environment.[6]

A trusting U.S. public assumes the government is protecting them from the profit motive of chemical companies by properly testing all toxins introduced into the environment. Al Gore, in his 1992 foreword to the new edition of *Silent Spring*, declared that nothing could be further from the truth. Gore warns that the entire EPA mandate to protect the environment and the consumer has degenerated into a total shambles: "The present system is a Faustian bargain—we get short-term gain at the expense of long-term tragedy. . . . Essentially, what we have inherited is a system of laws and loopholes, deadlines and delays, façades that barely disguise a wholesale failure of policy." Gore declares we are trading short-term economic benefit for future environmental catastrophe—the people are not being protected as they are supposed to be by the law. He insists that the EPA must be reformed.

The next question we must ask ourselves is, in the long run, do these chemicals even work? Are they truly worth it? "No responsible person contends that insect-borne disease should be ignored," Carson wrote in *Silent Spring*. "The question that has now urgently presented itself is whether it is either wise or responsible to attack the problem by methods that are rapidly making it worse." She proclaimed that the insects were actually winning the war. Darwin was right, said Carson, species adapt and evolve—meaning that ever more deadly toxins must be used as evolution defends itself by developing resistance. She scoffs at the notion that nature can be easily controlled with powerful chemicals and technology.

In fact, nature seems to adapt to almost anything chemists can conjure up, and pests have shown they can mutate within only a couple of years. "The insect enemy has been made stronger by our efforts. Even worse, we may have destroyed our very means of fighting." Carson says outright, "The insects are winning: We're on a pesticide treadmill. The insects adapt to the particular insecticide used . . . forcing us to find ever deadlier new ones. . . . Thus the chemical war is never won, and all life is caught in its violent crossfire." Neurotoxins like IMD are the next step up the spiral, and now the bees might very well be caught in the "violent crossfire."

PENNCAP-M, THE ULTIMATE WEAPON

It wouldn't be the first time insecticides have been accused of wiping out American bee colonies. In the 1990s, farmers began using Penncap-M in Nebraska, Colorado, North Carolina, and Washington to fight corn rootworms, a beetle that attacks the roots of the corn plant in its larval stage. Made by Cerexagri, Penncap-M, or methyl parathion, is a poison microencapsulated into tiny, pollen-size pellets. Worker bees gathered the toxic beads along with the corn pollen and carried the powerful neurotoxin home to their unsuspecting hives. The poison bead can even attach itself by static electricity to the hairs of the bee and make its way into the colony. Penncap-M was the ultimate bee-killer, a prime suspect for worsening the decline of pollinators before CCD came along.

Despite the known impact on bees, the growers, who don't need the honey bee because corn is wind-pollinated, kept using Penncap-M to fight their rootworms. Beekeepers in the affected areas were forced to move their hives out of state or far enough away from corn crops, while others were driven out of business by massive bee-kills. Today, apiaries must situate themselves far from treated cornfields, as the toxin was never removed from the market, despite its apparent disastrous impact. Sevin, or carbaryl, is another known pesticide responsible for catastrophic bee-kills. It, too, was never taken off the shelves. Fortunately, Penncap-M, like other organophosphates, is not used as much these days.

If Penncap-M and Sevin were barely regulated, IMD is literally a poster child for the whole rotten and broken system through which the EPA has released hundreds of toxins without proper environmental testing. Increasing insect resistance means new and more dangerous poisons must be continually invented, IMD being the latest entry on the chemical treadmill. With aphids and grubs becoming immune to older organophosphates that were themselves known to be carcinogenic, the economic need for a new, effective pesticide was enormous. Farmers needed it—and so did the chemical industry. IMD first had to be permitted for use in the U.S., however, and, given that it was a neurotoxin similar to nerve gas, food crop approval could prove to be difficult.

CHEMICAL COMPANY INFLUENCE ON THE U.S. GOVERNMENT

Besides the multimillion-dollar donations to universities and research institutes, corporations buy influence through campaign contributions and lobbying. In 2001, for example, Bayer spent $532,000 for their agricultural lobbying, with $600,000 spent the following year.[7] Most years it spent far less, but when it needs to, a large corporation will open the taps and hire several K Street law firms. Bayer and BASF are part of the chemical industry, one of the largest sectors that lobby the government and contribute to political campaigns and soft money groups. In 2006, the chemical and related industries spent over $6 million on U.S. campaigns, and earlier in 2000 gave over $11 million. But that's nothing compared to agribusiness. Through contributions from individuals, political action committees, and soft money, agribusiness is one of the largest funders, over $50 million a year according to Congressional records. Businesses don't give out that kind of money unless they are fairly sure it will garner influence in return.

The IMD story starts in the 1970s, when aphids and other bugs started becoming resistant to the initial insecticides. At the same time, some early toxins such as DDT, carbonates, and organophosphates were being banned or regulated for being carcinogenic in humans. This generated a strong effort to discover new chemicals, substances that would be safer to people and wildlife. The ultimate answer came in 1985 with Bayer's discovery of IMD, which worked by blocking an insect's nervous system but supposedly had little effect on humans or mammals. Aphids had meanwhile become resistant to the old carcinogenic pesticides and a new treatment was being requested by growers. EPA regulators let Bayer forgo the usual environmental tests that food crop approval requires and IMD was given its first "emergency exemption." IMD was eventually granted 163 emergency authorizations to be sold for food crop applications, a "time-limited tolerance," based solely on dire economic need. Environmental groups have charged that these temporary exemptions in practice became permanent, violating the intent of the law, with most extensions granted on a regular basis.

At first, the use of IMD and other neonicotinoids was limited, being approved crop by crop, state by state on emergency authorizations. The EPA would routinely grant the extensions under the Section 18 emergency clause of the Federal Insecticide, Fungicide and Rodenticide Act (see Appendix 4, FIFRA Section 18). The EPA does notify pesticide users that IMD is "highly toxic to honey bees" and that it should not be sprayed when bees are active.

Pesticide salesmen, however, often tell the growers they must spray early in the season, which is usually just before the bees arrive. Plus beekeepers worry that the real problem is that seeds painted with IMD—which are becoming the most popular— put out IMD in the nectar and pollen. So the EPA warning on IMD does little good. Despite known effects on honey bees, the EPA approvals, in effect, put economic considerations ahead of proper precaution for the environment. After 2004, IMD food crop, home and turf use soared when products containing the active ingredient diazinon were taken off the shelves.

Today, you can buy IMD for home or farm use in the form of MERIT (turf), GAUCHO (corn, cotton, potatoes), GAUCHO XT (cereals), GAUCHO MZ (potato seed piece treatment), GAUCHO GRANDE (cotton seed treatment), ADMIRE (potatoes, corn, grapes, vegetables, citrus), GENESIS XT (potatoes), PREMISE (termite control), PROVADO (fruits, vegetables), LEVERAGE (cotton), and CALYPSO (apple, pear, quince, crabapple). GENESIS XT, used on potatoes, is IMD combined with two kinds of fungicide, mancozeb and thiophanate, which might cause synergisms that increase the punch of the neurotoxin. Farmers drench their soil with some of these IMD products, they increasingly spray their fields with it, and seed companies now routinely paint the neurotoxin directly onto the seeds itself, allowing the systemic insecticide to permeate the plant, right up to the nectar. To control grubs, which cause unsightly yellow or dead patches of grass, golf courses use the IMD product MERIT, as do lawn chemical services. Lawn chemicals, in particular, contaminate flowers such as dandelions and clover, as well as lawn trees like lindens, where again they can affect bees.

If IMD and the neonicotinoids truly are the cause of the problem with the honey bee, their use is so widespread it would appear to be hopeless for man's second-best friend.

There is, however, a legal "out"—a legal trump card for the bees. If "relevant information" shows that "residues are not safe," *the permanent IMD authorizations could be revoked*. The 5-day feeding experiment of Dr. Colin et al., published in 2004, is enough data to show that IMD residues are indeed a "significant risk" to the honey bee even in trace sublethal doses of just 6 PPB. The French IMD research, and the fact that the old Section 18 exemptions closely match the states where CCD has appeared, certainly would seem to be strong enough data to trigger the suspension of all the food and feed crop authorizations. The burden of proof, legally, would then be on Bayer CropScience to meet the safety requirements and show that their product is indeed safe. It appears the honey bee may, in the future, have a regulation or two on its side.

But for now, the chemical companies rule the day.

THE CORPORATE FOX IN THE EPA HENHOUSE

The EPA, working under the Bush Administration, raised the tolerance levels for five major pesticides in 2002—violating the agency's own guidelines. One of them was IMD. As mentioned earlier, the aphids and other bugs, were now becoming resistant just as Darwin, Carson, and Gore would predict. A stronger dose of the neurotoxins were now needed, another step on Carson's "pesticide treadmill."

Thanks to the largesse of the Bush Administration's regulators, the chemical companies were suddenly able to recommend the use of far more IMD on certain crops. For example, where the previous safety level for blueberries, was set at 1 PPM residue, blueberries, could now have up to 3.5 PPM IMD. Between IMD being sprayed or used at about three times the ordinary rate on blueberries, the IMD-applied acres increasing by leaps and bounds, not to mention more and more seeds being painted with the toxin, the French research would indicate that honey bees in the U.S. would be profoundly affected within a year or two. That's exactly what happened.

In a phone interview, Hackenberg now says he saw the first cases of colony collapse disorder in his yards in 2004 and 2005 as did other keepers. Then, by 2006 and early 2007, colony collapse disorder swept the U.S.; but only in the 36 states where neonicotinoids had been given emergency authorization and was heavily used, or states with large migratory beekeeping operations.

When aphids and other pests began showing more and more resistance, the EPA interpreted safety standards so more insecticides could be used. They were limited by a law, however—the Food Quality Protection Act of 1996 (FQPA). An EPA task force recommendation for the execution of that law said whatever the chemical tolerance level for adults was, there had to be a safety factor of ten times beyond that for children.

The EPA simply set new tolerance levels by interpreting away the 10X safety factor protecting children and embryos for five major pesticides, including IMD. As charged by the NRDC, in a June 19, 2002, citing on the Federal Register: "EPA has violated the requirements of the FQPA [the Food Quality Protection Act of 1996] in establishing new tolerances for imidacloprid, mepiquat, bifenazate, zeta-cypermethrin, and diflubenzuron—With respect to all five pesticides, EPA failed to apply the children's 10X safety factor, acknowledge and consider farm children as a major identifiable subgroup, take into consideration reliable data concerning occupational exposure, or fully assess aggregate exposures. With respect to imidacloprid and mepiquat, EPA additionally failed to protect all infants and children and not just those within a certain percentile, and as a result left potentially more than a million children unprotected."[8]

The NRDC sued on the rights of parents to know that foods are safe for their children to eat. The problem for children and embryos in all this is that the Bush EPA is trying to avoid having the chemical companies do the critical DNT tests that should be performed. Although the EPA did receive a DNT test for IMD from Bayer in 2004, and it showed safety for mammals, the other neonics might fail the developmental neurotoxicity test. This is presumably why the EPA is now bending over backwards to help the chemical companies avoid the DNT tests even though it was originally the EPA's own scientist Makris who called for the research, as pointed out by the NRDC in their suit. "Studies by EPA staff scientist Dr. Makris show that DNT testing is more sensitive than other studies in measuring the effects of exposure on proper development of the brain and nervous system, and therefore DNT testing is more appropriate for protecting children's health. DNT testing is essential for pesticides. . . . "

Despite the EPA's own 10X Task Force recommendation and the studies showing the need for the DNT tests by Dr. Makris, the agency has only recently started to enforce the need for such testing. The EPA thus continues to endanger children who might be exposed to pesticides.

IMD is suspected of possibly having damaging human health effects, yet no studies of commercial products have so far been conducted. The *Journal of Pesticide Reform*, 2001 IMD fact sheet, noted that although certainly safer than earlier insecticides such as DDT and the organophosphates, the research shows that IMD particularly seems to affect the thyroid gland: "Chronic (long-term; lifetime) feeding studies with rats showed that the thyroid is especially sensitive to imidacloprid. Thyroid lesions were caused by doses of 17 milligrams per kilogram (mg/kg) of body weight per day in males. Slightly higher doses (25 mg/kg per day) reduced weight gain in females. At higher doses (100 mg/kg per day), effects included atrophy of the retina in females."

The *Journal* also reported that IMD studies have found reproductive problems such as low birth weight and abnormal skeletons in test animals. "Imidacloprid affects reproduction in a variety of ways. In pregnant rabbits, imidacloprid fed between the sixth and eighteenth days of pregnancy caused an increase in the frequency of miscarriages and an increase in the number of offspring with abnormal skeletons. These effects were observed at a dose of 72 mg/kg per day. In rats, a two-generation feeding study found that rats fed imidacloprid gave birth to smaller offspring. Their weight was reduced at a dose of 19 g/kg per day."

Although IMD does not appear to be carcinogenic in itself, in the field it is mixed with crystalline quartz silica, which allows the toxin to be delivered efficiently to its target insects. According to the International Agency for Cancer, crystalline quartz silica is "carcinogenic to humans." The U.S. National Toxicology Program agrees: crystalline quartz silica is "known to be a human carcinogen." Crystalline quartz silica can be found in the imidacloprid product Merit 0.5 G. The inert ingredient naphthalene, in the Bayer IMD product Leverage 2.7, has also been found by the National Toxicology Program as exhibiting "clear evidence of carcinogenic activity."

The problems IMD could possibly wreak on human health are concern enough. Now the concern is the honey bee. Tripling IMD, from 1 PPM to 3.5 PPM on blueberries, for example, could theoretically have an impact, as the French research showed disorientation at just 3-6 parts per billion in the nectar or pollen. Distracted by other world events, such as the war in Iraq, the public has never even heard that the application of some pesticides were increased, nor does it know how the Section 18 approvals have been handed out like candy over the years. The media has never properly informed the nation about any of this.

There are many other facts about the Bush EPA that the public knows little or nothing about. To make a long story short, the corporate fox was not only in charge of the EPA henhouse, he was using the henhouse to hold wild, all-night parties, with feathers flying everywhere. The inner workings of the EPA-lobbyist relationship were revealed by the Public Employees for Environmental Responsibility (PEER), an employee whistle-blowing group. According to meeting notes obtained by PEER on August

9, 2005, a significant meeting was held at the president's Office of Management and Budget with EPA officials.[9] Present were a former EPA assistant administrator of the Office of Prevention, Pesticides and Toxic Substances turned chemical company lobbyist, representatives of the pesticide industry association from Crop Life America, and Bayer CropScience. The meeting agenda was to go over a new, quick way to speed up the permanent approval process of pesticides. Goal number one was to create loopholes in testing regulations so that children could actually be used for chemical exposure experiments, as had been proposed earlier in a Florida program by the state and the American Chemical Council. Lured by a small cash payment and a gift, low-income parents would sign up for the program and knowingly let their children play in a room where they would be exposed to varying levels of organophosphate nerve agents. An October 2004 article in *The Washington Post*, entitled "Study of Pesticides and Children Stirs Protests," described the scheme, known ironically as CHEERS, the Children's Environmental Exposure Research Study:[10]

> *The EPA announced an investigation, partially funded by the American Chemical Council, of how 60 children in Duval County, Fla., absorb pesticides and other household chemicals.*
>
> *In exchange for participating for two years in the Children's Environmental Exposure Research Study, which involves infants and children up to age 3, the EPA will give each family using pesticides in their home $970, some children's clothing and a camcorder that parents can keep.*

Low-income parents would be given a camcorder and $970 if they would agree to regularly spray their child's room for two years. Every child had to be under the age of three, and there was no thought about the embryos of pregnant mothers getting contaminated in the process. The organophosphates which the American Chemical Council wanted to test on young children are all banned in England, Sweden, and Denmark.

Those at the OMB meeting in August all agreed to allow the child-experiment loopholes through the issuing of a new rule, which was soon accomplished. On June 23, 2006, PEER Executive Director Jeff Ruch lodged a mighty complaint against the striking shift in policy toward experimenting on children. From the PEER Web site press page:

The pesticide and chemical industries have been pushing hard for EPA to base its regulatory decisions upon human testing data, which cannot be collected on the same scale and using the high chemical concentrations that can be used on animals. In addition, the industry has explicitly lobbied for loopholes allowing use of children in tests, as rules require much greater protection for this vulnerable population absent compelling evidence that the protections are unneeded.

In January, EPA adopted a human testing rule that was hailed by the pesticide industry but decried by the public health community. Last month, 9,000 EPA scientists sent an extraordinary letter of protest objecting to pending agency approval of a cluster of powerful pesticides derived from nerve agents despite strong evidence of the harm posed, particularly to developing children and fetuses.

"Despite espousal of family values, the Bush administration is encouraging corporations to pay thousands of poor people both in this country and abroad to ingest commercial poisons and other chemicals in experiments that are designed to measure harm for financial rather

than public health reasons," added Ruch, noting that EPA has abolished its Office of Children's Health Protection and transferred review of these issues to its pesticide staff. "Our Environmental Protection Agency appears to be more concerned with protecting industry than us."

The testing of children fortunately never took place. Yet that was only the beginning, according to the whistle-blowing employees. PEER charges that chemical company lobbyists have been allowed to set policy and that science has been marginalized by political favors for the industry. PEER Executive Director Ruch states outright: "Our top public scientists are morally and professionally compromised by the Bush administration's partnership with the chemical industry."

In their letter, the 9,000 scientists warned that the EPA "risk assessments cannot state with confidence the degree to which any exposure of a fetus, infant or child to a pesticide will or will not adversely affect their neurological development." Even worse, the door is wide open to still more policy being set by industry lobbyists. The letter sadly concludes that politics have trumped science and that the chemical companies now have final say on all new regulations: "The prevailing belief among managers in the Pesticide and Toxics Programs [is] that regulatory decisions should only be made after reaching full consensus with the regulated pesticide and chemicals industry."

This is not the way a regulatory agency is supposed to work. An agency is not supposed to reach "full consensus" with the companies it is regulating—especially when the products in question are toxic chemicals. To add to this outrageous list of avoiding safety tests, arbitrarily raising tolerance levels, approving the use of children and pregnant mothers in chemical exposure experiments, pushing through chemicals known to be unsafe and pledging to abide by industry wishes on future regulations, the Bush EPA then took apart one of the most critical programs for public health in the country.

The EPA has a special library of pollution and test data that is used by staff scientists to approve or reject new chemicals. Without public notice, the agency dismembered and closed its library system, cutting off at the knees the EPA's own researchers—and those wishing to sue over illegal actions concerning approvals for toxins. In particular, on October 20, 2006, PEER charges the Office of Prevention, Pollution, and Toxic Substances (OPPTS) Library, in the EPA's Washington, D.C. headquarters, was closed without notice. "Budget pressure" was cited, even though the library was essential in the mandated review of all common chemicals on the market. Remember, the library's extensive documents were crucial to EPA scientists working on chemical approvals. The OPPTS Library included unique studies on children and pesticides—all now difficult or impossible to see, as the papers and monographs were thrown into boxes and are currently being stored in a basement cafeteria. Disorganized, the previously cataloged collection is now useless.

Ruch explained how the library closings effectively shut the door to meaningful research and regulation: "Without this research assistance, EPA scientists have fewer resources to conduct thorough analyses on hundreds of new chemicals for which companies are clamoring for agency approval to launch each year into the mainstream of American commerce. When confronted with new chemicals, EPA scientists often begin by looking at the effects of similar chemicals or analogues—a technique hampered by closing its library housing research on chemicals and their effects. . . . Given the tremendous public health risks, this is absolutely the last place EPA should be cutting." The closing of the OPPTS library without prior notification is, in fact, a violation of federal policy—OMB Circular A-130—which states that the public must be told whenever the government is "terminating significant information dissemination products."

The EPA claims to be digitizing all these documents, now in boxes, with a laborious page-by-page survey that will apparently take years. Yet the digitizing project has no budget, timetable, or plan for completion, and the EPA's own scientists can no longer access any of the material. It could be said the closing of the EPA libraries made far less of a stir than the Fascist book-burnings of the 1930s, but the result was very much the same—the documents were no longer a threat.

THE GRIM OUTLOOK FOR THE FUTURE

Each and every year chemicals to kill insects are applied to hundreds of millions of acres. In 1964, the year Rachel Carson died of cancer, 233 million pounds of pesticides were used in the U.S. In 1982, that had tripled to 612 million pounds of active ingredients. And in 1999, that figure had ballooned to an amazing five billion pounds of toxins being used to kill insects and weeds on U.S. crops, forests, lawns, and flowers, as well as in homes and buildings for termites, ants, fleas and other bugs, including bees, hornets, and wasps. As quoted in a March 2007 article in *News Target*, Mike Adams, executive director of the Consumer Wellness Center in Tuscon, Arizona, worries we may have passed the point of no return: "the fact that honey bees are now simply disappearing in huge numbers is a strong indicator that a key chemical burden threshold has been crossed. We may have unwittingly unleashed an agricultural Chernobyl."

The outlook for the future? Dismal. Even more pesticide use is predicted, along with a dramatic rise in chemicals throughout society. Keep in mind that, except for France, IMD is the most popular insecticide for Bayer in the U.S., Europe, and Asia, applied in greater amounts than any other toxin to kill bugs. Not only that, the patents are running out, which means other manufacturers can in some countries make cheap generic versions of IMD, spreading its use even further.

This is what the honey bee faces in the United States and around the world. This is the future we as consumers face. It is a grim prospect. Not only is pesticide use exploding faster than population growth, the government is for the most part ignoring the prime suspect for CCD at everyone's peril, even to the point of endangering the very food supply. It's not even about the money anymore. The old paradigm is obviously defending its very way of life.

In 2007, it is the kindly beekeepers who suddenly find themselves opposing the entire Establishment, an Establishment seemingly blinded by the passion of defending an idea—that agrochemists know what they're doing, that pesticides are fundamentally safe. Former ABF President David Hackenberg worries that beekeepers are "up against some of the most powerful people in the world."

THE BEEKEEPER RESPONSE IN THE U.S.

The beekeepers, led by Hackenberg and some others in an ad hoc manner, meanwhile tried to cope with the situation and form some kind of response. Hackenberg ended his March 2007 letter to the growers' associations with a plea to not spray before the bees arrive:

Even though we may "think" we know something about what is killing the bees, there is very little that will be done by regulatory agencies in [the] short term to help us.

We need the cooperation of our pollination customers for this. That is something individual growers can help with. I have already got word from my largest customer, Jasper Wyman and Sons Blueberry Co. that they will not use these products on blueberries and I wish to thank them for taking the lead. I am asking you as a grower to take a look at what you have used last year and what you might be using this year. If at all possible, please try to use something beside these products. I have attached a list of neonicotinoid products and their brand names.

If you as a grower feel you must use these products, please speak to me before honey bees are placed in your crops. We as beekeepers must do everything we can to minimize our exposure.

Since he got little practical help from Penn State, Hackenberg began asking himself some very pertinent questions: Why did CCD happen to his hives in November, several months after being near IMD? He realized that when the hive was working a commercial pollination job, contaminated pollen and nectar would be stored in the hive's honeycombs. This IMD-tainted food would be finally eaten only over the fall and winter, when cold weather prevented any member from leaving the hive for days at a time. Hackenberg writes:

[The bees] bring the pollen and nectar back to the hive and store it in their comb to use later. It is usually several months later when natural sources of pollen and nectar slow down in the field that the bees would use this store of pollen and nectar to raise brood that the symptoms appear. The young bees raised on this food may exhibit memory loss and impaired immune response.

What may finally kill the hive are two things: first, the loss of most of their adult bees because when "sick" bees leave the hive to collect food they do not return (disappearing disease) and second, the remaining young bees in the hive may have such a weakened immune system that normal pathogens found in the hive such as fungus easily overwhelm them. The result is a dead hive loaded with pathogens in the dead and dying brood left behind. Of course, these symptoms appear several months after exposure to neonicotinoids and up until recently the cause and effect appeared unrelated.

It should be noted that the bees concentrate IMD in nectar when they evaporate water to make honey within their bodies. Nectar is converted from 90–95% water to 18.5–19.5% water in honey. If the bee then eats the honey, it gets four to five times the IMD dose per gram than the original nectar could deliver. So the American bees are likely getting a far more potent punch from eating their honey than the French bees typically get from a dose direct from the nectar. Plus the American bees, in general, are more diseased and mite-ridden than the French bees, thanks to many operations mingling all together during pollination season. The U.S. honey bees seemed to be getting hit harder than their European cousins, and it could be the concentrated IMD in the honey stores.

Back in the fields, Hackenberg and fellow beekeepers were trying to avoid IMD contamination, but many growers refused to stop spraying, listening instead to the pesticide salesmen and scientists. Hackenberg said, "We've been telling them, just give us another ten days and our bees will be out of there. But the chemical people say, 'No, you've got to spray now.'" As a result, Hackenberg Apiaries tells its customers to look elsewhere for bees if they are using or plan to use IMD.

This strategy has already paid off. Hackenberg's hives have quickly climbed from a low of 800 all the way back to 2,400. Another keeper, Jim Aucker, of Millville, Pennsylvania, had 1,200 hives, got down to 250, and has since brought his colonies back to 600 strong. He is convinced, like Hackenberg, that IMD is the cause of colony collapse disorder.[11] Aucker has avoided pollination jobs on fields that use IMD and believes that is the reason he was able to bounce back some. In a phone interview, he said, "Once we started avoiding imidacloprid, the bees looked better." Hackenberg, however, did send his bees to California and is now back down to 1,200 hives.

Perhaps the most fortunate thing about colony collapse disorder is that bee colonies can be rebuilt rapidly, within a couple to a few months. If IMD is the cause, and commercial pollinators can keep their bees away from tainted crops and orchards, they might be able to avoid CCD and thrive. As in France, where the bees made a partial recovery, there are now these two anecdotal examples of the bees coming back in America, in which avoiding IMD appeared to be a factor.

THE RESPONSE FROM RESEARCHERS IN THE U.S.

The colony collapse disorder crisis in the U.S. was beginning to look like the early situation in Europe. The EPA and most university researchers continued to ignore the crucial 108-page IMD report from the government in France, only seriously considering the Bayer or BASF studies, and focused attention on other causes. Throughout 2007, Bayer and BASF continued to use favorable studies from agrochemists, toxicologists, and entomologists on IMD and fipronil, showing their safety for bees. The chemical companies also kept using the talking point that the bees had never returned to France, even though they had come back in the southwest of the country in 2005. Most U.S. entomologists and bee researchers, like their European counterparts, focused on non-man-made causes, such as viruses, bacteria, and parasites, or blamed it on the beekeepers in the way they managed, fed, and transported the bees. Other U.S. research, however, supports the idea that IMD is a suspect for CCD. One report from North Carolina showed that when a fungicide was combined with IMD, the neurotoxic effects were increased a *thousandfold*. This means that a very, very small amount of IMD, combined with the fungicide together in a product or through sequential applications, could have a detrimental effect. Fungicides and IMD are often used or even mixed together now.

In the April 24, 2007, issue of northwestern Michigan's Horticultural Research Station *Weekly Update*, beekeepers were warned directly about IMD, telling them to beware of neonicotinoid pesticides disrupting bee navigation:

> *As we mentioned last week, we have reported cases of colony collapse disorder (CCD) in our honey bee hives in the region. We also reported that neonicotinoid insecticides have been found in nectar and pollen in hives where bees have disappeared. The following recommendation has been issued from Dr. Zachary Huang, the MSU honey bee expert: Avoid using neonicotinoid insecticides near honeybees, if possible. If growers must rely on these chemistries, avoid using them during bloom or before bloom, as the pesticides are systemic and can be transported into nectar and pollen. . . . Recent evidence suggests neonicotinoids can impair honey bee learning and disrupt their homing abilities.*

THE GOVERNMENT RESPONDS?

As colony collapse disorder swept the U.S., Bayer continued to maintain its position on CCD not being linked to IMD. "We have done a significant amount of research on our products, and we are comfortable it is not the cause," said John Boyne, company spokesman, in a June 2007 AP report. Boyne reiterated that "a number of non-chemical causes may be to blame."

At the same time, a few in the government, like Senator Barbara Boxer, were aware that IMD might be a problem and included money for pesticide research funding. Emergency federal legislation, the Boxer/Thune Pollinator Protection Act, provides $89 million in research grants, in part to find out the cause of CCD. Without holding any hearings on the French experience, however, this five-year budget unnecessarily studies a multitude of other possibilities. In the end, the bill spends money on multiple theories and bee health, but allocates only one-ninth of $2 million a year to study pesticides in general. That's about $250,000 annually for research grants from the Secretary of Agriculture for pesticides. One area of concern, the synergistic effect between neonicotinoids and fungicides on bees, is not funded. Nor is the University of Florida's Jamie Ellis, who wondered if hive miticides might synergize with IMD-tainted nectar from painted seeds, causing immune problems and parasites.

This bill has been only partially allocated so far, due to tight budgets. On July 13, 2007, USDA Deputy Secretary Gale Buchanan announced an additional emergency CCD Research Action Plan, funded by redirecting several million department dollars. Here again, most of the money goes toward funding research on other causes, although some of this money *is* spent with the Penn State group to study sublethal doses of pesticide. This money, too, has been arriving at Katrina response speed, with $4 million due only at the end of August 2008!

The response from the government, as this book went to press, has been painfully slow, misdirected in many ways and completely inadequate to the looming catastrophe confronting us. There has, however, been a positive response to an apiary disaster relief bill that was proposed to Congress by the American Beekeeping Federation in early 2008. This legislation would bail out the beekeepers and pay them for every lost hive as Ontario and Manitoba do in Canada. Beekeepers would also receive tax breaks and carry-forwards for losses. Hopefully, this beekeeper bailout will pass in the U.S. Congress and be signed by the president by the time you read these words.

NATURE AND *60 MINUTES* COVER CCD

Colony collapse disorder began to garner great attention in the U.S. when the PBS television show *Nature* devoted a whole hour to the crisis in late October 2007, on the same night CBS's *60 Minutes* spent fifteen minutes on the subject. Although both broadcasts interviewed Dave Hackenberg, he says that PBS cut out all his comments on IMD (which he refers to as "neonicotinoids"). CBS News, to its credit, did not censor him, and on national television Hackenberg was able to state his concern, that he thinks insecticides are causing colony collapse disorder:

> *HACKENBERG: Well, basically, the chemical, the manufacturers of this product say it breaks down their immune system, causes memory loss, causes nervous system disorders. It causes the insects to quit feeding.*
>
> *KROFT: [narrating over film of the Bayer CropScience plant] Bayer CropScience, a leading manufacturer of neonicotinoids, denies that the pesticide is responsible for colony collapse, and it cites studies which support that conclusion. Other studies by the French government, and*

protests by French beekeepers, caused the pesticide to be partially banned there in 1999.

HACKENBERG: This product causes insects to lose their sense of navigation.

PETTIS: Well, if that's true, then we'll be able to find certain levels of different pesticides in those hives. And we haven't—we don't have that complete picture yet. We just don't have consistency that points us in that direction.[12]

What was not brought out in the broadcast was that the French found that as little as six parts per billion IMD disrupts foraging and eating. Nor did the broadcast mention the North Carolina study that showed a commonly used fungicide amplifies the effects of one of the neonics by a thousand times. Pettis's claim of inconsistency thus stood unchallenged. In truth, in the field, the bioavailability of IMD from multiple sources alone gets the contamination level beyond the sublethal dose needed, as the French studies found.

With the French research from 2003, only 6 parts per billion IMD is enough—easily gotten from nectar, pollen, leaves, and water in the field. The apparent inconsistency between the French and Bayer experiments seems, in fact, to be related to the bees being able to sense IMD above 20 PPB. As we have seen, that, and other technical factors, could very well account for a discrepancy. The critical point of the *60 Minutes* segment came when Dr. Pettis said of Hackenberg's worry that IMD was the cause, "Well, if that's true, then we'll be able to find certain levels of different pesticides in those hives. And we haven't. . . . We just don't have consistency." At Penn State, however, Dr. Chris Mullin has found IMD and many other pesticides in almost all pollen and beeswax samples studied.

Dr. Mullin was called and interviewed for this book in early 2008. So far Mullin has looked at 108 samples of pollen, bee bread and beeswax and screened them for up to 171 various pesticides. One sample contained seventeen different chemicals. Most ominously, only three out of the 108 samples were clean, with no detection of toxins.[13] In the phone interview, Dr. Mullin said Dr. Pettis's claim of inconsistency on *60 Minutes* came before his results were made, "that was a while back." He also said, "IMD is a concern," and that, in encapsulated form, it can last in the soil for ten years. Mullin also said there is more to learn and CCD is likely caused by many factors.

Before his new research on the samples, he had been quoted in *The Washington Post* discounting IMD as the culprit: "Extensive testing . . . has never proven these concentrations are high enough to harm bees." He still believes that, but, concurred that the synergistic effects from fungicides and other pesticides in the samples he looked at could magnify the potency of the IMD residues. Dr. Mullin also noted that much of the imidacloprid is excreted quickly and the excretions are removed from the hive by the colony, so IMD intoxication does wear off rapidly.

Mullin told the January 2008 conference in Sacramento there are trace amounts of IMD in the hive, confirmed by his new research at Penn State. Mullin's work has not been officially published yet, but it was revealed at a January 2008 beekeeper conference in California, and at the special San Diego CCD conference held a little earlier. At the same conference, Dr. Pettis revealed that test hives at Penn State would be exposed to pesticides as well as to IAPV, to see if the colonies can be made to collapse. The main question, however, remains: Will the dead IAPV hives or pesticide test hives show all the symptoms of CCD as well? In addition, Dr. Colin has noted it is relatively easy to feed honey bees IMD and, due to conditions, the disorientation will not appear. Hopefully, Pettis and Penn State will contact Dr. Colin and learn how to duplicate his IMD experiment exactly, and see if they get the same result.

WHERE DOES ALL THIS LEAVE US?

To sum up, it appears that, except for *60 Minutes*, the media is not quite keeping the powers-that-be honest, the chemical industry lobbyists have been given the key to the regulatory candy store by the Bush White House, the EPA is thoroughly politicized and compromised, the USDA is focusing on natural causes, rather than man-made ones, the universities have been increasingly privatized by chemical industry "largesse," the growers are mesmerized by the pesticide salesmen—and all the while the bees keep dying. Even the Democrats in Congress seem to have been led off the trail by the many red herrings left by scientific witnesses.

The facts appear to be held hostage by the supporters of chemical farming. They are worried that if IMD is the new DDT—and is seen as killing the bees—the public may insist on enforcing the regulatory tests and proper examination that hundreds of chemicals have so far avoided. And those required safety tests could prove to be a legal trump card, as IMD was approved without sublethal dose tests for bees. If thought to be unsafe, the authorizations can be withdrawn by the federal government. The burden of legal proof is then on Bayer CropScience to prove IMD safe, not on the environmentalists or beekeepers to prove that it is unsafe. Ignoring that 108-page Comité Scientifique et Technique report—which concludes that just 6 PPB IMD do disrupt foraging—is thus key to the strategy for keeping the chemical on the market. That research is new, qualified "relevant information" that claims IMD is not safe for bees, down to the lowest trace amounts. In short, as soon as that report is acknowledged, and a repeal process triggered, it would snowball and IMD would likely be removed from the market at some point.

All this stalling over testing and the successful slick public relations on IMD can only happen because the populace is still unaware of the facts. The loss of investigative journalism and a truly free press in America has now proved to be a catastrophic loss indeed, not just in the case of the bees but also, as Al Gore argues, in the case of global warming. As Carson proclaimed in 1962, however, the ultimate need for health and survival means that the public has the right to know yet another inconvenient truth, the truth about the bees—and decide for itself if "it wishes to continue on the present road."

As it was with DDT, America is clearly being kept in the dark when it comes to IMD and the other neonicotinoids. Gore made clear that the lobbyist/EPA fox is guarding the henhouse, or in this case the beehive—and all people can do is ask, "I wonder why all those bees keep disappearing?" The government is today officially dependent on that same fox to solve the mystery, to give us definitive scientific proof of the answer. Yet what happens when that answer means the fox's friends could no longer sell billions of dollars worth of products? Wouldn't the fox do anything to stop the truth from coming out? It appears to be a Catch-22 for the bees—and for the humans.

THE BIGGER PICTURE

How did we get to the point where the chemical industry is rewriting EPA regulations and the government acts as though environmental laws simply don't exist? Our present-day world seems to have forgotten *Silent Spring*'s warning: that the entire planet, and society itself, is threatened by the use and overuse of pesticides. The free rein given to corporations, through the control of the government by lobbyists, has gotten so bad it seems the underpinnings of civilization itself are coming apart—not just with the bees but in many different areas, from hundreds of "dead zones" in the ocean to global warming, the economy unraveling, and much, much more.

If all this is true, are we facing our very own human version of colony collapse disorder? Doesn't the collapse of the beehive tell us something about the fragility of our own human hive? Could the dead bees be merely a symptom of a deeper problem, an indicator that something is terribly wrong in our supposedly democratic, scientific society?

The missing bees bring up all sorts of disturbing questions, including ones about ourselves.

Nine

Civilization Collapse Disorder

The disappearance of the bees nonetheless has mythic depth. It captures intuitions people have about the human condition. A hive is an organism, like a nation. It may be made up of individuals, but it produces results beyond the imagination of any one of its members. To think of one unraveling is profoundly unsettling.
—Joel Garreau, Washington Post article,
"Honey, I'm Gone!" (June 1, 2007)

ARE THE DYING HONEY BEES A METAPHOR FOR OUR OWN SPECIES? Does colony collapse disorder portend something similar for humanity's hive—could the world develop our own "Civilization Collapse Disorder"? Of course this is not to say that commuters will one day drive off to work in the morning and never come back. Might our complicated human society, however, suffer a breakdown in one part of its functionality, causing a chain reaction that leads to a collapse of civilization as we know it?

Already high food prices and scarcity have led to food riots in West Bengal and Mexico, while India, Yemen, and Burkina Faso have also seen unrest. Modern society depends on a bountiful food supply. In *Collapse: How Societies Choose to Fail or Succeed*, historian Jared Diamond tells the story of the total destruction of several previous societies as well as some that managed to avoid ruination.

Diamond found that collapse was the result of cultures failing to adapt to new challenges, or even trying to adapt. The status quo is maintained and unconscious social suicide is the result. He wrote his book in the hope that our modern world will step back, learn from history, and consider more carefully where we are headed in the future. According to Diamond, the eight factors which have historically contributed to the collapse of past cultures are:

1. Deforestation and habitat destruction
2. Degradation
3. Crises involving water
4. Overhunting
5. Overfishing
6. Destructive impact of new species to a fragile ecosystem
7. Human population growth
8. Increased impact of humans on an individual basis (lifestyle, customs)

Diamond also lists four new factors that could contribute to the weakening and collapse of present and future societies, including the buildup of chemicals:

1. Man-made climate change
2. Accumulation of poisonous chemicals
3. Energy crisis
4. Increasing human population exhausts photosynthetic capacity to produce enough food

Although environmental degradation can cause the extinction of whole civilizations, Diamond states that "it would be absurd to claim that environmental damage must be a major factor in all collapses: the collapse of the Soviet Union is a modern counterexample, and the destruction of Carthage by Rome in 146 BC is an ancient one. It's obviously true that military or economic factors alone may suffice."[1] A collapse of a civilization can come in five different ways or combinations thereof: (1) environmental damage, (2) climatic change, (3) hostile neighbors, (4) loss of trading partners, and (5) the society's own responses to its environmental problem. Diamond specifically tells the story of how several historical cultures were destroyed, including:

- Easter Island (environmental exploitation)

- The Polynesians of Pitcairn Island (environmental damage plus loss of trade)

- The Anasazi of the Southwestern U.S. (environmental damage plus drought)

- The Maya (hostile neighbors, environmental damage, climate)

- The Greenland Norse (environmental damage, loss of trading partners, climate change, hostile neighbors, plus unwillingness to change in the face of social collapse)

Professor William Rees, coauthor of *Our Ecological Footprint*, felt that the most significant lesson in *Collapse* is that societies can survive if they learn how to be flexible and adapt to the new situation. Rees illuminates how our present world is unconsciously headed down the failure/suicide path, in that economics today still trumps environmental protection:[2]

Human behaviour towards the ecosphere has become dysfunctional and now arguably threatens our own long-term security. The real problem is that the modern world remains in the sway of a dangerously illusory cultural myth . . . most governments and international agencies seem to believe that the human enterprise is somehow "decoupling" from the environment, and so is poised for unlimited expansion. Jared Diamond's new book, Collapse, *confronts this contradiction head-on.*

Author Malcolm Gladwell, writer of *The Tipping Point* and *Blink,* made another point. He said that by concentrating on the breakdown of the ability of the ecosystem to support the population, Diamond was showing that environment trumps culture, something historians usually miss. Americans in particular may feel safe and secure because their nation has a strong cultural tradition of freedom and democracy—but history shows that values mean little when the ecosystems supporting the society are wiped out. In his January 2005 review of *Collapse* for *The New Yorker,* Gladwell wrote in "The Vanishing,":

Diamond's distinction between social and biological survival is a critical one, because too often we blur the two, or assume that biological survival is contingent on the strength of our civilizational values. . . . The fact is, though, that we can be law-abiding and peace-loving and tolerant and inventive and committed to freedom and true to our own values and still behave in ways that are biologically suicidal.

COULD TODAY'S INDUSTRIAL CIVILIZATION COLLAPSE?

So, can collapse happen to us? Certainly our present global civilization is already threatened by ongoing environmental damage, as the making of the almighty dollar in the easiest way possible continues to trump reason and the pleas of environmentalists. The Law of Unintended Consequences rules everywhere. Obvious examples are the hundreds of dead zones in the ocean and dying coral reefs almost everywhere, the growing Ozone Hole, rampant deforestation, carcinogenic compounds in our food, pollution from fossil fuels, and of course global warming, which threatens to change the very map of the world. Now the bees are suffering from colony collapse disorder and that, too, may be man-made.

A large part of the planetary crisis we're in is that so many things are going wrong at the same time. If we don't shift now, the world in a few decades could be suffering from multiple hits, weakening the ability of the global economy to withstand the increased hurricanes and storms from global warming, as well as the rising sea levels, while vast forest fires destroy the landscape and plunging river levels force nuclear and coal plants to close. Energy costs and electric bills would become prohibitive, and wars over resources would be commonplace, sucking ever more human and monetary capital into a quickening whirlpool of horror and revenge.

The declining catch of seafood, the growing price of grain and meat, and the end of commercial pollination would meanwhile bring an end to a varied diet full of protein for all but the wealthiest, degrading the health and strength of the planet's eight billion people. Chemical agriculture, on a declining curve of production, and beset by the drought, storms, and floods brought on by global warming, would be decimated by the increase in energy costs, making it difficult for farmers or even agribusiness to borrow seed money or to afford nitrogen fertilizer.

With billions more poor people, not enough affordable food for even the middle class, wars for resources raging, and massive super-storms like Hurricanes Katrina and Rita destroying the economy of the U.S. and other nations, Diamond would have to agree that the factors for a collapse of global civilization are all here right now. In fact, this imploding world of the future would fail in eleven out of the twelve factors cited by Diamond in *Collapse*, which include chemical contamination. Colony collapse disorder thus sets off all sorts of alarm bells in people's minds because the threat of a collapse of our own human hive is now so real—and perhaps not so far away. The missing bees then truly do appear as the beginning of the apocalyptic futures so often depicted in science fiction movies and Stephen King novels.

As Diamond revealed, however, we can choose to adapt, we can choose success—or we can acquiesce to failure. And if we are to adapt, if we are to change, we must use science to do it. Real science. Science uncorrupted by crony capitalism. Science that regenerates and restores the environment, rather than diminishing it. We need to use science to find the solutions to all these emergencies. And to find the right answer in science or anything else, guess what you have to ask?

The right question.

THE DANGERS OF ANTHROPOCENTRIC THINKING

So what is really behind all these multiple crises? How did we ever get into such a mess? Were scientists basically overconfident and not thinking long-term? Or were they instead trapped in an old paradigm, a pre-ecology worldview that sees a machine-like Clockwork Universe, the Newtonian universe where man is the center and all nature is here to exploit for economic gain? Nature in the nineteenth century was something to be conquered, something to be controlled. Man-made causes of planet-wide disasters like global warming or the dying bees are strongly resisted, for in the anthropocentric worldview, man is justified in manipulating Nature on a macro scale. Man-made causes for global warming or the missing bees thus represent a threatening paradigm anomaly, a true challenge to the whole anthropocentric/mechanistic worldview. So the studies showing these problems to be man-made are irrationally resisted and countered with theories blaming natural causes.

In *Silent Spring*, Rachel Carson declared that the entire anthropocentric notion that man could control nature is hazardous to our health. The anthropocentric worldview is a concept made obsolete by ecology, which teaches us that man is not the center of the universe. If anything, the center would have to be the living biosphere around us, existing in a fragile, interconnected balance. Rather than endlessly exploiting nature, ecological science shows that we need to respect the biosphere, that we ourselves depend on it for life, and that the biosphere could sicken and die like any other living being. There is today a whole new level of awareness in ecology, beyond the old anthropocentric universe. This is not to say there can't be such things as economic development and wise use of resources—but from now on there must be a new ethic in harvesting the bounty of nature. We must discover how to live in harmony with the biosphere while creating wealth, how to restore the environment rather than destroy it. We must respect the Law of Unintended Consequences by always using The Principle of Precaution.

It is not science or development itself that is bad, but rather that the old, pre-ecology paradigm was limited in its modeling from the beginning. Technology and the conquest of nature was the answer to everything. Now co-opted by industry dollars, the old mechanistic thinking has led itself—and the world—into a series of technological dead ends. Pesticides, global warming, agricultural pollution of the oceans, overdevelopment of the land, overfishing, governments run by corporate lobbyists, unsustainable economics, a coming reduction in the production of oil, built-in inefficiencies everywhere—the list of dead ends goes on and on.

Civilization as we know it can only take so many hits, so many Category 4 and 5 hurricanes destroying oil rigs, so many summer droughts shutting down nuclear and coal power plants (as has already occurred in Europe). There are already two billion people who live in abject poverty, who live on soil so poor that subsistence farming gives them an average of only one meal a day. Throughout all these crises, most people in the industrialized world ignore the dilemma caused by the old machine-model science, acting as though their own lives are not in danger. These dead ends are catching up to humanity, however, and starting to synergize in terrible ways. Civilization is, according to several different perspectives, living on borrowed time, borrowed money, and a borrowed environment. It appears it's time to pay the piper, and none of us are going to like the ruinous bill.

It would be a wonderful irony if the global concern about the bees eventually led to a paradigm shift on pesticides and the environment, waking people up to the current crisis of chemical farming and how the government and corporations are bamboozling them. It would become another major tipping point, adding to the political tipping points on global warming, chemical pollution, corporate responsibility, media accountability, and so on. The momentum for deep change could suddenly be there. Then the crisis of the honey bee would certainly be a historic wake-up call—and would have helped save us in the end from our own human CCD.

THE MECHANISTIC DILEMMA

So if we want to avoid the nightmare of Civilization Collapse Disorder, where do we start? Insecticide bans? Global warming? Dead zones in the ocean? Corporate reregulation? Global poverty? The truth is all of these problems have a single paradigmatic cause: the old pre-ecology science, which views everything through the model of a machine. As pointed out by thinkers from William Barrett to Fritjof Capra to Ken Wilber, mechanistic thinking is the underlying problem. The fatal flaw of the old worldview, of the Clockwork Universe, is that it is trying to understand life through an analogy that does not itself possess life. A clock cannot explain a flower, or the birds and the bees, or the fragility of an ecosystem. Life, biology, and ecology are far more complex than a simple clock mechanism.

When you get right down to it, the world will never get itself out of this "Mechanistic Dilemma" unless it completes the shift to ecological science and the new interconnected, biological models of nature. Trying to solve each of the symptoms separately will take far too long, and then the old paradigm remains in control of the institutions and governments of the world. Without completing the paradigm shift, the mechanistic worldview will still be in a position to obstruct change and even create new disasters, complicating an otherwise workable future with new dead-end technologies and concepts.

The man-made causes afflicting our planet will continue to be ignored by the mechanists at a furious pace, just so the anomalies don't expose the utter falsity of the anthropocentric worldview. Just as the Catholic Church refused to accept the reality of the heliocentric system until 1751, 208 years after Copernicus revealed the obvious truth, the mechanists are prepared to dig in their heels and defend their paradigm to the bitter end. Consciously shifting the paradigm and addressing the root cause of the dilemma, rather than just the symptoms, is the ultimate cure for Civilization Collapse Disorder.

THE PUBLIC HAS TO WAKE UP

However we decide to tackle them, the multiple crises must be solved as soon as possible. Everything has to happen simultaneously, which will actually create a synergy and positive reinforcement for the new paradigm solutions. Just as global warming and global poverty must be addressed immediately, the pesticide situation appears to be a crisis that cannot wait. We must become active on many different fronts at once. Avoiding the human version of CCD means reinventing most of society and science, from economics to energy to agriculture and education and beyond. They are all huge, institutional changes.

For example, the EPA and the FDA, and similar government entities around the world, have literally been getting away with murder—bureaucratic murder in the form of not requiring all the mandated safety tests for dangerous chemicals, thus exposing the public to likely carcinogens and endocrine disruptors. Through the use of loopholes, the FDA does not even test for residues for many of these poisons, the Law of Unintended Consequences be damned. This must be changed immediately, for people are currently ingesting unknown amounts of toxins of many kinds.

For example, the FDA does not always test for all chemical residue—some chemicals are not on the list of toxins to monitor. Why is IMD not on the list? Because the EPA has never given permanent food or feed crop approval status to IMD, nor to the hundreds of other chemicals that are given "emergency" waivers. Clearly, little thought is given to human health by this rigged system—never mind the health of the bees.

Once the regulatory system fails, the public has to demand a ban through other means. The public has to force the change, reform that happens only through the political process and the courts. For the public to become active, however, people must first know the facts that are being kept from them. The public, as Rachel Carson said, has the right to know. As of now, most people simply don't understand the hazards of pesticides and herbicides for the environment and their family's health. Or they would not be doing what they do every single day—which is using pesticides everywhere, seemingly anytime they are suggested by commercial advertising. This includes fly strips, bug sprays, lawn products, garden sprays, and extermination products.

Carson said we need to totally rethink how chemicals are tested for human safety, especially for diseases like cancer and more subtle problems. For the last forty-five years, *Silent Spring* has inspired a scientific revolution in toxicology, leading to many key realizations—including the discovery that toxins must be studied in combination for their synergistic effects, not just one at a time. Chemicals must also be tested for long-term safety and extensively for low-dose physical, reproductive, and mental problems, especially developmental problems for fetuses. While high doses are lethal and cause immediate death, low doses can hijack the development of embryos and cause new, hidden problems. Although all this is now known, the EPA and the chemical industry lobbyists continue to stall DNT testing as long as they can, to the detriment of public health—and the environment.

And then there's cancer, especially from earlier pesticides. According to the American Cancer Society, men in the U.S. now have a 45% chance of cancer in their lifetime and women 38%.[3] Pesticides, especially ones from decades ago, are likely a major factor boosting this high rate. Meanwhile some very disturbing trends are beginning to emerge in the environment at large, oddities that have been tied to the use of pesticides.

It was discovered in 2002 that the weed killer atrazine in water runoff causes frogs to become hermaphrodites, to be both male and female. This effect occurs at levels *30,000 times* below the lethal dose. A 2001 study of historical birth data and DDT use meanwhile found that 15% of all infant mortality in the United States during the 1950s and 1960s could be linked to low-dose effects of that chlorine-based insecticide.[4] In general, low doses of many chemicals can disrupt the signals that run the mind, the body, and the reproductive system. This means using novel and toxic chemicals for farming, landscaping, and lawn maintenance could be far more hazardous than we thought. If true, it also means the safety levels we have today are too high and should be lowered as research demands, while the testing tools are hopelessly out of date. To find out more, visit the Web sites of the NRDC, the Sierra Club, Beyond Pesticides, the Pesticide Action Network, and RefuseToBuyChemLawn.org.

The low-dose issue in particular raises still more disturbing questions about the whole EPA/FDA health system. Even today, we don't have a lot of the tools needed to ensure safety, for the sub-lethal doses are so low and difficult to detect and the possibility of signal disruption and disease are so enormous. There is a huge gap between the proven science on low-dose effects and the old public health standards for chemicals. Not to mention the outright corruption of the system in the revolving door between the employment of lobbyists, regulators, and industry management.

Under the federal pesticide law, the Federal Insecticide, Fungicide, and Rodenticide Act (FIFRA), the EPA is given authority over pesticides—but it merely requires the EPA find that a chemical poses "no *unreasonable* risk," a term that can be subjectively interpreted. The EPA is moreover allowed to weigh the economic benefits against the risks, tipping the scales in favor of industry. Then the agency avoids having full tests through temporary authorizations, relying on the manufacturer's initial trial data. The use of emergency authorizations must be reserved for true emergencies, not as a legal loophole allowing truckloads of new products to avoid the tests they are supposed to undergo.

Rachel Carson explained in *Silent Spring* that nature evolved over hundreds of millions of years to reach the fruitful balance of the present. Using ever-more-lethal chemicals to battle insects and increase farming yields threatens to undo that delicate balance, even with low doses—and so a different way must be sought. Unfortunately, this barrage of poison affects good insects as well as bad. Not only bees, but beneficial bugs like earthworms and lacewings are also wiped out by the toxins that end up in the environment. The balance of nature that took hundreds of millions of years to evolve beneficial insects like the honey bee can in no way cope with the flood of chemicals being thrown at it. Remember how delicate and sensitive the honey bee genome is? Although hardier individual pests may adapt and thus become resistant, the ecosystem as a whole is thrown off, with bees, birds, predaceous mites, and spiders dying from increased applications, thus removing natural predators from the sprayed fields. There is no free lunch, especially with pesticides. But there is the Law of Unintended Consequences. There's also Murphy's Law: "If anything can go wrong, it will." That certainly seems to be at work here as well.

Right now, it's often left up to environmental groups like the Natural Resources Defense Council or the Pesticide Action Network to defend the public interest and sue the EPA to do the proper testing or take the product off the market. A lawsuit, unfortunately, takes several years and the industry is in the meantime free to spray the new crops, often with illegally increased tolerance levels. States, moreover, have preemption laws, which prevent local governments from passing antipesticide ordinances more stringent than state tolerance levels. In short, the system is rigged in favor of the corporations, which, as we have seen, are enormous campaign contributors and mount huge lobbying efforts. The Congress typically takes little or no action in this area, although there is hope with a new Congress.

There is even less protection from the EPA for residential use than there is for agriculture. None of the chemicals mentioned above have been studied properly for synergistic effects, for example, although they are certainly applied together, and sometimes even mixed together. Oftentimes, synergistic effects amplify the potency or detrimental side effects of a pesticide treatment. Bee-keepers recently began to worry that "Triple Stack" Corn, corn treated with Roundup, YieldGard Corn Borer, and YieldGard Rootworm, is especially problematic for bees that encounter the wind-swept pollen.[5] Triple Stack Corn is therefore another area that requires immediate research.

Testing, however, is done primarily by the manufacturer themselves. And even when chemicals show risk, the EPA may not ban their use. For example, tests that have been done show that of thirty commonly used lawn chemicals, nineteen appear to cause cancer, thirteen are suspected of creating birth defects, twenty-one are linked to reproductive problems, fifteen affect the nervous system, twenty-six can lead to liver or kidney disease, and eleven could disrupt hormones.[6] Yet the EPA declares them all safe for home use.

ORGANIC, BIOLOGICAL CONTROL OF INSECTS IS THE SOLUTION

Carson pulled her punches and suggested more careful use of pesticides while alternatives are phased in. All of the current techniques of organic farmers, however, were not known in 1962. Today, on the other hand, the biological and organic methods of insect control are very well known and extremely effective. With higher organic prices, organic farming is now more profitable than conventional agriculture. There is no scientific or economic reason preventing most conventional chemical farmers from converting to organic methods. Yet the government, which first created the agrochemical industry after World War II, does little to help shift farmers away from chemical farming. We must realize that the underlying anthropocentric notion that nature can be controlled, that nature can be continually battered by toxins, endless development, and pollution flies in the face of the Law of Unintended Consequences. We need to adapt to nature, not the other way around.

We can start the struggle with a clarion call to protect the environment—by enacting a global suspension of IMD until it is proved safe for bees and children. There must be an enormous political effort on several fronts to change the way things work—or the bees will just be the beginning of our problems. In fact, with so many brewing disasters—from global warming to a widening war—the true story of the bees, the breakdown of EPA regulation of pesticides, and the failure of chemical farming get no attention. As in France, a vast coalition and visible protest may be necessary. Bayer CropScience is not going to let its number-one insecticide be suspended from use without a fight.

It would mean farmers could no longer control aphids with IMD, nor could golf courses and homeowners spray tons of the stuff to keep down grubs. Unless totally banned, it should be noted that IMD and Fipronil are permanently approved by the EPA for use in homes for termites, fleas and ant control, which would not be affected by any suspension of IMD for food crops. If imidacloprid and other neonicotinoids could not be sold to farmers, the chemical companies would no doubt predict disaster.

Fortunately, there are today solid biological alternatives to IMD and the others. Organic farming and gardening have themselves been evolving since 1962, and the insect solutions for farmers, gardeners, and homeowners are very reliable. Following reform of the EPA, USDA, and FDA, the government would have to revamp agriculture and pest control along the lines of the new advances. Homeowners, meanwhile, should be looking for ways to switch to organic lawn maintenance and organic gardening. The concept of "lawn" itself needs a paradigm shift: move away from solid mats of monoculture Kentucky bluegrass and, instead, encourage botanical diversity—more clovers, mints, plantains, and dandelions to feed the bees. It will look a little different, but it will be more in harmony with nature.

Whether through political activism and participation, or through active changes in one's own life and occupation, the starting point to saving the bees is to get IMD out of the ecosystem until testing proves it safe, as was done in France. Science must respect the Law of Unintended Consequences and be guided by the Principle of Precaution. Everyone has to pitch in, learn the new solutions, and really change. As with global warming, solving CCD apparently means becoming more aware of society's relationship with the insect world and how we can change our own individual lives. Just as energy conservation begins at home, saving the bees thus means changing the way we buy food, exterminate insects in our buildings, and treat our home lawns. Perhaps IMD will be proven perfectly safe for bees, and not a "significant risk," as the French found. Until that day, however, under the FIFRA law, its use must be suspended and lots of things have to change.

It will not be quick or easy. We must all join together and start on a strong effort to stop the way things are going. For right now, civilization is on the failure-suicide path. We must change our direction soon—before it is too late. As Jared Diamond showed in *Collapse*, the choice is up to us. Civilization today exhibits eleven of the twelve factors for failure, and the buildup of toxic chemicals is one of those eleven. We can choose the status quo and thus failure, or take the path of adaptation and success. If IMD is seen by the public as the prime suspect behind colony collapse disorder, it could very well be the thing that brings the paradigm shift to a global tipping point. Before a worldview is given up, however, people must feel secure that the new paradigm actually works—that they can change their habits as well as their thoughts and not be betrayed by reality. They must know that the new science is not only real, but superior, on a wholly different level. And they must understand thoroughly how it all works.

We need to switch from chemicals to natural techniques and controls, but it must be done carefully. Replacing conventional chemical methods with biological controls and organic farming methods can cause economic and yield issues if not transitioned correctly. A mass transition to organic must all be thought out beforehand and fully funded by the U.S. Congress, as well as governments around the world. There is no lack of knowledge about how to do this. We have today not only the examples of Australia and New Zealand, where there is no CCD, but also the 12,000 organic farmers in the United States. We must study those methods further and make available all information to every grower and turf manager on the planet.

The waiting is over. The time to change is now if we want to avoid waking up to a spring without bees.

Ten

The Farmer Solution

*We allow the chemical death rain to fall as though there were no
alternative, whereas in fact there are many, and our ingenuity
could soon discover many more if given opportunity.*
—RACHEL CARSON, *SILENT SPRING*, 1962

IN THE 1960S, RACHEL CARSON PREDICTED THAT HUMAN
INGENUITY WOULD SOON DISCOVER MANY SAFE AND NAT-
URAL ALTERNATIVES TO PESTICIDES. She was right. Today,
just about every major pest has an organic, natural solution,
with no need for harsh chemicals. The wonderful thing about a
successful biological control is that the pests cannot evolve and
become resistant to the attack, for they are up against evolution
itself in the form of their specific natural predator. For example,
aphids are eaten up voraciously by lacewing larvae, and that's
been going on for millions of years. With chemicals, however,
succeeding generations of insects can quickly become immune
to powerful toxins, turning them into "super-bugs." Stronger
doses or more applications are needed which, in turn, cause
even more adaptation and resistance. Biological controls take
the pest problem out of the dangerous spiral of growing toxicity,
what Carson called the "pesticide treadmill." A bug can't evolve
against its own natural predator, or rather it could, but it might
take a million years.

The Chinese ideogram, or pictogram, for crisis actually means "crisis-opportunity": within every crisis is a hidden opportunity to improve things; you just have to be able to see it. So within the CCD crisis is a hidden opportunity, the chance for U.S. agriculture to shift more toward organic farming, to forgo the insecticides and herbicides altogether.

With organic methods and biological controls, the Law of Unintended Consequences is far, far less likely to be violated, meaning few problems and virtually no catastrophes. So let's take agriculture quickly in this direction! The USDA has the ability through its extension agent system to accomplish the conversion of growers to organic and IPM, starting with the largest users of IMD such as almonds and blueberries. Australia and New Zealand, where there is no CCD, have IMD "time-outs," to prevent insect resistance to the poison, as well as many other programs that would be helpful for the USDA to study. Extension agents need to be trained in organic methods, have soil checked for IMD residues, and help farmers transition to biological controls.

In almost every region, farmers converting to organic methods successfully get high enough yields without using chemicals of *any* kind. They even have a greater profit than their conventional neighbors because they are receiving higher prices for their goods, plus they don't ever have to buy expensive chemical fertilizers, herbicides, or pesticides. To an organic farmer, the key to managing pests, besides some safe, organic sprays, powders, and essential oils, is to make sure their soil is healthy and that natural predators are present. Healthy soil is key to all organic farming.

Chemical farming tries to control nature by repeatedly blasting fields with powerful toxins, but this ends up killing the beneficial microorganisms and bacteria that make soil healthy in the first place. Natural predators, such as birds and other bugs like spiders, are also removed from the ecosystem by the sprays and painted seeds (birds eating whole seeds painted with pesticides can die). Earthworms, for example, are very susceptible to IMD and many other pesticides. With hot, unhealthy soil and no natural predators, no earthworms or other "beneficials," crops are even more dependent on chemicals and artificial fertilizers to generate high yields. Even worse, the pests then develop resistance and additional, stronger applications are needed again. It's a vicious cycle, slowly degenerating the whole system.

Organic farming is the antidote to all this. By using composted manure to fertilize and annually restore the health of their fields, and by ensuring that natural predators have a safe home in interspersed strips of brush and woodlands, organic farmers actually *regenerate* the environment. The health of the whole system, biologically and economically, is continually increasing—instead of slowly spiraling downwards.

Beyond Organic: Regenerative Agriculture

Besides new biological controls, organic farmers today possess powerful new knowledge, garnered from their own experience and the comprehensive research of soil scientists. We now know exactly how soil works, something that was not understood as little as twenty-five years ago. Researchers such as Dr. George Bird have shown that there are entire ecosystems within every shovelful of soil, billions and billions of microorganisms and bacteria that interact together, creating the balance that we know as healthy, fertile soil. Take away one link in this chain reaction of life-forms, and the entire system starts to degenerate. Conversely, add compost and other items, and one can regenerate even dead soil, restoring its fertility and ability to create large agricultural yields. (See Appendix 6: Farmer Solutions.)

Organic farming has actually evolved in the last two decades toward a new approach: low-till or no-till "Regenerative Agriculture." Developed first by The Rodale Institute at their Experimental Farm in Kutztown, Pennsylvania, Regenerative Agriculture is now taught in universities around the world and used extensively in certified organic food production.[1] Systematizing all the new advances in soil science, biological insect controls, and farm design, regenerative farming consciously restores the local environment through its operation. It is a whole-system approach, planned out in advance to promote regeneration.

By reducing the compacting of soil through low-till or no-till methods, moreover, not only does soil health improve, but the climate crisis is addressed in two ways. Less fossil fuel is being used as there is less need for tractors, especially big, diesel-guzzling tractors. Lighter tilling, meanwhile, releases far less methane from plowed soil into the atmosphere. Methane is a more potent greenhouse gas than carbon dioxide, and its reduction is critical for planetary survival. An additional benefit is that the reduced tractor time means lower fuel costs and higher profit for the farmer.

Regenerative farm design is always careful to have adjoining brush and wildlands, so that natural predators—and pollinators—have a healthy habitat. These tiny little workers help the farmer control pests in the field, and their salary requirements are zero. Regenerative farm design depends on the following:

- Proper farmland assessments and design

- Renewable energy feasibility studies, planning, and project management

- Woodland management designed to restore trees, brush, and open space

- Wildlife habitat regeneration and management

- Reduced water harvesting

- Natural storm-water treatment systems to prevent runoff of nutrients

- Sustainable and organic agriculture that encourages natural predators and healthy soil

Regenerative farmers restore the environment as they operate, sometimes even bringing fish back to waters where there were none, or expanding wetland habitats. American Quaker farmers have a saying: "If you want to live and thrive, let the spider run alive." This goes not only for the spiders, but also the birds, wasps, hornets, wild bees, beneficial mites, nematodes, and a host of other organisms. Once a farm goes regenerative, the adjoining wildlands flourish with natural predators, and that alone typically relieves some of the need for insecticides. With regenerative farm design, the old-fashioned way of farming is making a huge comeback, supported by organic food sales increasing in popularity by 20% each and every year. The public clearly wants organic products.

HEDGEROWS SHOULD BE PLANTED BY FARMERS

Since nearby woodlands and hedgerows also provide a habitat for wild native bees, these should be brought back to the immense agricultural fields that stretch from California's Central Valley to the Atlantic Coast of the U.S. In 2002, Dr. Robbin Thorp, emeritus professor of entomology at UC Davis, and Dr. Claire Kremen, a conservation biologist at UC Berkeley, published a study on the effect of native bees on California watermelon pollination.[2] They found that, because woods and brush were always nearby, organic watermelon fields tucked into the hills were nicely pollinated by bumblebees and other native species. Down in the Central Valley, however, the long stretches of monoculture fields, with no woodlands left, meant that the native bees had no place to live. Farmers had to rent hives for the pollen-hungry fruit, which require 1,000 grains of pollen just to fertilize one flower. That's a lot of work, even for the bees. Kremen chose watermelon to study for that reason. If native bees can pollinate that crop, they can succeed on any other. The research thus produced dramatic results, showing that native bees, if given a chance, can pollinate crops that now require commercial honey bees.

Kremen has several recommendations. Farmers should first of all think of the cost of managing the native bee population as something that will offset their need to rent expensive commercial hives. Appropriate habitat needs to be provided. Full Belly Farms in California's Central Valley, an organic operation that worked with Dr. Kremen, has planted hedgerows of native shrubbery to expand their local natives, and now other operations in Yolo and Solano counties are also planting hedgerows. In addition, cover crops like rye and clover feed the bees when they flower, and these both should be expanded, while roadsides and ditches could be employed to make bee-nesting areas or restore beneficial native plants.

Dr. Kremen most of all urges farmers to reduce their use of pesticides or, if they have to spray, do it at night when the bees are not in the air. She asks growers to stop and consider the bottom line. Bees are necessary if they want their crops to be profitable. With the end of inexpensive commercial pollinators and the decline of natural pollinators, farmers now must see that native bee management is critical to their livelihood. Any cost incurred to nurture native bees will be paid back in lower commercial pollinator costs, as growers will need to rent fewer hives for their fields with hedgerows.

At some point in the near future, it seems the system must turn to organic methods or collapse from lack of pollinators. It does not pay to use pesticides to the point where the ability of your local region to produce a bountiful crop disappears. Growers are going to have to come together and work as a community to reduce chemicals and bring their pollinator access back to normal. Without bees, their yields could plunge as much as 90%. If one farmer in a valley sprays IMD or some other toxin, and the bees decide that field is the *fleur de jour*, it eventually impacts the yields and pollination costs of their entire region. So it pays to come together and cooperate. This would be a change in attitude in many places, as modern farmers tend to be competitive and are not used to doing too many things together. Reducing pesticide use is not going to come without effort. The fact of the matter is that organic methods are often less capital-intensive but more labor-intensive.

THE APHID LION: THE LACEWING FLY

Sometimes farm design, native predators, and healthy soil are not enough to prevent an onslaught of voracious bugs. That's when organic/regenerative farmers reach into their bag of tricks. IMD is most often used to poison aphids, for example, but organic growers know aphids are actually easy to manage with natural methods. Perhaps the most straightforward technique is to buy and release ladybugs or, better yet, green lacewings, a predator whose nickname is "The Aphid Lion." Lacewings are voracious and feast upon aphids, expanding their own population until the aphids are all eaten. Then, with no aphids left, the lacewing population itself subsides.

Cornell University does much organic research, and in a report entitled *Biological Control: A Guide to Natural Enemies in North America* by Catherine Weeden, Anthony Shelton, and Michael Hoffman, the lacewings are discussed: "These lacewing larvae are considered generalist beneficials but are best known as aphid predators. The larvae are sometimes called aphid lions, and have been reported to eat between 100 and 600 aphids each, although they may have difficulty finding prey in crops with hairy or sticky leaves. . . . The lacewing (scientific name *Chrysopidae carnea*) is considered an important aphid predator in Russian and Egyptian cotton crops, German sugar beets, and European vineyards. The North Carolina State University Center for IPM considers it an important natural enemy of long-tailed mealybug. . . . " As we saw, the lacewings in Australia and New Zealand are so successful there are few serious aphid outbreaks, and less IMD is therefore applied. Much less. Another biological control under study for soybean aphids are stingless wasps from China, or *Binodoxys communis*. Still more organic answers for aphids include Safer's Soap Solution (an organic control), Sunspray Horticultural Oil, and an organic product named Neem. All of these methods, and more, are used on large organic farms every day.

OTHER BIOLOGICAL CONTROLS FOR PESTS

Whiteflies are another problem, not only for agriculture but horticulture as well. IMD is used to kill this pest in greenhouses where flowers are grown, and on crops as well. The biological control here is the tiny parasitoid wasp *Encarsia formosa*, which attacks the whiteflies by laying eggs inside of them. Growers using *Encarsia* have shown that no pesticide was needed for poinsettias and that costs were comparable to using chemicals to control the pest.[3] The wasp control also works for tomatoes.

Root weevils or rootworms afflict cranberries, berries, and citrus. Certain species of nematodes, which are tiny roundworms, can be used as biological controls for a host of plants, including cranberries, which are now sprayed with IMD or use pesticide soil drenches to combat pests. The little worms are sprayed and applied in a variety of ways, killing many different types of problem insects within twenty-four to forty-eight hours.[4] In contrast, the nematodes find their way into the host insect body and release a symbiotic bacteria that rapidly multiplies and quickly kills the infected host. Beneficial species of nematodes are used which do not affect mammals, just insects. These are one of the most common beneficials, but growers must learn how to use them. Growers are familiar with pesticide use; they must now learn best practices in using biologicial controls. For example, nematodes are living organisms, thus they cannot be stored or left in hot vehicles. Although it is initially a lot of new information to absorb, and going biological means thinking about pest management in different ways, there are many advantages besides helping the bees and the environment—including cost, pesticide residues on consumer products, and protecting one's own health.

Flea beetles are another concern for corn and other crops where IMD is used. Here too nematodes are effective against flea beetles, as are *Microctonus vittatae Muesebeck*, a native braconid wasp which sterilizes the female flea beetle and kills the adult flea beetle.[5] Using regenerative farm design and maintaining brush strips and nearby wildlands will help keep native populations of the flea beetle's natural predators, but if that fails about a billion nematodes per acre will usually control the flea beetle. These pests can also be knocked back with botanical pesticides including Neem, rotenone, pyrethrin, and sabadilla, or some combination thereof.

A MASSIVE USDA PROGRAM TO HELP GROWERS TRANSITION TO ORGANIC

For every agricultural insect pest, there is now an organic solution. IMD, in particular, can be easily replaced by various biological controls or through such things as natural insecticidal soaps and sprays. The key is to first have healthy soil and to create a regenerative farm design that brings natural insect predators back to the field. Instead of poisoning these little farmhands, organic management nurtures the way nature is used to working. By going a little deeper into the truly wonderful and fascinating world of how soil actually works, and how each pest has a natural enemy, the farmer can learn how to combat the insect nemesis—and not harm a single bee in the process. Although it is not possible in this book to cover all the many organic solutions, for more information, go to *NewFarm.org*, a Webzine from the Rodale Institute. There's even an online wholesale Organic Price Index on that site, so farmers can see how much organic products are fetching in their area (see Appendix 6: Farmer Solutions).

If 12,000 farmers in the U.S. can successfully farm organically, so can all the others. We have to finally get off the pesticide treadmill. There should be a massive USDA program aiding the change from pesticides to integrated pest management and organic farming. This program must be adopted and disseminated by all of the land grant institutions. This should include the following:

- Use of the Web to train and aid growers wishing to transition to Certified Organic. Many farmers want to switch but are daunted by the extra paperwork on field inputs and operations in general. If the USDA put that paperwork online for everyone and automated it as much as possible, it could make a big difference.

- Economic aid to fully carry the grower over the full transition period. Right now the grower has to bear the financial burdens of transitioning to organic. The government should pick up some of the cost.

- Many more extension agents could be fully trained in organic methods in order to aid farmers in the mass changeover. Organic agriculture institutes and certain universities are there to help train the new extension corps.

- The Internet should be used to help train personnel and farmers alike in the latest biological controls. There could be video clips of successful farmers who switched, telling their stories of how they use biological controls instead of insecticides.

- The USDA Farm Report could include the prices of wholesale organic commodities, so that growers can constantly compare the price of conventional foods with organic ones.

- The USDA could partner with organic agriculture institutes and broadcast their own television show on regenerative farming, perhaps over RFD-TV, the satellite farming channel.

- Organic Community-Supported Agriculture groups, CSAs, could be supported more to nurture small local growers, reducing the use of fossil fuel to truck food long distances.

Beyond switching farmers to organic methods and integrated pest management, we must change the way we have structured some parts of our society to be dependent on chemicals, especially IMD. In the final analysis, saving the bees means that all of us will likely have to change our lifestyles a little—it's not just the farmers and the beekeepers. Families, for example, can buy organic produce, supporting the switch to chemical-free agriculture—although they may have to band together and buy in bulk to afford it.

But buying organic is only part of the solution. We must also change what we're doing in a number of different areas, specifically in the way we care for our homes, lawns, and gardens. We now know that chemical lawn care may also be a possible danger to the bees because the MERIT product contains IMD. And if bees are in danger, we must also ask, what are we doing to our own health, to our children's health? Home insect control and lawn care is where we come into closest contact with herbicides and insecticides, and it's where the greatest danger to our families often lies. It's time to become better informed and take action.

Eleven

Taking Your Home and Lawn Organic

A lawn is nature under totalitarian rule.
—Michael Pollan, *Second Nature*

After agriculture and horticulture, the next biggest use for IMD is to kill grubs on lawns and golf courses. The lawn and garden industry is a $35 billion industry, with pesticides and fertilizers making up a major part of the revenue stream, over $9 billion annually for pesticides alone. Beyond just IMD, seventy-eight million U.S. homes use insecticides in the house or outside. It may surprise you to learn that chemically maintained lawns in the U.S. use more pesticides per acre than any food crop. The National Academy of Sciences reports that three to ten pounds per acre of pesticides were applied annually on residential lawns and gardens, compared to about two pounds per acre of soybeans. Each and every year, homeowners apply at least ninety million pounds of pesticide to lawns in the United States. The home lawn chemical industry is big business.

Americans in particular can get obsessed with their lawns, often equating a green lawn with upstanding behavior and morality. To many, it's a status symbol, like their automobile.

Whatever the reason, the trend for greener, more perfect lawns has gotten intense in recent years, as new, sophisticated marketing programs target the homeowner, landscaper, and golf course superintendent. While this has been an economic boon to chemical marketeers, the toll on health and the environment is only now being understood. Unwittingly, homeowners are violating the Law of Unintended Consequences on a daily basis and putting their family and even their pets at risk.

With large marketing campaigns by the pesticide industry, home use of lawn chemicals soared 42% between 1998 and 2001 and now represents the only growth sector of the U.S. market. Groups have recently organized to fight back against their use. In Boston, the Toxics Action Center has targeted the ChemLawn company in a nationwide boycott called "Refuse to Use Chem-Lawn." The Center accuses ChemLawn of pollution, of using known carcinogens, and of not informing potential customers about the true hazards that come with their service. All of the chemicals sprayed or injected by ChemLawn have been shown to adversely impact water quality, aquatic life-forms, and non-target insects, says the Toxics Action Center. Another group, the National Coalition for Pesticide-Free Lawns, meanwhile asks that homeowners use nontoxic alternatives on their yards and wants nurseries to stock nontoxic lawn care products. They furthermore request that the public demand protection from pesticide use for solely aesthetic reasons.

The Toxics Action Center states that ChemLawn will use over thirty different chemicals on a lawn; some of them are banned for food crops, or have been declared illegal overseas for being too hazardous. A homeowner is not even told to be wary of exposure after application, as a farm worker is. Children, of course, run barefoot all over a lawn and get a dermal dose that could affect them in several deleterious ways, from brain cancer and asthma to learning disabilities. While people are putting out birdseed in the backyard to attract feathered friends, they are hurting the birds, themselves, their children, and likely the bees with the chemicals they spray in the front yard.

Insecticides are also applied in and around the home to control termites, fleas, and ants. IMD and fipronil are permanently approved as insecticides for these pests, although the honey bee is likely not threatened by indoor or underground use of IMD as it seems to be by agricultural use or for turf management. Again, there are organic methods that can be used as alternatives to chemicals. Prevention of termites, fleas, and ants is key to success. Buildings must be made tight enough to stop entry of termites, and inspection and early detection is critical. Boric acid, in the form of treating wood with borate sprays, can control termites by interfering with feeding, but inform yourself fully before using any treatment and apply carefully. In addition, the fungus *Metarhizium anisopliae* has been used successfully by commercial pest control services to destroy above-ground colonies of drywood, powderpost, and subterranean termites.

Ants can be controlled with orange oil and other natural means, while there are essential oil remedies for fleas that seem to be effective, from pennroyal oil, eucalyptus oil, rosemary oil to citronella. See if these treatments can replace your pet's flea collar, which might contain fipronil or Sevin. A cloth with a light oil can be used to apply it to a dog's coat, while a cat can have a drop placed behind its neck, where it cannot lick. Boric acid solutions can be used to remove fleas from rugs, but should be applied carefully and only after reading instructions. For cockroaches, Natural Castile Peppermint Lavender Soap can repel invasion, but here again cleaning up the premises and removing food and water is key to control.

Try these natural methods first and see if they work in your situation. They just might do the trick, and then you can avoid the chemicals.

CHILDREN, PETS, AND LAWN PESTICIDES

So what are some of the unintended consequences, the side-effects on your family's health? Because they roll around in the grass and the carpets and get a large dose through their skin, children and pets are the most in danger from use of lawn chemicals. Sadly, those who appear to be affected the worst are exactly the parts of the population that the EPA never thought to include in its safety tests. The embryos of pregnant women, as well as infants and children are most at risk from the toxic soup applied to lawns, as are the aged and the chronically ill, yet these populations were never tested. Chemicals can also suppress the immune system, increasing susceptibility to cancer and other diseases, especially in the sick and elderly, so they are at increased risk as well.

Once a chemical has been applied to a lawn, there is little escape for those in the house. Research has found that because of drift and track-in, the weedkiller 2,4-D and the insecticide carbaryl can contaminate air, dust, and carpets inside a home, rapidly reaching rates ten times higher than pre-application levels.[1] In short, if you spray it outside, it's bound to get inside. The common herbicide 2,4-D is suspected of being carcinogenic and of causing non-Hodgkin's lymphoma. It was the active ingredient in the infamous Agent Orange, responsible for many veteran and civilian health problems during and after the Vietnam War. Weed-and-feed mixtures usually contain IMD and 2, 4-D together, and are especially popular. Since these chemicals are not subject to rain or sunlight when they get indoors, chemicals can persist for years in a carpet, where they might actually accumulate. Maybe that's why the Centers for Disease Control and Prevention report of July 2005 found 2, 4-D in 25% of blood samples taken in 2001–02, reflecting its widespread home use and resulting pollution.

Children are far more susceptible to exposure to pesticides than adults. Childhood leukemia is seven times as likely to occur if lawn chemicals are used, according to the *Journal of the National Cancer Institute,* while other studies have found that asthma can develop.[2] A 2004 National Institute of Environmental Health Sciences study discovered that herbicide and insecticide exposure in a child's first year created a significantly higher risk of asthma compared to a control group. Children exposed to herbicides develop asthma by the age of five, four and a half times the normal rate, while insecticides raised the risk nearly two and a half times. The Law of Unintended Consequences is a harsh mistress.

Pesticides have also been linked to hyperactivity, developmental delays, behavioral disorders, and motor dysfunction.[3] A report called *In Harm's Way: Toxic Threats to Child Development* by the Greater Boston Physicians for Social Responsibility found that by measuring blood levels of chemicals in children and correlating that to schoolwork, lawn chemicals were closely related to test scores. It typically takes but a few weeks to dramatically reduce the learning disabilities of many of these contaminated children. As a neurotoxin, the spraying of IMD could theoretically add to a learning disability problem.

If the honey bee is getting intoxicated after sipping just a trace amount of IMD, how does putting a powerful neurotoxin on your own lawn affect your child's ability to learn and remember? Well, we don't know exactly because, again, the *developmental neurotoxicity tests on IMD have never been done, even though one of the metabolites has been shown to affect the nervous systems of mammals.* This is why the Physicians for Social

Responsibility and the Natural Resources Defense Council have teamed up to sue the EPA over those DNT tests for IMD. Dr. Ted Schettler, one of the authors of *In Harm's Way*, said, "The urgency of this issue is underscored by the fact that between 5 and 10 percent of American schoolchildren have learning disabilities, and an equivalent amount have ADHD (Attention Deficit Hyperactivity Disorder)." The other primary author, Dr. Jill Stein, added, "We risk needless and irreversible harm to current and future generations if we fail to overhaul our flawed regulatory system."

The smaller the organism, the stronger the potential impact for the same size dose. While that rule certainly applies to children, it is especially true for the even-smaller denizens of the yard and neighborhood. Of thirty commonly used pesticides, eleven are toxic to bees, sixteen to birds, and twenty-four to fish, not to mention the effect some of these poisons have on pets. Canine lymphoma, for instance, is said to double in dogs exposed to herbicide-treated lawns and gardens, while bladder cancer in certain breeds can increase by four to seven times.[4]

WATER CONTAMINATION

Besides all the health and environmental problems the desire for a green lawn can lead to is the simple matter of watering all that grass. In the East, municipalities on the average use 30% of their water for residential lawns, while in the drier West the figure is an astounding 60%. Given increasing drought in a world that is warming, and the water shortages that are already occurring, it is clear that this cannot continue. Plus that much watering, in turn, means contamination of water aquifers and entire watersheds, as the toxins are leached into groundwater or run off in storms. Out of thirty common lawn pesticides, seventeen have been discovered in groundwater. Runoff, especially of 2, 4-D herbicide, causes widespread pollution in streams and shallow groundwater, according to *Health Effects of 30 Commonly Used Lawn Pesticides* by the Beyond Pesticides organization.

An estimated 15% of all fertilizer use in the U.S. goes to lawns. In 1990, three million tons of nitrates were applied. In fact, Americans use as much fertilizer on their lawns as India does on all its food crops combined. IMD, the most popular insecticide of all, is now actually mixed into weed-and-feed fertilizers for home use. Watering and rainstorms wash the whole chemical soup into drains and watersheds, leading to all sorts of environmental problems and sometimes outright chemical disasters.[5] Well documented are the effects of chemical fertilizers running off and creating algae blooms, depleting oxygen, and killing rivers and lakes. When combined with all the agricultural use of nitrates and agrochemicals, hundreds of "dead zones" develop at river outlets in places like the Gulf of Mexico and Chesapeake Bay, waters totally devoid of life-giving oxygen. According to the Northern Gulf of Mexico Hypoxia Study, the dead zone in the gulf was 7,900 square miles in 2007, up from an average of 5,200 square miles—thanks to all the additional nitrates from extra corn plantings for ethanol. It's ironic that a supposed solution for global warming is thus causing this larger and larger part of the gulf to die every year. This is yet another confirmation that The Law of Unintended Consequences must be thought through before large fixes are made to the planet.

ARE YOU PART OF THE PROBLEM, OR THE SOLUTION?

We can all, as individuals, follow the Principle of Precaution and take responsibility for our own lives. Taking your lawn organic, and talking to your neighbors about it, are critical for many different reasons, but they are especially needed to remove the most suspect chemicals from the nearby environment, the bees' environment, and your home environment. For all the reasons given above, community drives to take as many lawns organic as possible will hopefully become the norm. This shall not be easy, as the public does not usually respond to change easily or quickly.

Fortunately, organic lawn care looks like a business about to boom. A National Gardening Association survey finds that while only 5% of homeowners use organic methods for their yards and gardens, another 21% say they plan to switch over. That is a huge change due to happen soon. In response to the growing organic shift, Lowe's and Home Depot, along with Sears, now carry organic products in their gardening sections. Even Scott's Miracle-Gro has come out with an organic fertilizer and an organic potting mix. In an April 2006 article, "Turf Wars," *The Wall Street Journal* reported on the organic trend: "Marblehead, Mass., recently converted 15,000 acres of athletic fields to organic care. Even Walt Disney World has reduced its use of traditional pesticides by 70% since the 1990s and is using all-natural composts in some areas of the park. . . . Homeowners are going organic as well: Ms. Delcore said she used to pay a pro to douse her lawn with pesticides, but got worried after nearby flowers started dying. She fired the lawn-care company and now she's ready to give organics a shot."

A lawn owner's number-one enemy is grubs. As mentioned earlier, if their populations are allowed to get too large, grubs can cause unsightly dead or yellow patches of grass. When organic soil maintenance doesn't reduce or eliminate the grubs—and Cornell researchers found that 82% of the time, nothing needs to be done for lawn grubs—organic landscapers reach into their bag of tricks. "Milky spore," a natural bacteria, is one long-term solution to grubs, but these populations can take years to grow. The main biological control for grubs, simply added to the soil once every two or three years, are nematodes, which almost always do the job. Swimming on water particles going down into the soil, these tiny little creatures voraciously attack lawn grubs, releasing their lethal bacteria into their victim's body. After three weeks, if applied correctly in the evening, nematode sprays will have severely depleted the lawn pests. Nematodes not only control grubs but also many other destructive beetles and chafers. Like lacewings for aphids, nematodes for grubs are an effective and inexpensive insect solution. (See Appendix 7: Organic Home and Lawn Solutions.)

Communities have now started to outlaw pesticides. Over seventy Canadian cities have now banned pesticide use altogether in residential and commercial landscaping. In 2005, the Canadian Supreme Court upheld a 2003 Toronto ban, setting a precedent for the other towns, which had already passed similar ordinances but were waiting for court approval to implement them. *The Toronto Star* reports: "The decision means the pesticide industry has exhausted all legal avenues in its attempts to strike down the city's bylaw, which restricts the use of pesticides on lawns and gardens. . . . As of Sept. 1 this year, commercial applicators could face a $225 ticket for non-compliance." That's in Canada. In the U.S., half the states now require commercial applicators to notify neighbors or apartment building managers every time pesticides are used, or for schools to notify parents, letting everyone know that people and pets should stay out of the sprayed areas for at least twenty-four hours. Warning signs are required after applications, now often seen on golf courses, which must close for the day after spraying. Over a dozen towns, including Lawrence, Kansas, and Chatham, New Jersey, have parks that are pesticide-free (and thus IMD-free). Thirty-three states and several hundred school districts now also protect children from chemicals in various ways. New York City meanwhile requires the phasing out of the worst pesticides on city-owned or leased land, and makes all commercial landscapers notify the neighborhood before applying some chemicals to lawns.

How to Manage Organic Turf

The good news is that you don't need chemicals to have a lawn—learning basic organic soil management and some simple methods will keep your grass green and healthy. The Natural Yard Care Program in Seattle has a Web site teaching homeowners and landscapers how to maintain a "natural" lawn. The site lists five steps to natural yard care:

1. Build healthy soil.
2. Plant right for your site.
3. Practice smart watering.
4. Think twice before using pesticides.
5. Practice natural lawn care.

Healthy soil is the key to organic lawns. Learn how to use compost. If your organic matter level is below 5%, put on a quarter-inch layer of finished compost in the fall. Find out what soil pH is all about. And don't use the usual bags of lawn fertilizer. Sometimes those will include herbicide and insecticide, even IMD. In any case, the nitrates run off too heavily, unlike nitrogen from compost, which degrades far more thoroughly and does not normally pose a runoff issue.

Another, simpler technique is to get a mulching mower. As you mow, the lawn clippings are mulched and added to the lawn as green fertilizer, providing at least two pounds of nitrogen per

1,000 square feet of lawn a year—without any pollution at all. Rather than making the ground toxic and discouraging earthworms and other beneficials, natural nutrient products such as fish, kelp, and corn gluten meal encourage the good microbes and organisms. Earthworms are a sign of healthy soil, as are a host of beneficial microorganisms and bacteria. To the regenerative soil scientist, they are the "bioindicators" of healthy soil, true in organic farming and in lawn care. If a lawn has been managed with chemicals for years, there may not be much life left in it, and tilth could be less than 2–3% (the tilth is the rich, active part of dirt, most of which is otherwise inert). If your soil is this depleted, it will take tilling, heavier composting, and the addition of organic matter to regenerate the topsoil.

All of this will convert the micronutrients in the soil so they are readily available for plant life. No runoff should ever reach your local streams and lakes because it has been naturally absorbed and utilized, although phosphates in some of the organic fertilizers can escape. Always follow the directions and only use when necessary. Studies have shown that organic fertilizers out perform chemical ones, for they regenerate soil, rather than degrading it and making it dependent on hot, chemical inputs. An added advantage: because healthy organic soil holds moisture far better, it is more resistant to drought than chemically maintained turf.

Using compost alone will likely give you a good soil pH. The normal range is from 5.5 to 7 pH. That is when the microorganisms in the earth work best. You usually don't have to add something like lime, but all soils are different. Learn how to test the soil with a kit. Talk to someone local doing organic management. Aerating can help if the soils have been compacted, as they often are. The best method is a rented machine which takes out a dime-sized hole. Grass seed grows well in these holes.

Many homeowners unknowingly overwater their lawns. This is not necessary and actually is counterproductive to a healthy, natural lawn. Average grounds require only around an inch of water a week. You should water only when it does not rain enough. Put a can, like a tuna can, beneath the sprinkler to see how much water you are using, keeping it to that recommended inch per week. Keep in mind that once you see runoff, you are wasting water.

You can also transition to species of grass and plants that do not use as much water or nutrients, especially in drier regions. This switch can cut watering needs dramatically. Also plant different varieties. Some may do well, others not—but having just one type of grass or plant can lead to one disease or pest damaging most of your yard. Also accept a little plant and lawn damage; it's only natural. Blasting the whole yard with chemicals because of one grub patch or weed is simply not necessary. If a plant or tree has a chronic problem, it should be replaced with a hardier type. You can also overseed bare spots in the fall at night to maintain a lush look. Think of planting a bee garden, and provide a bee house or habitat for them and other pollinators (see more on bee gardens and houses in Chapter 14).

It may take several seasons to switch a chemically maintained lawn to an organic one. It will require weed-pulling and perhaps twice as much in cost the first year or so. After a while, however, the cost will be less—and the worry about your health will be nonexistent. If you are on well water, or if you have pets, children, or concern about your own health and, of course, that of the bees—it pays to go organic and be pesticide-free. Depending on rain, soil types, and the kinds of products used, it can take a few years for the chemicals in soil to leach out.

If you are going to use an "organic" lawn care service, however, beware. Many lawn services say they are "green," natural, or even organic. Organic lawn care is not a legal term with certain standards, as certified organic is in food products. TruGreen Chem-Lawn has "natural organic" and "natural fertilizer" options, but these programs are nothing more than fertilizer applications with little analysis and no useful work toward soil health, as outlined above. The boycott group Refuse To Buy ChemLawn says if there are weeds or insect pests, the TruGreen service does not have a real alternative to pesticides, *and they may use them.*

On their Web site, Beyond Pesticides publishes the following guidelines in hiring a lawn service, reproduced with permission here:

1. Do not simply take the company's marketing claims at face value; find out what products (and their active ingredients) will be used—they will speak for themselves.

2. Investigate the toxicity and environmental effects of each ingredient. There is at least one fertilizer on the market that bills itself as "natural based," but in reality, this product contains a small percentage of composted chicken manure mixed with a large percentage of synthetic, petroleum-based fertilizer. Be cautious of the word "organic"—one definition of organic is any class of chemicals containing carbon, which most pesticides contain.

3. Question the service people you contact. When a service provider asserts that he or she has an alternative lawn care or indoor pest control service, find out the specifics of their program—an integrated pest management program is only as good as the principles of the person providing it. It is important to know the components of a good IPM program.

Here are a few questions to get you started:

• What products do they consider acceptable?

• Do they monitor for pests (good) or spray on a fixed schedule (bad)?

• Do they attempt to determine the cause of a pest problem and fix it (good) or do they treat the symptoms only (bad)?

• Do they perform yearly soil tests?

• Do they keep records of their monitoring results?

• What training do they have in alternative services?

• Is most of their business in chemically based programs or alternative ones?

• Make sure you read the fine print on any contract or literature: some companies will choose to use "plant protection chemicals" (pesticides) if a "special situation" arises. Get what you want in writing, and hold them to their commitment.

• Be wary of "green consumer" claims. Growing consumer interest in environmental issues has encouraged many companies to pursue environmentally sound or "green" images. There are a growing number of reputable companies. Unfortunately, often businesses only change their image and not their product or service! The best defense against false claims is to look at labels closely and to question salespeople with a critical ear.

Since there are no actual standards, no certification for organic lawn care, the Northeast Organic Farmers Association created a set of protocols for turf similar to the organic standards in agriculture. The NOFA site is at www.organiclandcare.net. If you live in the Northeast, NOFA also supplies a list of trained lawn services that meet their certification requirements. The NOFA book on the subject is called *Standards for Organic Land Care: Practices for Design and Maintenance of Ecological Landscapes* and is also available at the same Web site.

Taking your lawn organic will not only help protect the bees, but also the birds, the butterflies, your pets, the health and development of your children—and of course the health of you and your spouse. It is essential that organic turf management and true organic lawn services continue to expand and replace the chemicals we use today.

Farmers, homeowners, and landscapers, however, are not the only ones that need to change their ways in order to save our pollinators. As we have seen, the management of golf courses—and their massive use of pesticides and IMD—must also be transformed. Fortunately, thanks to progress in agriculture and in lawn care, the bees have a new ally—in the shape of a rising organic trend that is changing the direction of the game.

Twelve
Organic Golf, Anyone?

*Golf is so popular simply because it is the best game
in the world at which to be bad.*
—A. A. MILNE

BESIDES THE IMD USE IN AGRICULTURE AND ON LAWNS,
ANOTHER MAJOR PROBLEM FOR THE HONEY BEE APPEARS
TO BE THE MASSIVE USE OF INSECTICIDES AT GOLF
COURSES. Yes, the Law of Unintended Consequences must even
be considered for those who like to chase the little white ball.
That's because the amount of pesticides and fertilizers applied
to keep fairways and tees green is nothing less than astonishing.
The Pesticide Action Network states that pesticides in general,
both herbicides and insecticides, are applied at rates ranging
from four to seven times greater than the amounts used by farmers on crops. Around nine million pounds of pesticides are used
every year on U.S. golf courses, an average of 6.5 pounds per acre
annually. As always, IMD is in the mix, adding to its environmental bioavailability for the honey bee.

Beyond IMD and the possible link to CCD, there is the issue
of water quality. Watering of turf causes great runoff or leaching of
chemicals. Contamination of drinking supplies, wells, and underground aquifers has thus become an enormous problem. Many
golf courses have had to halt construction or have been blocked
altogether by neighborhood protest groups over this issue.

Due to water contamination on Long Island, the attorney general of New York State put out a report in 1991 entitled "Toxic Fairways: Risking Groundwater Contamination from Pesticides on Long Island Golf Courses." The report found that the average Long Island golf course used an astounding *18 pounds of pesticides per treated acre per year.* That's around six times the annual 2.7 pounds per treated acre per year that farmers apply to agricultural crops.

Once more, what is sprayed outside on a golf course often ends up getting inside—where it is ingested or gets into the body through dermal exposure. Since more and more courses are built as the center of new housing developments, this problem has increased. An article in *The Green Guide,* published by National Geographic, explained this in 1997: "A 1996 study published in *Environmental Science and Technology* showed that as much as three percent of the 'dislodgeable' turf residues (the portion of the herbicide that does not adhere to the turf) of the herbicides 2,4-D and dicamba that were sprayed on grass were later found in carpet dust, ready to be taken up on the hands of infants and children playing on the floor." The article also noted the plight of Laurie Harris and her young children, who lived on a golf course in Colorado. Worried about aerial drift of pesticides, she got the course managers to let her know when spraying would occur so she could get the children indoors and shut the windows.[1]

GOLF COURSE SUPERINTENDENTS HAVE THEIR OWN GOLF HAZARD: CANCER

If the chemicals sprayed on golf courses are so dangerous, wouldn't groundskeepers show a higher rate of cancers associated with pesticides? In fact, one study showed exactly that. "Golf course superintendents died from cancer more often than the general public," concluded Dr. Burton Kross and colleagues in a University of Iowa report.[2] Using a sample of 618 superintendents, Dr. Kross discovered that those who manage turf for a living matched the rates for rare diseases that pesticide applicators suffer from. Urging the superintendents and their workers to "minimize their exposure potential to pesticides," the authors found a 23% rise in non-Hodgkin's lymphoma, a 29% jump in prostate cancer, a 17% increase in cancer of the large intestine, and 20% growth in brain and nervous system cancers. Nationally, non-Hodgkin's lymphoma, a rare blood disease, has risen 83% between 1973 and 1998. Something is causing this dramatic increase, and the chemicals used to manage turf might be a major factor. There is no study of golfers themselves comparing time spent on courses to rates of cancer, nor is there a study looking at cancer rates for child and teenage golfers.[3]

State and federal laws, in fact, permit many hazards in the application of pesticides, noting that there is not a 100% claim of safety or no risk at all. Children, meanwhile, are not properly accounted for in tolerance levels, or pollution through drift and runoff. Companies can even declare many of the most dangerous chemicals proprietary—and not disclose them at all as an ingredient on the product label. The EPA designation of safety thus means little. In fact, the EPA is currently charged with conducting a deep investigation of the safety of three dozen of the most common pesticides—but the research by the Bush EPA has gone at a glacial pace.

GOLF: BAD FOR YOUR HEALTH AND FOR THE ENVIRONMENT?

Golf today has become a game fraught with uncertainty, as multiple applications of toxins—especially in the spring—create so many variables. Have the chemicals washed off enough? Are shoes tracking in dangerous residues and depositing them on carpets? Is drift causing cancer among children living in neighborhoods adjacent to golf courses? Is a course safe for younger golfers to enter? Are the superintendents actually monitoring the levels of pesticides and herbicides on the course and in the environment as they spray?

Up until recently, it was thought a golf course was a wise use of land, that it was ecologically sound. A golf course does preserve open space in areas that would otherwise be developed, and it does offer a recreational sport in harmony with a suburban region. It used to be that inclusion of a golf course in a planned housing development would help win public and planning commission approval. Pesticide runoff and contamination of local wells and aquifers now end up being the first order of business at planning boards, as concerns from many groups are raised. Fertilizer runoff is typically next on the list, for the extra nutrients create all sorts of local water problems. On Long Island, some courses were built atop old sand dunes, allowing leaching straight through to the water table. Water quality and contamination underground are notoriously difficult to predict, with approval battles becoming a court fight between experts.

NOT A DROP TO SPARE

The Utah Division of Water Rights estimates that an eighteen-hole course uses about a million gallons of H_2O a day. An average family by comparison uses 325,900 gallons a year. With around a hundred golf courses in Utah, 100 million gallons daily is being used just to keep those fairways and tees green.[4] *World Watch* magazine estimates that, every day, golf courses use 2.5 billion gallons of water globally.

Natural habitat is also destroyed by the development of golf courses, as wildlands and wetlands are replaced by manicured lawns. Bees, in particular, cannot live on a manicured lawn. Plus the cutting of trees is one of the major impacts from golf course development. Native bees often nest in trees.

Golf courses are furthermore allowed to use chemicals banned for residential use, including the highly neurotoxic insecticide chlorpyrifos (Dursban). When Dursban was outlawed for home use, the EPA ignored the great concern over children's exposure to chlorpyrifos, as well as the hazards posed to workers, allowing continued use for golf course maintenance. Given the drift and track-in problems, this is very shortsighted.

Golf courses are being rapidly developed in many countries around the world, especially in Asia by the Japanese. Wildly popular in Japan, golf has become part of the social/corporate ladder to success. There are over 2,000 courses, with a total area exceeding the size of Tokyo.[5] Groups opposed to further development, however, have halted the construction of over 700 Japanese golf courses since 1988. So the developers went to Thailand, Malaysia, and other nations to build, where the land is cheap, the environmental regulations are weak, and the opposition is unorganized.

In Thailand, over 200 golf courses have used up water that is desperately needed by farmers. The Royal Irrigation Department discovered thirteen golf courses that were actually diverting water in violation of the law.[6] Farmers soon lost out, however, when they were forbidden to grow a second crop of rice in a drought year—while the golf courses were not restricted at all. Malaysian developments have meanwhile gobbled up huge swaths of rainforest for 165 facilities. Indonesia has seen over ninety courses built, in one case displacing 1,000 families to begin construction. Today China, Myanmar, Laos, and Cambodia are the countries that are being developed by the corporate golf industry, with a "golf-resort-plus-casino" design being brought to Southeast Asia. In Vietnam, the average worker would have to work 100 years for the $30,000 it takes to pay the corporate fee at the Japanese-owned Song Be Golf Resort in Ho Chi Minh City.

KILLING BEES FOR SPORT?

Since nearly all of the golf courses in the world use pesticides and IMD in massive amounts, the spread of golf around the planet could be making its own contribution to the bee problem in far-flung areas. The pests being managed, of course, eventually grow resistant to the standard dose, requiring stronger applications. Unfortunately, golf too is on the "pesticide treadmill."

Using insecticides and herbicides to raise enough food so everyone can eat at least has the possibility of being a rational argument. Yet to poison the planet, wildlife, and ourselves for a sport makes no sense at all—especially if we don't have to. After all, golf existed before pesticides and all those fertilizers were ever invented. Ask yourself: If groundskeepers could maintain green turf back then without chemicals, why can't they now?

The answer is: Of course they can. It's just grass.

A transitionary step has been organized by Audubon International with its Audubon Cooperative Sanctuary Program, or ACSP, pledged to by 2,100 of the 16,000 golf courses in the U.S. The program creates bird-nesting areas and restores habitat while reducing pesticide use through an integrated pest management (IPM) program. Increased natural habitat also encourages local natural insect predators like birds, which feast on grubs, as well as certain species of spiders and wasps that control pests. In a survey, 82% of the facilities reduced their pesticide use, and 75% lowered their spending on chemicals. The program also works to reduce water use and has been successful at that as well. One town, Eufala,

Alabama, was so inspired by ACSP that the entire community went green, as residents passed an environmental plan for city properties that integrated many aspects of the Audubon approach.

The Audubon Society, however, still condones chemical use in its program by recommending integrated pest management. IPM can reduce chemical volume, but it nevertheless allows massive amounts of toxins. The Audubon program also does not require notification of pesticide application to golfers or workers by its 2,100 course members. The ACSP is thus only a half-measure, and not a very effective one at that.

SUE FOR ORGANIC GOLF

The real answer is "organic golf." Grass can be grown quite easily with tried-and-true organic methods—no pesticides required. As mentioned earlier, organized neighborhood groups have formed over the last decade or so, often using water quality laws in long, drawn-out court battles to force change upon developers. In the end, many new facilities have had to agree to forgo herbicides and insecticides entirely. As a result, today there are golf course superintendents who are managing without any chemicals at all. With this early success, organic golf is a growing trend, though perhaps not growing rapidly enough. Developers and superintendents have been forced to admit that organic turf management really does work, much to the chagrin of the chemical companies. They cannot rebut reality itself, no matter how hard their marketing departments may repeatedly make the attempt. As Mark Twain once said, "Fewer things are harder to put up with than a good example."

Enjoying higher altitudes and thus fewer weeds and insects, the Applewood course in Golden, Colorado, has seen no need for any pesticide use at all. Maintenance workers, for example, learned to pull weeds by hand rather than spray. It wasn't that difficult to change over, once a knowledgeable organic turf manager was in charge. Besides operating pesticide-free, by planting less water-intensive types of grasses and redesigning the landscape plan, Applewood was actually able to cut its water use from 100 million gallons to just 40 million gallons a year.[7] Berry and currant bushes were meanwhile planted to absorb whatever fertilizers were applied, and tall native wheatgrass was grown to provide a lush habitat for wildlife and natural pest predators. Applewood has been very successful.

Another organic golf course is the Resort at Squaw Creek near Lake Tahoe. Superintendent Mike Carlson says, "We've learned to deal with a lot of things, like not always having a lush course. But we just try to educate the public that that's the way it's supposed to look. We can do as good a job, if not better, without the chemicals." And Arnold Palmer himself is managing a pesticide-free course in Presidio National Park in San Francisco, using it as a model for the rest of the world.[8]

On Long Island, where water quality is a paramount issue, organic golf allows recreation without pollution. An activist group, the Long Island Neighborhood Network, sued the developers of a proposed new golf course, using water quality regulations to block construction. After two years of struggle and negotiations, the builders finally agreed to use organic land care for the grounds. *Newsday* reported in 2000: "With the ambitious goal of setting a new standard for organic premier golf courses, Suffolk lawmakers have approved a project for pesticide-free courses in Yaphank. . . . The idea, according to Assistant County Attorney Robert Garfinkle, is to prove to developers that 'they can build and maintain chemical-free golf courses' that are economically viable." The Neighborhood Network has since supported another new organic golf course on Long Island, the Sebonack Golf Club, near Peconic Bay in Southampton. Neal Lewis, executive director of the Neighborhood Network, said, "this golf course will be the first on Long Island to be 100% pesticide-free, and we intend to hold it out as an example to be followed for all types of lawns."

The group Beyond Pesticides recently put together a set of guidelines called "Environmental Principles for Golf Courses in the United States." Joining with other national environmental organizations and the industry to develop organic standards, the principles find areas of agreement including planning and siting, design, construction, and maintenance. A problem lies in that the golf course association still denies any problems with pesticides and the principles directly ask that superintendents immediately stop using chlorpyrifos, or Dursban, a chemical already banned in homes as being too hazardous. The document advocates "maintenance practices that promote the long-range health of the turf and support environmental objectives . . . [including] introduction of natural pest enemies . . . soil aerification techniques . . . reduced fertilization, limited play on sensitive turf areas, reduced watering, etc." The guidelines end with the admonition that, "chemical control strategies should be utilized only when other strategies are inadequate."[9]

Although the main golf course association of the U.S. is a partner in the "Environmental Principles" with Beyond Pesticides, most of the member courses do not follow the more significant guidelines, for they continue to believe that pesticides are safe. Control by the chemical industry of the sport is simply too strong a legacy to overcome—at least anytime soon. Legislation and court action over water quality seem to be the only real solution that can clean up the game of golf and bring actual elimination of IMD and other harmful toxins. The chemical industry is not about to step aside. It is prepared to fight to the end and has been battling all along against environmental pressure and any new regulations. Court action is unfortunate, yet it appears to be the only effective way at this time to bring change.

THE BENEFITS OF
ORGANIC GOLF

One of the benefits of organic golf will be that the greens and fairways will become a showcase for organic soil management. The lush shape of golf greens is the ideal homeowners envision when they think about turf. It's a big reason why the whole lawn craze got started in the first place in the 1950s and '60s. Going organic on the golf course will naturally make people think about switching their own grass over. Organic golf could thus raise awareness about alternatives more than anything else.

Another benefit to organic golf is the cheaper maintenance costs for the facility: Cheaper biological controls and soil management can handle insects and weeds, while lawn clippings through a mulching mower can replace nitrate fertilizers. No more expensive purchases of costly chemicals and fertilizers. No more days lost to the twenty-four-hour closure after chemical applications. No more legal bills fighting environmentalists and neighborhood groups over water quality. No more penalties from the state for inadequate signage warning golfers of chemical applications. No more extra liability insurance for worker pesticide accidents. No more bad image as an uncaring polluter, either. And no more having to pay workers extra salary to come in the next morning after a spraying to dispose of birds that might have died during the night. Although the first couple of years transitioning to organic management may be double or more in costs, after that the natural balance of healthy soil is reached expenses plunge. Adding up all of the above, it clearly pays for facilities to offer organic golf instead of chemical golf.

Then, of course, there are the added health benefits, reducing potential cancer and the possiblity of horrendous accidents and local water contamination. How much is it worth to reduce or eliminate those concerns? The Kross et al. study showed it is the golf superintendents themselves that suffer the most from cancer. Since they are the ones who mostly decide how the course is managed, superintendents are increasingly looking into taking the step from chemical turf to truly organic land care.

They must first, however, educate themselves. They must, in their hearts and minds, see that they can make this change—even if it means an old dog is going to have to learn some new tricks. Because in the end, the bees—and the poor beekeepers—are going to need all the help they can get. And although it may not have been obvious at first, the beekeepers apparently need the golf course superintendents—and the golfers themselves—to give them a hand.

Organic golf, anyone?

Thirteen

The Beekeeper Solution

If I did one thing in my life, I hope I did something for earth.
—MARLENE NOEL
(THE FIRST TO THINK OF USING OIL
OF WINTERGREEN WITH BEES)

BEYOND REPLACING IMD AND THE NEONICOTINOIDS WITH
NATURAL METHODS, THERE IS ANOTHER CRITICAL PESTI-
CIDE ISSUE THAT MUST BE ADDRESSED: the *Varroa destructor*
mites that are plaguing the honey bee. Commercial beekeepers
use miticides which might be synergizing with traces of IMD—
creating a chemical cocktail more potent than IMD alone, possibly adding to CCD and the loss of immunity. There has not been
much research in this area, so here, too, the Law of Unintended
Consequences rules. More important, the varroa mites are now
nearly resistant to all approved miticides. Beekeeper David Webb
of Florida confirms that the miticides simply don't work anymore.
Much stronger doses of miticide are being applied in recent years
anyway, increasing the susceptibility of the hive to disease and
cold weather.

More research needs to be done on the point of synergistic
effects, yet why not eliminate chemical miticides altogether if
an organic solution works just as well or better? Getting all the
chemical miticides and antibiotics out of the hive might even

help keepers avoid some CCD, just by raising the level of immunity and making stronger hives. The beekeepers would finally get off their own insecticide treadmill, where the mites become ever more resistant to stronger and stronger doses. What, then, is the alternative to Apistan and Checkmite+, as well as for antibiotics used for disease?

THE FORMIC ACID FUMIGATOR

In the 1970s, European beekeepers used formic acid, a readily available organic acid, to rid their hives of pests. In the late 1990s, beekeeper David Vander Dussen began experimenting with formic acid and eventually formed a company called NOD Apiary Products in Frankford, Ontario. Passing the difficult tests for approval to market a product to beekeepers, NOD Apiary's product is called Mite Away II and can be purchased from the company in Canada and the U.S. NOD also carries other innovative products, easing the task of working a large yard.

CEO Vander Dussen says the testing shows hives can be clear of mites for 4 to 5 months and longer. Another treatment may then be necessary. Canada has clearly benefited from the introduction of the Mite Away II product. David Vander Dussen, in fact, is the proud recipient of the first $100,000 Premier's Award of Excellence for Agri-Food Innovation.

Placing paper pads dosed with formic acid inside the hive creates powerful vapors, very small molecules that penetrate the soft cuticle of the mite (instead of skin, bugs have cuticles covering their body). Formic acid is a powerful, hazardous organic acid and widely available. A varroa mite exposed to the vapors of a diluted formic acid solution quickly dies. The mite eggs and offspring also die, even deep within the capped brood cells of the hive, where the female is attacking the larvae and laying her own eggs. A handful of newly hatched bees may also be killed by the fumigation, yet these are quickly replaced by the queen who can lay 1,000 to 2,000 eggs per day. Adult bees older than forty-eight hours are not affected and the hive can be cleansed of mites.

At West Virginia University, Dr. James Amrine began studying the use of formic acid and posted his research and recommendations on the Internet. He devised a 50% formic acid solution injected onto paper pads. Annoyed by the harsh fumes, the bees will beat their wings incessantly to rid the hive of the gases. In this way, all of the nooks and crannies of the hive box are penetrated by the small molecules of formic acid, even the capped brood cell. Like Vander Dussen, Amrine found the mites die but the colony's adult bees do not.

Air temperature affects what dilution rate should be used. If the acid vapors are too strong, the hive will be killed, says the WVU entomologist. Beekeepers should note that Amrine's formic acid fumigator approach is not approved for sale on the market, and he is not selling it in any way. For information and the Web site address, see Appendix 8.

How does this occur? Why would varroa and the young bees die from formic acid vapors but not the adults? Amrine found that the adult bee has a physical defense to the formic acid that *Varroa destructor* does not. Twenty-four to forty-eight hours after it is born, the honey bee begins to develop a layer of "cement" over the surface of its cuticle. It is this cement layer that prevents death from the formic acid, postulates Amrine.

Young bees—and the mites—don't have the cement in their cuticle, and so they die from the small acid molecules penetrating their body. In fact, a successful treatment with formic acid is indicated by the handful of dead honey bee hatchlings found in front of the hive. David Vander Dussen, on the other hand, believes it is the fumes themselves that overcome the hatchlings, not the lack of the cement layer in the cuticle.

The good news is that it would take *Varroa destructor* perhaps a million years to evolve over its cuticle a cement layer. Resistance to formic acid by *Varroa* will therefore probably never occur, while neurotoxin resistance can emerge after just two to four years of use.

Be forewarned, however, that the use of formic acid fumigation alone can lead to the death of the queen, for the powerful gases cover up the royal pheromone. Bees communicate by pheromones, and are constantly touching each other's mouths to receive and transmit scents. There are worker bee pheromones, drone pheromones, brood pheromones, and queen bee pheromones. If the queen pheromones are covered up, her large shape makes her appear as an invader to the colony—and the hive attacks and kills her.

ESSENTIAL OILS SEEM TO CONTROL MITES, IMPROVE BEE HEALTH

Vander Dussen says in tandem with the formic acid treatments, Canadian keepers use Thymol, made from oil of thyme, as a way to control mites. Thymol is the active ingredient in ApiGuard, a gel that releases the oil over several weeks following honey flow, which is made by Vita. This oil is not used in the spring, however, as it can interfere with the Queen's egg laying. Between the Mite Away II treatments and ApiGuard, beekeepers are able to control their mites naturally, a huge improvement over the chemical miticide treadmill.

Still more important discoveries concerning essential oils and the honey bee have apparently been made in recent years. These are mentioned here, although more research is certainly required, as with most areas of bee health.

One evening in Maryland in 1995, beekeeper Bob Noel told his sister Marlene, a nurse, of the terrible problem he was having with the varroa mites and the viruses they cause. His hives were dying, and the chemicals he used to treat for mites were known to be hazardous. He didn't want to use the chemicals. Knowing she was a nurse and knowledgeable about many things, he asked, "Do you have anything that would kill 'em?" Without a word, she got up and returned with a bottle of wintergreen oil. "Here," she said, "this will work." Looking at the bottle, Bob asked, "How do you use it?" "You'll figure it out," Marlene replied. Before she died of cancer in 1998, Marlene said she hoped that her attempt to heal the bees would be the one thing she had done to help the Earth. Could that hope have been fulfilled?

Noel started experimenting with the wintergreen oil, mixing it with a honey-water mixture and feeding it to his affected hives. It killed the mites in application at a satisfying rate of 97%. This solution is even passed down to the brood in its capped cell, killing the female varroa mite as it tries to attack a larva. Results were very positive, with hundreds of dead mites the very next day on the hive bottom. He kept working with essential oils and it seemed to him that wintergreen "grease patties," a mixture of vegetable shortening, wintergreen oil, and salt were effective at killing *Varroa destructor*.

CAN ESSENTIAL OILS KILL MITES?

Noel sent out a letter to fifteen universities, detailing his discoveries. Penn State called, but never came to observe his operation. Dr. James Amrine, however, replied and arrived within two days to see for himself.

Amrine was skeptical at first but, upon seeing the results decided he had better conduct his own treatments. He put together a team of researchers to help him, including Terry Stasny and Robert Skidmore of WVU. So began a partnership between Noel and Amrine, as the two set out to perfect the natural elimination of *Varroa destructor* through wintergreen. Beekeeper David Webb in Florida, for example, now uses an ordinary grease gun to inject wintergreen and shortening straight into the hive entrance, the quickest and easiest way to treat a large yard. In a phone interview, Webb said he has begun to depend on wintergreen to help control the mites after, or even in place of, formic acid treatments. As wintergreen oil is not on the approved list of marketable products for beekeeping, Amrine and Noel went in another direction, one that now seems very promising.

OIL OF LEMONGRASS: LOVE POTION NO. 9 FOR THE HONEY BEE?

In the course of working with wintergreen oil, and trying to get the bees to eat all of their medicine, Noel and Amrine discovered that mixing oil of lemongrass into the grease patty would cause the hive to quickly eat up the wintergreen dose. It was also discovered that spearmint oil, which *does* happen to be on the approved list, seemed to make the hive stronger, seemed to somehow improve the health of the honey bee. This is exactly what was needed for bee yards beset by weak colonies with low immunity.

A new product, the feeding stimulant Honey-B-Healthy, was thus born, a combination of spearmint and lemongrass oils. Although it has never been independently tested beyond Dr. Amrine's and Robert Noel's research, it is now starting to be used by many apiaries, especially in Canada. Beekeepers agree that Honey-B-Healthy has helped their hives, and that their bees are highly attracted to it.

As soon as honey bees smell spearmint/lemongrass, they fly over to it and start gorging on it. It's an amazing phenomenon to watch, like Love Potion No. 9 for bees. According to Dr. Amrine, the components of lemongrass oil mimic worker bee "Nasanoff gland" pheromones. It was love at first bite, for pheromones are the active parts of scent that ignite the sexual drive. The hive would literally dive into the grease patties in a pheromone frenzy. The constant mingling of the colony then spread the healing grease everywhere.

Feeding syrup containing spearmint and lemongrass oils seems to greatly boost bee development and produce healthy colonies. "The bees will enthusiastically eat the Honey-B-Healthy," Dr. Amrine said. "It seems to combat pathogens and give the honey bees an edge in improving their health. It doesn't kill bacteria, but it apparently stops their invasion of the bees. Also the grease gets on the bees and simply makes it harder for the mites to try to hitch a ride.

"African people used lemongrass to manage honey bees for the last several thousand years. They deserve the original credit for that. We mix it with spearmint, and it helps the bees resist the pathogens the mites carry, possibly by boosting the bees' immune systems," explains Dr. Amrine. "The underlying mechanisms of action of essential oils are poorly understood. There are various reports that state they are 'cytophylactic,' meaning they actively stimulate the immune system to help fight off pathogens. We treat declining honey bees with Honey-B-Healthy, and within twenty-one days, one brood cycle, we see improvement."[1]

HOW COULD SPEARMINT OIL RAISE IMMUNITY AND FIGHT DISEASE?

Although full independent testing must still be done, the main effect of Amrine and Noel's Honey-B-Healthy is that it seems to improve bee health. Amrine hypothesizes that the mid-gut cells in the stomach are fortified by the oils through a cytophylactic effect, that the cell walls are somehow protected by the spearmint and lemongrass.

Viruses (including IAPV), *Nosema,* and most bee diseases carried by the varroa mite are known to attack the bee by penetrating the mid-gut cell, where the parasites and pathogens begin their reproductive process. The oils' protective effect might perhaps explain how Honey-B-Healthy could be effective against both viruses and *Nosema.* Also remember that the genome map showed that there is a genetic weakness for detoxification enzymes in the honey bee stomach. Essential oils in the stomach might also be helping to directly weaken or inhibit these different organisms and viruses, making up for that genetic void.

More studies are needed, however, to prove that the mid-gut cell wall is indeed being strengthened, and to better understand the huge number of compounds that are at work in the essential oils. Lemongrass oil has 72 chemical compounds, while spearmint has 122. Many of these are not well known.

The lemongrass-pheromone match is so powerful, Honey-B-Healthy can even be used as a "lure" to make the bees move their hives. Just as remarkable is that it actually can be used as a replacement for tobacco smoke, which is used by beekeepers to calm the hive. With smoke, the bees think there is a fire and immediately begin gorging themselves on honey so they can fly a long distance and start a new colony. They are too busy to sting and defend the hive.

With a Honey-B-Healthy spray, the bees don't sting because everything, including the beekeeper, smells like a worker bee! "I use Honey-B-Healthy in a solution of corn syrup or sugar water in place of smoke, working with my bees," says beekeeper John Slawter of Aurora, West Virginia. "The swarms are much easier to hive with this solution. Bees remain calmer during normal yard work using this spray."

USING HONEY-B-HEALTHY DURING FORMIC ACID TREATMENTS

Amrine and Noel say they made further discoveries when they began using Honey-B-Healthy during formic acid treatments. Specifically, lemongrass has a real benefit in formic acid fumigation by dramatically lowering the percent of queen deaths.

Paper wads and grease patties of Honey-B-Healthy are used in tandem with the formic acid treatment, and quickly spread the essential oil mixture throughout the hive, and all over the queen herself as the bees go into a lemongrass-induced frenzy.

Instead of the queen being attacked 1 in 5 times, however, it is left alone when the formic vapors hit. Dr. Amrine theorizes that since lemongrass oil mimics the worker bee pheromone so closely, the queen—instead of smelling like nothing—smells like a worker bee. So she is never attacked and survives the fumigation process almost every time. Queen bee deaths in the final analysis were down from 25% to 5% or less, certainly worth the loss given that Armine claims that 97% of the varroa are eliminated by the formic acid vapors.

These are not independent scientific results, however, just company testing. More scientific research needs to be done on these new methods to convince the main scientific communities in the United States. Provinces in Canada, however, are already so impressed from beekeeper experience they are spreading the word about the essential oils, the formic acid fumigator method, and the ready-to-use Mite Away II product from NOD Apiary.

Final testing of the process was very impressive. Killing the mites on the adult bees is one thing, but being able to penetrate the brood cell, where the female varroa lay their eggs, is far more difficult. You have to be able to penetrate the cap on the brood cell without completely killing the hive. Vapors of 50% formic acid are able to do that, for they are very small molecules, as are some of the essential oil compounds. Chemical miticides such as Apistan or Checkmite+ kill anywhere from 25% to 60–70% or so of the total mites, depending on resistance, and virtually none in the brood cells. The most recent Florida results in October 2007 for the formic acid fumigator combined with Honey-B-Healthy at the bee yard of beekeeper Harry Mallow were as follows:

MITE MORTALITY FROM FORMIC ACID TREATMENTS

HIVES	Number Mites Alive	Number Dead	Total Mites	% Mortality
40 Control Hives	1481	25	1506	1.66%
5 Treated hives, 10/8-9/2007	7	438	445	98.42%

These are truly hopeful numbers, as they are for a single treatment of formic acid with the combination of spearmint and lemongrass oils. The beekeepers using it claim that a second treatment two to three weeks later typically results in a near 100% mite kill for most hives, lasting to a year. If these results are accurate, the use of formic acid fumigation, together with the essential oils, is a significant breakthrough in the control of Varroa destructor, and can replace the increasingly useless chemical miticides.

ESSENTIAL OILS ALSO SEEM TO BUILD HIVE IMMUNITY AND HAVE OTHER USES

Unfortunately, bees are often reinfected by wild bees or nearby hives, yet wintergreen and lemongrass grease patties and Honey-

B-Healthy in some syrup will keep the mites down for a while and seem to build hive immunity. Although wintergreen oil cannot be sold, beekeepers can buy it on their own and use it.

Beekeeper Becky DeWitt of Kitzmiller, Maryland, said, "I really do believe in Honey-B-Healthy, along with regular use of wintergreen grease patties—they are the backbone of reviving and sustaining honey bees at my apiary here in the mountains of Maryland. They work wonders in combating the varroa mite. The Honey-B-Healthy maintains the colonies' health while the wintergreen grease patties control the mites."

If all these new methods truly do work, and keepers started using them, it could start to make a real difference for the industry. The African Acarological Society and the National Agronomic Institute of Tunisia recently gave Dr. Amrine a Special Recognition Award. And in 2006, Dr. Amrine was selected "Researcher of the Year" by the Florida State Beekeepers for his multiple breakthroughs and helping apiaries there with their *Varroa destructor* infestations.

Hopefully, this information about farming, lawn and garden, and new beekeeper methods will help reduce the use of the chemicals that are harmful to bees, while encouraging the restoration of native bee populations. We can go one step further, however, and get proactive.

We can all feed the bees.

Fourteen

Plant a Bee Garden and They Will Come

When the bee comes to your house, let her have beer; you may want to visit the bee's house some day.
—Congo Proverb

Besides switching your own life to organic living, beyond calling your representatives and demanding that IMD use be suspended, and beyond contributing to efforts to save the honey bee on the international and national scene, there are many other things you can do to help bring the bees back. The bees need your aid on the local, state, and city level. Yes, even if you are in a city, you can help save little winged lives. As we saw earlier, the French found the urban bees were producing more honey than the rural bees.

Here are some things that can be very helpful in bringing back the bees.

Plant a Bee Garden, Rural or Urban

Concerned about colony collapse disorder, Burt's Bees, a company selling natural bee products, decided to give away free seed packets for bee gardens at their Web site. After filling 50,000 requests, they ran out—but millions of additional flowers will be available for the bees because of the program. You can order bee garden seed packets at PlanBeeCentral.com or get some at your local nursery, based on the flower list given below.

Planting a bee garden is not hard. Just start with a variety of flowering plants, fruits, and vegetables, a diversity that will bloom throughout spring, summer, and fall. If you are in a city, use a window planter or your roof. The bees, assuming there are any left in your area, will arrive and feed on the nectar and pollen. And any garden vegetables, mints, or fruit will, in turn, be well pollinated for your efforts. Just don't use any insecticides or herbicides, and be aware that some seeds may be "painted" with chemicals! Try to get organic seeds and learn how to work with the physical and biological controls used in organic gardening. Go to PlanBeeCentral for more info.

Flowers that are blue, purple, and yellow especially attract bees, while flowers with no tubes or short tubes are easier for most bees to gather pollen and drink nectar. Daisies are good for bees, as are cosmos, zinnias, and dahlias. "Double" varieties, which have been bred to grow extra petals instead of anthers, make little nectar and so don't generally make good flowers to plant. Plant "single" varieties only. Mints are excellent and provide leaves for sweet tea.

Sunflowers are good for native bees, while short-tongued bees enjoy the shallow flowers of buttercup, goldenrods, valerian, mustards, asters, yarrow (*Achillea sp.*), and Queen Anne's lace. Long-tongued bees look for herbs like sage (salvia), mint, oregano, and lavender, along with native plants such as *Nepeta* (catnip) and *Stachys* (lamb's ear). Long-tongued bumblebees love hidden nectar spurs, as in monkshood, larkspur, delphinium, bergamot, jewelweed, mimulus, columbine, blue and yellow penstemons, false dragonhead, and snapdragon. Also try solanaceous-type (tomato-type) flowers—including tomato, nightshade, eggplant, and potato, along with bell-shaped flowers like *Arctostaphyls* (bearberry) and blueberry.

Think about how you can use the native and perennial wildflowers that grow naturally in your area. Local flowers are adapted to the local climate and generally need less water and care than imported new-breed flowers—which often are all show and provide little nectar for our tiny friends. "Heirloom" seeds have been popular lately, including black-eyed Susans, lupines, cosmos, and mint. These older varieties have more nectar than today's hybrids. Check with your local university or extension for more information on plants for your locality. Try to have at least ten bee-friendly plants or trees in your garden.

Here is a partial list of the flowers bees like:

ANNUALS

Asters	Calliopsis	Clover
Marigolds	Poppies	Sunflowers
	Zinnias	

PERENNIALS

Buttercups	Clematis	Cosmos
Crocuses	Dahlias	Echinacea
English	Ivy Foxglove	Geraniums
Germander	Globe Thistle	Hollyhocks
Hyacinth	Rock Cress	Roses
Sedum	Snowdrops	Squills
Tansy	Yellow Hyssop	

GARDEN PLANTS

Blackberries	Cantaloupe	Cucumbers
Gourds	Peppers	Pumpkins
Raspberries	Squash	Strawberries
Watermelons	Wild Garlic	

HERBS

Bee Balm	Borage	Catnip
Coriander/Cilantro		Fennel
Lavender	Mints	Rosemary
Sage	Thyme	

SHRUBS

Blueberry	Butterfly Bush	Button Bush
Honeysuckle	Indigo	Privet

TREES

Alder	American Holly	Basswood
Black Gum	Black Locust	Buckeyes
Catalpa	Eastern Redbud	
Fruit Trees *(especially Crabapples)*		
Golden Rain Tree	Hawthorns	Hazels
Linden *(very attractive to bees)*		
Magnolia	Maples	Mountain Ash
Sycamore	Tulip Poplar	Willows

Once you have the flowers, fruits, and vegetables planted, you're halfway there. You will soon have a "floral island," a pollinator paradise that will help restore nature's balance.

If many, many people create these bee oases all around their local area, a network of floral islands will flourish—an enormous help, as bees usually only fly two to three miles from their nest or hive. If people all over your state do the same, the network—and the bee population—grows. It's not just the bees, either. Some insect pollinators, such as the monarch butterfly, migrate hundreds of miles along "nectar corridors." They will be stopping at your pesticide-free floral island for a nectar break, along with migrating bird species. It's organic fast food for wildlife tourists. In fact, you'll be attracting a lot of watchable wildlife along the way, so get your camera, zoom lens, and binoculars ready!

THE MAGIC BEE TREE: THE SILVER LINDEN

If we really want to feed the bees, there is one special thing we can do. We can all plant as many silver linden trees as we can for the rest of our lives, and urge our schools and communities to do the same. It's called a "silver" linden because it has dark, radiant green leaves on top, with a striking silver beneath. Shimmering in the breeze, it's quite a visual effect. The yellow-white flowers bloom in late June to early July and are extremely fragrant and attractive to bees.

This is therefore a tree that not only provides shade, conserving energy for homes, and cleans carbon out of the air—as all trees do—but it also feeds the bees perhaps better than any other living plant. In the U.S., silver lindens go well in city or country, except for the deep South, California, and the Northwest. It is a beautiful shade tree with attractive light gray, smooth bark. Lindens are pollution tolerant and so grow well in urban areas. It likes moist, well-drained alkaline soil and does its best in full sun. They can reach 50 feet to 90 feet with up to a 35-foot spread across. They have good heat resistance, can withstand drought, and have few pests.

So think of planting some of these magic bee trees in your backyard or organize your community to undertake a silver linden tree planting drive. It's perhaps the nicest thing you can do for a bee. Maybe some of you will become Johnny or Joni Lindenseeds and plant hundreds of them. The bees and other pollinators would be thrilled.

Making Bee Habitats

Now you need to do some other things, so the bees stick around. Many times it is not the lack of flowers but the scarcity of good nesting sites that limits the bee populations, especially as more and more development takes place. Often wild bees live in solitary nests, which they need in order to escape from predators or to mate in. Leave some bare ground for ground-nesting bees—a well-kept lawn is impossible for most to nest in. Don't leave just mulched areas and lawn; give the ground-nesters some dirt.

Also leave some dead wood or branches around for bees to move into. You can even drill various-sized holes in the wood to help them out. Have a dead tree on your rural property? Don't cut it down—get your drill out instead and make a bee apartment house. Bees like to squat in old wood-boring beetle burrows in these dead trees—and with your 5/16-inch bit, you can help them along by pretending you are a wood-boring beetle yourself. The woodpeckers coming to the dead trees will provide good bird-watching opportunities; they are always hungry as fastidious foresters remove dead trees before the beetles get there. If you can't stand having a dead tree, try to tolerate living with some dead branches. These can be great habitat for mason and leafcutter bees. Drill them up, then tie the branches together and lean them up against a shed. See if someone moves in.

If wild mason bees are present, you can also leave a foot-high cone of mud, kept wet by a pan of water at the base of the cone. Industrious mason bees will roll up mud balls and fly nearby to build their mud houses. Then they will return every year, slowly increasing in number. Bees also need water, so keep a dripping faucet, a bowl, or a birdbath holding stones for them to land on. Mason bees are so efficient at pollination, they are being looked at by farmers as a possible last resort replacement for honey bees.

Build a healthy thriving habitat, and the bees will come. Make nesting opportunities, pollen, water and nectar, and open ground available, and within a year or two, the garden will be buzzing with activity.

Put Up a Bee House

You can also put together a "bee house," which is simply a block of wood with an overhanging roof. Drill holes in the block for solitary wild bees to live in and mount your simple bee house on a post. These are fun to make with children. Or you can simply buy a mason bee house, which is sold by Gardens Alive. Do not worry about stinging by hole-nesting bees; they only sting if they are grabbed, and do not defend the holes.

To make a bee house, you'll need drill bits of different sizes. For mason bees, such as the blue orchard bee, a 5/16-inch bit will create the right size hole. Get scrap lumber and go 3 to 5 inches in. Do not drill all the way through. In early spring, nail the bee house up in under eaves or in other protected spots. Another way to make a bee house is take large paper or plastic straws, bundle them up, and glue them to the bottom of a paper milk carton or into coffee cans. Find safe dry, shady places for these quickie bee condos, and soon you will have some buzzing tenants.

Make impromptu bumblebee nests by filling dry, plastic, one-gallon milk cartons with cotton or insulation; then place them with the opening down in a sheltered area. If you do several in mid-March, there is a good chance that a young bumblebee queen will find one and start her colony. This convenient bumblebee nest then can be temporarily capped and moved into blueberries or tomatoes for pollination. You also might want to consider a "bat house" and birdhouses. Help those pollinators out too.

Don't Use Pesticides
in Your Bee Garden!

Remember that if aphids are ever a problem in your bee garden, use the lacewings mentioned for farmers, water spray, or the soaps. Encourage birds with birdbaths and feeders, and let spiders build their webs to catch grasshoppers, crickets, and other problem pests (bees are sometimes able to avoid spiderwebs). It's actually fun to create your own backyard ecosystem and see how it interacts and matures.

Bee Stings Are Rare

Many people are afraid of getting stung by a bee, and some must avoid bee stings altogether due to profound allergic reactions. Everyone remembers getting stung, so it is natural to fear it. Yet most of the time bees are simply looking for nectar, pollen, and water, or a place to live. They are not looking to sting you. Do watch out in the southern U.S., South America, and Central America for Africanized honey bees, however, as they easily swarm, although they are not really deserving of the name killer bees. They will defend their hives more aggressively than European honey bees, but their sting does not contain a more potent punch.

Repeal Anti-Beekeeping Ordinances

Of course, if you really want to get into it, get a hive, a queen bee package, and start your own honey bee colony. The added benefit, besides experiencing the joy of beekeeping, will be pounds of honey. Be aware, however, that some cities and towns have anti-beekeeping ordinances. These laws should now be repealed. There is no practical reason why beekeepers cannot have hives in suburban or even urban areas. Even Manhattan has a beekeeper's club, with quite a few colonies maintained on rooftops. Find out what the local laws are before you purchase anything. Some states have passed laws protecting beekeepers.

In Oklahoma, for example, the town of Bethany passed an ordinance banning beekeeping after a woman was stung and needed hospitalization. A state law, however, had been passed in 2005, stating that apiaries can be regulated and zoned by towns, but not banned. The Oklahoma State Beekeeping Association and the Oklahoma Agriculture, Food and Forestry Department countered at the council hearing with the words of the 2005 Apiary Act. "We need bees," explained AFF Department spokesman Jack Carson. "This law was passed . . . to prevent cities from trying to do this."

Find out if your town has an anti-beekeeping ordinance and ask that it be reversed, especially in light of the current CCD crisis. Even if you don't want to start a hive yourself, it will allow others to do so later on. Here's some other things you can do to help:

- Encourage highway departments, cities, and towns to plant mints and lindens and other bee-friendly flowering plants in the medians and rights-of-way. Mints and catnip have essential oils that help fight the mites.

- If honey bees make a problem hive in your house, call a beekeeper, not an exterminator.

- Write letters to the editor to tell everyone in your town about what they can do.

- Ask your local newspaper to do a story on all of the above.

BEES ACTUALLY THRIVE IN URBAN AREAS

Out of all this concern over the honey bee came a surprising discovery. In 2005, the beekeepers in France began a program to locate hives atop buildings in urban areas, and quickly realized that the city bees did better and made more honey than their country cousins. Apparently the warmer temperatures in the towns and cities allowed the bees to be active for longer periods and gather more nectar and pollen, which was readily available in parks, lawns, gardens, and flower boxes, which are usually not sprayed with chemicals. For example, 350,000 bees now live quite happily on the roof of a grand hotel in Montpellier, producing 150 kilograms of honey per year.[1] Fifty communities have signed up for this successful UNAF program. Similar programs should be started in every nation.

Another thing you can do—make sure your town develops according to the principles of smart growth and leaves open space and bee-friendly wildlands in between. Also agitate to stop spraying of pesticides on government and large commercial landscaped areas. And encourage the planting of wildflowers and silver linden trees along roadsides and in parklands to feed the bees.

But that's just the beginning of what you can do to help the bees. Now that you've created a bee-friendly environment at home, it's time to go to Washington. . . .

Fifteen

Plan Bee

"It's better to bee safe than to bee sorry"
—Motto of Plan Bee

Addressing the issue of the vanishing bees requires a multi-level approach, from scientific research to legislation to revocation of the approvals for the neonicotinoids, especially the popular bestseller IMD. Approving all that IMD use without doing the sublethal test for bees, especially when the research shows it can accumulate in the soil, ignored the Principle of Precaution, and now the Law of Unintended Consequences has come back to haunt us as our food supply threatens to collapse. If the science is "inconclusive," err on the side of caution.

The French looked at the science and, being under less corporate influence than in U.S. society, decided to suspend IMD use on sunflowers and corn and rescind the "temporary" marketing authorizations the chemical had been given. France applied the Principle of Precaution and now so should the rest of the world. Let the chemical industry show that all neurotoxins are safe for bees before they are used massively on food and feed crops.

Let there be an end to the abuse of the temporary or emergency exemptions for toxic chemicals of all kinds, but especially right now for IMD and all the neurotoxins. That won't be easy.

The bees are up against a lot in the U.S. and around the world. It is going to take a massive amount of organizing, publicity, and politicking to save them—but it appears the will and thus the energy is there. It is going to take a lot of people doing a lot of different things to save the bees. It is going to take energy, time, and money. It is going to take leadership, determination, and courage.

We can do it. We have the knowledge and the solutions to live, farm, and work without using so many pesticides. Given that "It's better to bee safe than to bee sorry," carefully reducing or removing these chemicals from the environment is the prudent thing to do. With the natural insect solutions in hand, and with IMD and the neonicotinoids the prime suspects as the cause of CCD, the only course of action is clear. If the beekeepers and French researchers are right, until they are proved safe it is time to suspend use of IMD on food crops, feed crops, and turf.

For just about every pest control problem, there is now an organic alternative at hand. With biological controls, essential oils, insect soaps, and natural insecticides, the organic beekeepers, farmers, and landscapers of today have an arsenal of tools that can deal effectively with bugs of all kinds. So the answers are already available—no fundamental research required—although no doubt studies to tweak the organic methods for the largest farms would prove very useful. In short, IMD use can be suspended and natural alternatives put in its place without causing massive economic harm to farmers, or forcing them to give up planting certain crops. As we have seen, IMD or the other neonicotinoids are simply not needed in most cases. Nor are the chemical miticides necessary for in-hive mite control.

Knowing all that we have so far discovered about insecticides, the bees, and the powers-that-be, if she were still alive today, what would Rachel Carson be urging us to do? We have to believe

Carson would say it's clear that "Plan A"—deploying IMD and fipronil as the ultimate bug-killers—is going down the wrong road, a dangerous road. It's time to go to "Plan Bee." Carson would have no doubt wanted us to change and adapt, rather than continue the status quo. She would say it's time to suspend the use of the other neonics, IMD and fipronil, around the world until they are proved safe. And, she would say, it's also time to reform the government agencies that regulate pesticides, the EPA and the FDA in the U.S. and counterpart agencies around the world. Carson would proclaim that neither the public, nor the bees, are being protected as the law requires. In fact, they are being victimized.

The exacting French research from the Comité Scientifique et Technique is, at the least, scientific "relevant information" that IMD poses an "unreasonable risk"—with its conclusion stating that sublethal doses are a significant risk to the honey bee. Only this 2003 report is needed to tripwire the Federal Insecticide, Fungicide, and Rodenticide Act in the U.S., nothing more. That is likely why top U.S. entomologists act as though the French report does not even exist. Acknowledging the Comité Scientifique et Technique report means acknowledging that IMD poses an "unreasonable risk" to bees, and must therefore have its emergency authorizations revoked. The 2003 French report, plus Dr. Colin's semi-field study showing profound impacts from just 6 PPB OF IMD, show that IMD must now be considered the prime suspect behind Colony Collapse Disorder.

Most CCD research at this point is primarily a stalling tactic by the government, universities, and industry. It's time for action. Plan Bee is a campaign to raise awareness and force the issue politically and legally. Beyond the request that the EPA rescind the emergency authorizations for IMD, the campaign has the following goals:

ORGANIZE A GLOBAL COALITION OF BEEKEEPERS, ENVIRONMENTALISTS, AND CONSUMERS

As in Europe, beekeeper, environmental, and consumer groups must form a political coalition to force government agencies to adhere to the law as written and protect the populace and the bees. Right now the beekeepers in the U.S. and Canada are not allied with the environmental groups. Consumers, meanwhile, have their own powerful organizations, and they, too, would likely join the coalition as the public's pocketbook takes a severe hit if food prices soar from CCD. Everyone needs to get together behind Plan Bee's agenda and force the issue to the Congress, the White House, the media, and the world.

START A GLOBAL AWARENESS CAMPAIGN ON IMD AND FIPRONIL

The world needs to be educated on IMD, fipronil, Penncap-M, and other toxins that could be affecting the bees. People are simply not aware of the problems, or the politicians would already be getting pressured to make changes.

We must assist the media in reporting on IMD and the Plan Bee movement to suspend use of the toxin until the required safety tests are finally conducted. Don't let them present half the story and repeat the theme that the missing bees are a complete mystery. Remember both the French bees and Hackenberg's bees came back when IMD was taken off the menu.

The French apparently have the solid data on IMD and fipronil, but it seems the media, the government, the universities, and the chemical industry will try to continue the spin for these pesticides for as long as possible. Big chemical companies don't want the focus to be on man-made chemicals, any more than

Big Oil wants the public to think global warming is man-made. It's not just IMD and fipronil either; there needs to be awareness about the other neonicotinoids as well, such as thiacloprid (CALYPSO), dinotefuran (VENOM), acetamiprid (ASSAIL, INTRUDER, ADJUST), thiamethoxam (ACTARA, PLATINUM, HELIX, CRUISER, ADAGE, MERIDIAN, CENTRIC, FLAG-SHIP), and clothianidin (PONCHO, TITAN, CLUTCH, BELAY, ARENA). Given the research and beekeeper experience, none of these should be used on food and feed crops until sublethal doses and possible synergisms are proved safe for bees.

CREATE LEGISLATION TO BE PASSED IN THE U.S. CONGRESS

The first piece of legislation must be one that bails out the bee-keepers. They have been the ones who suffered the most, taking the brunt of decisions to approve neurotoxins without safety tests for bees. The bailout can be fashioned after drought relief bills, as well as the beekeeper relief programs in Manitoba and Ontario, which pay apiaries $85 for each dead hive. The Apiary Disaster Recovery Act, it could be called, should give the bee-keepers compensation for each lost hive as well as tax breaks and tax carry-forwards. Another idea is to pay apiaries twenty-five cents for every pound of honey produced. This economic relief will allow the apiaries, especially the biggest ones, to weather the storm. If the cause of CCD *does* prove to be IMD, and the permanent approvals are revoked, within two to three years soil residues should return in most areas to levels that won't decimate the migratory honey bee.

Testimony must be given before Congress by the beekeepers, environmentalists, and the lawyers from the NRDC. Legislation must be crafted that not only closes the loopholes but finally protects the bees. Legislation should enforce "time-outs" on all insecticides and herbicides, as in Australia and New Zealand, so organisms do not grow resistant to them so quickly. The USDA at the same time must go into high gear and teach the new organic solutions and biological controls to farmers. There must be funding for research into using essential oils for mite and disease control, formic acid, mite control, a huge USDA Organic Conversion Program, USDA extension agents trained in organic methods and integrated pest management, who work with the large-scale growers of almonds, blueberries, and the main crops that use IMD, to teach them all how to farm without chemicals. There is a lot of work to be done, but fortunately most of the organic solutions have been known for years if not decades, and can be implemented immediately.

SUSPEND USE OF IMD
FOR FOOD CROPS AND TURF

Until the skipped environmental tests prove IMD, fipronil, and other chemicals safe for bees, their use on food and feed crops should be suspended in the U.S. and throughout the world. Under the U.S. FIFRA law and FQPA regulations, the French Comité Scientifique et Technique report is "relevant information" that fulfills the IMD suspension trigger, showing that this product poses "an unreasonable risk" to bees and the permanent approvals for IMD and approvals for all the neonicotinoids should be revoked. This would allow soil to eventually return to normal. Attorney Aaron Colangelo of the NRDC also notes that "someone who is harmed by the emergency exemption could sue EPA for approving the pesticide use in violation of FIFRA." This could obviously apply to the beekeepers, and might be used to help undo the permanent approvals for IMD and the other neonics.

Any safety tests for permanent food crop approval or continued turf management approval must be independently conducted, not through the compromised EPA, USDA, or U.S. universities—nor, of course, through the companies involved. During the Bush Administration, the EPA has bent over backwards, kowtowing to the demands of industry and their K Street lobbyists. The FDA does not even test food for the residues of some chemicals, if it was allowed under a temporary authorization, letting it slip by that usual requirement. It appears to be crony capitalism, using bureaucracy and rules to favor chemical companies over beekeepers and consumers.

All of these violations of the law and the public trust must be ended permanently. The EPA must now go back and properly test all chemicals that have been given temporary authorizations, starting with the most commonly used. Pesticide laws in general must be reformed, as it does not work to have the EPA use the principle of unreasonable risk in its decision-making. Do the insecticide neurotoxins pass independent neurotoxicity tests or not? Are the thousands of new chemicals safe or not? What are the sublethal effects of the compounds and their metabolites? The supposed economic benefits should not matter if a toxin is unsafe for the bees or for human consumption, even at trace levels. Plus the FDA must start testing all food for IMD contamination, and look for residues of other toxins and metabolites that regulators have let slip by. Business as usual is not an option anymore. The bees have awakened the pesticide issue all over again. The French studies on IMD mean that the burden of proof is now on government and the industry to show that IMD is indeed safe for bees, down to just a few parts per billion.

ENFORCE THE REGULATIONS ALREADY ON THE BOOKS

The NRDC, the EDF, and other environmental and consumer groups, along with the beekeepers, must work toward the permanent end of business as usual at the EPA and FDA, where chemicals are thrust upon the public without proper testing, and where concepts like precaution sound, well, French. For starters, let's get the content of the Office of Prevention, Pollution, and Toxic Substances (OPPTS) Library in EPA's Washington head-quarter reorganized, a project which will no doubt take years to finish. EPA's own scientists as well as outside scholars have been hamstrung by the closure of this central resource for study.

Section 18 authorizations for toxic chemicals must be ended except in cases of true emergencies, as they present such poten-tial for abuse. Nor does it make any sense to give something so likely to be a hazard a pass in the first place. Make all chemicals go through the rigorous testing for permanent authorization, including the DNT test. Repeal permanent authorizations of IMD and the neonics first, using the Comité Scientifique et Technique report on sublethal doses causing CCD.

Plan Bee also calls for special pesticide testing for honey bees. Tests designed to discover lethal doses are important, but CCD shows that comprehensive testing for sublethal exposures, and for multiple exposure through bioavailability in the field, must be undertaken as well. Sublethal doses may also lower the immune system of the bee, or sicken the caretaker bees, or affect the func-tion of the queen. It's not just IMD, either. Sevin, Penncap-M, and the other neonicotinoids should be tested for bee safety. All of these possibilities must now, for the first time, be com-prehensively tested. The burden of proof must be placed back squarely on the shoulders of the chemical manufacturers. It is time for corporations and governments to stop using the public and the bees as guinea pigs in an uncontrolled, worldwide field experiment. Great change is needed. K Street and an unregulated industry must be stopped before the harm is irrevocable.

RESEARCH BIOLOGICAL CONTROLS AND ORGANIC METHODS

Funding for research to improve beekeeping and fight pests without chemicals of any kind must be increased. This should include mite and bacteria control programs using essential oils and organic acids. Penn State and other schools are to be commended for distributing recommendations to beekeepers on how to deal with the multiple crises that are confronting them. The next step, however, is to quickly establish what is effective and what can be done rapidly to help beekeepers deal with everything, from their mites to CCD, and then send out an army of well-trained USDA extension agents to help them get started.

PASS LOCAL BANS OF CHEMICALS OR CHEMICAL FERTILIZERS

Push for a local ban of pesticides on lawns, as has been accomplished in many Canadian municipalities. Or press for neighborhood pesticide application requirements. In New York State, counties can pass a simple resolution to abide by new state notification regulations. You can let neighbors know about Web sites like Beyond Pesticides and the Pesticide Action Network to get information, and show them some of the information in this book.

FORM NEIGHBORHOOD ORGANIC LAWN/SAVE THE BEES GROUPS

Neighborhood groups can organize against the marketing campaigns of chemical lawn services, which typically sell a toxic stew of over thirty substances that they apply. The groups can talk to neighbors about their chemical use. Homeowners should examine all the old insecticides they have stored and carefully dispose of the ones containing IMD or fipronil at their local county hazardous waste drop-off station. Remember that IMD, or imidacloprid, can be included in various products, including fertilizer and termite control treatments. Let your neighbors know about the alternatives discussed earlier, such as essential oils, borate sprays, and pyrethin dusts.

A similar effort to promote natural methods must take place in landscaping and lawn maintenance for homes and golf courses. Golf course superintendents should look at the cancer statistics for their profession and make the change for their own good health. In addition, regional and town planners should find out whether they are using IMD or fipronil on their own properties and immediately transition to organic soil management and biological controls to fight grubs and other pests.

Most important of all, don't use any more pesticides—or herbicides—on your lawn and especially in your garden. Lawn chemicals are often the largest contamination source in local areas—and the runoff into regional watersheds is atrocious, helping to cause enormous dead zones in bays, estuaries, and oceans. Ban IMD on your own lawn.

If millions do this, it would have a real impact. Learn how to use organic biological controls and methods instead. The truth is, the bees love dandelions and clover, and eliminating them with herbicides is thus part of the problem. What you can do instead is leave some dandelions and clover for the bees, and then pull them up by hand or with a garden tool after the pollinators are done with them. It might be more work than spraying, but that's a small price to pay in order for you and your lawn to live in harmony with nature.

In most towns, you can now switch from a chemical lawn service to an organic service, which will keep your lawn green through soil management and organic methods. Make sure your neighbors understand the difference between the lawn services that say they are organic, and still use chemicals, and the services that use no chemicals at all. Not only will the bees appreciate you switching to organic, so will the birds—and so will your children.

As we saw earlier, the Physicians for Social Responsibility in Boston found that when the lawn chemicals are stopped, blood levels of toxins in the children of the house rapidly go down and learning disabilities can disappear. As a result of studies like this, state and local governments are banning spraying on playgrounds, school grounds, and even on land near schools. If millions stop using lawn chemicals, and if hundreds of thousands make bee gardens, the tide would begin to turn, for the bees—and for us. So pitch in.

Also, if European honey bees make a problem hive in your house or on your property and they present a danger, rather than calling an exterminator, notify a local beekeeper. Many will gladly come and lure them away to their own hives without harming them. There is no reason to exterminate perfectly good honey bees (which are the furry little golden bees).

SUE FOR ORGANIC GOLF

Through federal and sometimes state water laws, there is now legal precedent in the U.S. for halting the construction of new golf courses unless they are managed organically. Potential groundwater and surface water contamination by pesticide run-off and leaching can derail developer plans for chemical golf and quickly force them to agree to no use of pesticides. Agitate also to require current courses to switch to organic management with these laws. Besides cleaning up the environment, organic golf will showcase the methods homeowners can use to go natural with their own lawns organically.

Although there has never been a study on frequent golfers and higher rates of certain diseases like non-Hodgkin's lymphoma, which indicate pesticide causality, it has been shown that golf course superintendents do have higher rates of NHL. Non-Hodgkin's has also been found in higher numbers among pesticide applicators. So it is not just about the bees. Reducing pesticide use of all kinds is a good idea from a public health point of view, as well as a golfer's point of view.

Have the USDA Start a Massive Organic Conversion Program

So that farmers do not suffer economically from making mistakes in the transition process to certified organic, growers must be taught how to reduce or eliminate their use of pesticides through safer, natural means. In partnership with the organic grower groups, Plan Bee calls for the implementation of a massive, ten-year USDA program to convert conventional farms to organic methods and biological controls of aphids and other pests. The economics are there for the farmers to switch anyhow, as the organic food market grows at 20% each and every year and organic is more profitable than conventional farming.

Extension agents should also teach how to cultivate wild bees and beneficial species through hedgerows, woodlands, and organic soil management. This can help relieve the immediate pollination crisis, especially in California's Central Valley, where nearly all natural habitat has been removed.

All of the above, from the awareness campaign to the hedgerows and support of the revocation of approvals for IMD, must be done simultaneously, and will require coordination. A Web site, PlanBeeCentral.com, will serve as a clearinghouse and blog in order to let everyone unite, organize, and, together, save the bees.

COMMUNITY DRIVES TO PLANT BEE GARDENS AND SILVER LINDEN TREES

Communities everywhere should plant bee gardens and silver linden trees to feed the bees that remain. Schools, town boards, city councils, or citizen activists can start the bee garden and linden tree drive. The Arbor Day Foundation could join in and offer silver lindens to everyone for free on Arbor Day. The goal should be to plant a million bee gardens and 500,000 linden trees a year in the U.S. That could really make a difference for native bee populations, as well as the populations of other pollinators. Just make sure the lindens are not ever treated with pesticides and are managed organically.

CONSCIOUSLY SHIFT THE PARADIGM

Begin dialogs on the difference between machine-model and biological-model science. Expose the falsity of the anthropocentric view by educating the people you know. To stave off the return of the overuse of pesticides and improper regulation, and to start moving the world in a new direction, people must strive to shift the paradigm.

Begin dialogs of all kinds with neighbors, blogs, scientists, letters to the editor, and in neighborhood groups. Talk about the differences between machine models and biological models in science, and why man-made causes of global crises show that the anthropocentric worldview has major flaws. Tell how Rachael Carson predicted the disappearance of bees. Discover for yourself the history of the new ecological science and how it is a shift equal to a second Copernican revolution. Become versed in the new thinking, so you help build a workable future in your own community for your children, and your children's children.

THE ULTIMATE FATE OF OUR WORLD IS UP TO YOU

It's a simple choice. It's either let the corporations continue their grip on government, the media, and universities, and let them maintain the status quo—or make sure your family always gets to eat an affordable and varied diet. You decide what you should do. And if you decide to become active, don't just do the little things from the list above; attempt some Big Picture change as well, some paradigm-shifting. That's when things could get *really* interesting. In the end, the old paradigm—and all its dark nooks and crannies—must be exposed to the light of day, completing the shift to a new, more ecologically aware science and society. The bees, after all, with their co-evolution with flowering plants, made civilization possible in the first place. Now it's time for civilization to return the favor—and in so doing, humanity will find its way out of the Mechanistic Dilemma and chart a new direction for the future.

Plan Bee must be started as soon as possible. Many of the largest beekeeping operations are on the verge of economic disaster from the CCD crisis, and although they love the business, bankruptcy looms. Now colony collapse disorder has struck again. The loss of commercial pollinators like David Hackenberg would be devastating to American agriculture and the overall economy, and would take years to rebuild, perhaps decades. If we ignore the plight of the bees for too long, if we shrug off what seems a vague threat of future disaster, it may be too late. The loss of the bees could even push civilization itself closer to disaster as CCD and soaring food prices just might be the straw that breaks the middle class's back. Then colony collapse disorder could help precipitate Civilization Collapse Disorder, as the economy and ecosystems fall apart from the increasing breakdowns caused by the Mechanistic Dilemma.

What would Rachel do? Clearly Rachel Carson would tell us that Plan Bee must be put into effect. She would tell us that saving the bees will be lots of work, cause great controversy, and will take the courage to go up against the combined might of the Establishment, but we must finally suspend the use of IMD and—hopefully—shift the paradigm.

Carson would remind us that the beekeepers and environmentalists have one very powerful ally on their side: the truth. She would say the public has the right to know the truth about IMD. For many reasons, the public will demand a different way, that we turn toward biological controls, and move massive numbers of farmers and beekeepers to organic management. The public will finally demand that the paradigm does indeed change, that science and society move beyond the mirage of the old anthropocentric thinking, which believes that nature is meant to be controlled by man, and with brute force. We cannot continue to violate the Law of Unintended Consequences.

Here again are Carson's words near the end of *Silent Spring*:

We stand now where two roads diverge . . . the road we have long been traveling is deceptively easy, a smooth superhighway on which we progress with great speed, but at its end lies disaster. The other fork of the road, the one "less traveled by," offers our last, our only chance to reach a destination that assures the preservation of our earth.

The choice, after all, is ours to make. If, having endured much, we have at last asserted our "right to know," and if, knowing, we have concluded that we are being asked to take senseless and frightening risks, then we should no longer accept the counsel of those who tell us that we must fill our world with poisonous chemicals; we should look about and see what other course is open to us.

A truly extraordinary variety of alternatives to the chemical control of insects is available. . . . They are biological solutions, based on understanding of the living organisms they seek to control. . . .

Only by taking account of such life forces . . . can we hope to achieve a reasonable accommodation between the insect hordes and ourselves.

Forty-five years ago, when *Silent Spring* implored us to avoid disaster, to phase out pesticides, and go to biological controls, we did not listen. Will we heed her warning this time? Or ignore her once again—at our ultimate peril?

There is no more time to lose. We are now forced to make the choice: do we consciously try to bring to an end the Mechanistic Dilemma, or will we continue to stick our heads in the sand and fundamentally ignore it? Do we remain on the road of the status quo, of no change, on the road to failure and collapse? Will things just go on as before—and then colony collapse disorder and all the other technological dead ends inevitably set the stage for Civilization Collapse Disorder?

Or will society finally see the big picture? Will we shift the paradigm to biological-model science, transcend the Mechanistic Dilemma, and choose the road of change—the road to planetary survival?

The choice is yours. Make it fast.

Appendix 1

NOTES

Chapter 1: To Bee or Not to Bee

[1] "Bee fossil is a honey of a find," *USA Today* October 29, 2006.

[2] The "Pollen Jocks" in the *Bee Movie* were males doing the glorious job of pollinating. This is the reverse of nature, where all the pollen gathering is done by females.

[3] Karl von Frisch, *The Dance Language and Orientation of Bees,* Cambridge, MA. The Belknap Press of Harvard University Press, 1967.

[4] J. D. Evans, K. Aronstein, Y. P. Chen, C. Hetru, J, L. Imler, H. Jiang§, M. Kanost, G. J. Thompson, Z. Zou, and D. Hultmark, "Immune pathways and defense mechanisms in honey bees *Apis mellifera,*" *Insect Molecular Biology.* 2006, 15 (5), 645–656.

[5] C. Claudianos, H. Ranson, R. M. Johnson, S. Biswas, M. A. Schuler, M. R. Berenbaum, R. Feyereisen, and J. G. Oakeshott, "A deficit of detoxification enzymes: pesticide sensitivity and environmental response in the honey bee," *Insect Mol Biol.* October 2006, 15(5): 615–636.

[6] *Bees In America: How The Honey bee Shaped A Nation,* Tammy Horn, Univ. of Kentucky, 2003.

[7] R. A. Morse, N.W. Calderone,"The Value of Honey Bees as Pollinators of US Crops in 2000," Cornell University, 2000.

[8] Sharon Levy, "The Vanishing" *On Earth,* Summer 2006, NRDC.

[9] M. Watanabe, "Pollination worries rise as honey bees decline," *Science*, vol. 265, August 26, 1994.

Chapter 2: Colony Collapse Disorder

[1] Letter to Growers from David Hackenberg, Hackenberg Apiaries, March 2007.

[2] Susan Milius, "Not-So-Elementary Bee Mystery," *Science News,* July 28, 2007; Vol. 172, No. 4, p. 56.

[3] Apiary Inspectors of America 2006-2007 estimated loss, according to David Hackenberg in March 2008.

[4] A caller told entomologist May Berenbaum the bee rapture theory on a radio show.

[5] 30% CCD rate in 2006-7, Apiary Inspectors of America, 36% in 2007-8 is recent USDA survey.

[6] State list compiled from book survey, AIA.

[7] Corinne Purtill, "Mysterious Bee Deaths Threaten Agriculture," *Arizona Republic*, April 17, 2007.

[8] "Beekeeper's hives still OK," *The Paris News*, June 4, 2007.

[9] "State of the Birds," National Audubon Society, June 14, 2007.

[10] "Unexplained 'White Nose' Disease Killing Northeast Bats" *Environment News Service*, January 31, 2008.

CHAPTER 3: THE POTENTIAL IMPACT OF COLONY COLLAPSE DISORDER

[1] Alexei Barrionuevo, "Honey bees Vanish, Leaving Keepers in Peril," *New York Times*, February 27, 2007.

[2] *ibid.*

[3] Agriculture Department Statement, April, 2007.

[4] "Declining honey bees a 'threat' to food supply," Associated Press, May 2, 2007.

[5] 30% die-off rate in 2006–7, Apiary Inspectors of America.

[6] Jared Diamond, *Collapse: How Societies Choose to Fail or Succeed*, Viking Adult, 2004. Diamond lists shrinking food supply as one of several main factors for the collapsed societies he studied.

[7] M. Watanabe, "Pollination worries rise as honey bees decline," *Science*, vol. 265, 1994-08-26.

CHAPTER 4: IT'S NOT THE CELL PHONES . . .

[1] Joel Garreau, "Honey, I'm Gone!" *Washington Post*, June 2007.

[2] Geoffrey Lean, "Are Mobile Phones Wiping Out Our Bees?" *The Independent*, April 15, 2007.

[3] Eric Sylvers, "Case of the disappearing bees creates a buzz," *International Herald Tribune*, April 22, 2007.

[4] Kimmel, Kuhn, "Can Electromagnetic Exposure Cause a Change in Behaviour?" Landau University, 2006.

[5] Mae-Wan Ho, "Mobile Phones and Vanishing Bees," ISIS Press Release Institute of Science in Society, April 25, 2007.

[6] Joel Garreau, "Honey, I'm Gone!" *Washington Post*, June 2007.

[7] *ibid.*

[8] Eric Sylvers, "Case of the disappearing bees creates a buzz," *International Herald Tribune*, April 22, 2007.

Chapter 5: It's Not the Mites or a Virus . . .

[1] Corinne Purtill, "Mysterious Bee Deaths Threaten Agriculture," *Arizona Republic*, April 17, 2007.

[2] Jeff Pettis, "A Scientific Note On Varroa Destructor Resistance to Coumaphos in the United States," *Apidologie*, September 1, 2003.

[3] M. Higes, R. Martin, A. Meana, "*Nosema ceranae*, a new microsporidian parasite in honey bees in Europe," *Journal of Invertebrate Pathology* 92: 93-95 (2006).

[4] "No Organic Bee Losses," *Information Liberation*, May 10, 2007. There needs to be a scientific survey of organic beekeepers in remote areas compared to the CCD rates of migratory operations, as well as the amount of neonicotinoids in the hive and in the bee itself.

[5] Judy Chen, USDA ARS note from researchers, November 19, 2007.

[6] Leigh Dayton, "Bee acquittal stings journal," *The Australian*, November 21, 2007.

[7] Juliet Eilperin, "Study Points to Virus in Collapse of Honey bee Colonies," *Washington Post*, September 7, 2007.

Chapter 6: The French Say They Know Why

[1] A.K. Jones, V. Raymond-Delpech, S.H. Thany, M. Gauthier, and D.B. Sattelle. "The nicotinic acetylcholine receptor gene family of the honey bee, *Apis mellifera*." *Genome Res.* 2006, 16(11), 1422-30.

[2] "Imidaclopride utilisé en enrobage de semences (Gaucho) et troubles des abeilles," *Rapport final,* September 18, 2003.

[3] "Uniform principles for ensuring health protection for workers when

re-entering treated crops following the application of plant protection products," Krebs et al. *Nachrichtenbl. Deut. Pflanzenschutzd.* 52, 5-9, 2000.

4 J. M. Bonmatin, P. A. Marchand, R. Charvet, I. Moineau, E.R. Bengsch, and M.E. Colin. "Quantification of imidacloprid uptake in maize crops," J *Agric Food Chem.* 53 (13): 5336-41, June 29, 2005.

5 Marie-Pierre Chauzat, Jean-Paul Faucon, Anne-Claire Martel, Julie Lachaize, Nicolas Cougoule, and Michel Aubert, "A Survey of Pesticide Residues in Pollen Loads," *Agence Française de Sécurité Sanitaire des Aliments*, 2002.

6 R. Schmuck, R. Schoning, A. Stork, and O. Schramel. "Risk posed to honey bees (*Apis mellifera L*, Hymenoptera) by an imidacloprid seed dressing of sunflowers," Pest Manag Sci. 2001, 57(3), 225-38.

7 Dick Lehnert, "Imidacloprid Resistance Appearing After 11 Years," Spudman, Insecticide Resistance Action Committee (IRAC) Guidelines.

CHAPTER 7: THE RETURN OF THE BEES!

1 "Imidaclopride utilisé en enrobage de semences (Gaucho) et troubles des abeilles," *Rapport final*, September 18, 2003.

2 Agence France Presse, April 21, 2004.

3 M. E. Colin, J. M. Bonmatin, I. Moineau, C. Gaimon, S. Brun, J. P. Vermandere. "A Method to Quantify and Analyze the Foraging Activity of Honey Bees: Relevance to the Sublethal Effects Induced by Systemic Insecticides," Arch. Environ. Contam. Toxicol. 47, 387–395 (2004).

4 "Imidacloprid Ban Update," British Beekeepers Association, October 2005.

5 UNAF Press Release, January 23, 2006.

6 "Imidacloprid Ban Update," British Beekeepers Association, October 2005.

7 London Beekeepers: Update: December 10, 2005 [condensed]:Estimate the following seed treatment use of IMD in U.K.: Straight imidacloprid seed dressing: Sugar beet 114,948 ha; Beta-cyfluthrin/imidacloprid mixture: OSR 311,620 ha; Linseed 22,821 ha; OSR or linseed grown on set-aside 31,815 ha; (29,537

ha OSR), Bitertanol/fuberidazole/imidacloprid mixture: Cereals 196,568 ha; Fuberidazole-imidacloprid-triadimenol mixture: Cereals 33,963 ha; Imidacloprid/tebuconazole/triazoxide mixture: Cereals 12,468 ha.

[8] "Are BC's bee colonies the latest to die-off?" *Straight* magazine, August 16, 2007.

[9] Australia and New Zealand: "Animal Residue Data Sheet—Imidacloprid," Australian Pesticides and Veterinary Medicines Authority. *Lettuce Leaf,* Issue 12, October 2003, "Integrated Pest and Disease Management (IPM) for outdoor lettuce— Final Report," G. Walker, P. Workman, M. Stufkens, P. Wright, J. Fletcher, C. Curtis, F. Mac-Donald, S. Winkler, S. Qureshi, M. Walker, D. James, S. Davis, August 2005, MAF Sustainable Farming Fund. "The soybean aphid, Aphis glycines, present in Australia," Murray J. Fletcher, Agricultural Scientific Collections Unit, Orange Agricultural Institute and Peter Desborough, Grafton Agricultural Research and Advisory Station. "Pesticide use in the Ord River Irrigation Area, Western Australia, and Risk Assessment of Off-site Impact using Pesticide Impact Rating Index (PIRI)," Danni Oliver and Rai Kookana, CSIRO Land and Water Technical Report, July 2005. "Prospects for extending the use of Australian Lacewings in biological control," T. R. New, *Acta Zoologica Academiae Scientiarum Hungaricae* 48 (Suppl. 2), pp. 209–216, 2002.

Chapter 8: America in the Dark

[1] CNN transcript, May 19, 2007.

[2] Juliet Eilperin, "Study Points to Virus in Collapse of Honey bee Colonies," *Washington Post,* September 7, 2007.

[3] Penn State Lehigh Web site, Faculty Support page.

[4] Lawrence Soley, *Leasing The Ivory Tower: The Corporate Takeover of Academia,* South End Press, 1999.

[5] Doan Family Farm Testimony, House Subcommittee on Horticulture and Organic Agriculture, March 22, 2007.

[6] Jennifer Lee, "Popular Pesticide Faulted For Frog's Sexual Abnormalities," *New York Times,* June 16, 2003.

[7] The Center for Responsive Politics maintains an online database of contributions and lobbying records.

[8] Federal Register: June 19, 2002, Volume 67, Number 118, Page 41628-41635.

[9] "Pesticide Industry Plotted Bush Human Testing Policy," PEER press release, May 30, 2006.

[10] Juliet Eilperin, "Study of Pesticides and Children Stirs Protests," The *Washington Post*, October 30, 2004.

[11] "Scientists Examine Cause of Bee Die-Off," Associated Press, June 14, 2007. (Hackenberg avoids IMD, colonies back to 2,400, Aucker back to 600).

[12] *60 Minutes* transcript, October 28, 2007.

[13] Bob Krauter, "Colony collapse creates buzz at bee conference," *Capital Press*, January 11, 2008.

CHAPTER 9: CIVILIZATION COLLAPSE DISORDER

[1] Jared Diamond, *Collapse: How Societies Choose to Fail or Succeed*, Viking Adult, 2005.

[2] W. Rees, "Contemplating the Abyss," *Nature*, January 6, 2005, 433, 15–16.

[3] A. Jemal, R. Siegel, E. Ward, Y. Hao, J. Xu, T. Murray, M. J. Thun, C. A. Cancer, J. Clin. "Cancer statistics, 2008," 58(2):71-96. E-pub Feb. 20, 2008. Department of Epidemiology and Surveillance Research, American Cancer Society. Lifetime chance of getting invasive cancer 45% in U.S. men, 38% in U.S. women.

[4] M. P. Longnecker, M. A. Klebanoff, H, Zhou, J. W. Brock. "Association between maternal serum concentration of the DDT metabolite DDE and preterm and small-for-gestational-age babies at birth." *The Lancet*, 2001, 358:110-114.

[5] Phone interview with David Hackenberg, February 5, 2008.

[6] Beyond Pesticides Factsheet, 2005. *Health Effects of 30 Commonly Used Lawn Pesticides.*

CHAPTER 10: THE FARMER SOLUTION

[1] More regenerative agriculture info can be found at www.newfarm. org.

[2] "Crop pollination from native bees at risk from agricultural intensification," Kremen and Thorp, UCD, Stanford University, 2002.

[3] R. G. Van Driesche and S. Lyon, Department of Entomology, University of Massachusetts, Amherst, MA, March 2003.

[4] Nematodes for purchase can be found at this Web site: www2.oardc. ohio-state.edu/nematodes/nematode_suppliers.htm

[5] "Farmscaping to Enhance Biological Control (Summary)" National Sustainable Agriculture Information Service.

CHAPTER 11: TAKING YOUR HOME AND LAWN ORGANIC

[1] M. Sears, C. Bowhey, H. Bruan, and G. Stephenson. "Dislodgeable residues and persistence of diazinon, chlorpyrifos, and isophenphos following their application to turfgrass," *Pest. Sci.* 20:223-231,1987.

[2] M. T. Salam, et al., "Early Life Environmental Risk Factors for Asthma: Findings from the Children's Health Study," *Environ. Health Perspectives* 112(6): 760, 2004.

[3] T. Shettler, et al. "Known and Suspected Developmental Neurotoxicants," *In Harms Way: Toxic Threats to Child Development*, Cambridge, MA: Greater Boston Physicians for Social Responsibility; Guillette et al., 1998. "An Anthropological Approach to the Evaluation of Preschool Children Exposed to Pesticides in Mexico," *Environ. Health Perspectives* 106(6); Warren Porter, "Do Pesticides Affect Learning and Behavior? The neuro-endocrine-immune connection," *Pesticides And You* 21(4): 11-15. Beyond Pesticides, Washington, D.C. (Overview of Dr. Porter's findings published in *Environ. Health Perspectives and Toxicology and Industrial Health*.) 2000.

[4] Lawrence Glickman et al, "Herbicide exposure and the risk of transitional cell carcinoma of the urinary bladder in Scottish Terriers," *Journal of the American Veterinary Medical Association* 224(8):1290-1297; 2004. H. Hayes et al., "Case-control study of canine malignant lymphoma: positive association with dog owner's use of 2, 4-D acid herbicides," *Journal of the National Cancer Institute*, 83(17):1226, 1991.

[5] Although the chemical companies insist that their products are safe if used according to directions, Robert Van Den Bosch has pages of chemical incidents and disasters from pesticides that were "properly applied" in his book *The Pesticide Conspiracy*.

Chapter 12: Organic Golf, Anyone?

[1] "Golf's Green Handicap," *Green Guide* 37, National Geographic, March 21, 1997.

[2] R. H. Snyder, J. B. Sartain, J. L. Cisar, and C. J. Borgert. "Dislodgeable residues of fenamiphos applied to turfgrass and implications for golfer exposure," *Soil and Crop Science Society of Florida Proceedings*, vol 58:51-57. 1999.

[3] Kross et al., "Proportionate Mortality Study of Golf Course Superintendents," *American Journal of Industrial Medicine* n. 29, 501-6, May 1996.

[4] Utah Division of Water Rights.

[5] "Chasing The Little White Ball," *New Internationalist.*

[6] GAG'M Newsletter, May 1994

[7] "What Price Green?" *Canyon County Zephyr.*

[8] "Golf's Green Handicap," *Green Guide* 37, National Geographic, March 21, 1997

[9] "Environmental Principles for Golf Courses in the United States." Beyond Pesticides.

Chapter 13: The Beekeeper Solution

[1] "Using Spearmint and Lemongrass to Protect Bees from Mites That Threaten Hives" *Science Daily,* May 19, 2007.

Chapter 14: Plant a Bee Garden and They Will Come

[1] UNAF Press Release, 2006.

Appendix 2

Beekeeper Letter to EU Commissioner

16 November 2006
Mr Markos Kyprianou
Commissioner of Health and
Consumer Protection
EUROPEAN COMMISSION
DG Health and Consumer
Protection
B-1049 BRUSSELS

Pesticides and bees protection: the case of Imidacloprid, Fipronil, Thiamethoxam and Clothianidin

Dear Commissioner,

The signatories of this letter are representatives of beekeeper associations, consumers and environmental organisations. Moved by the current situation of beekeeping in Europe, they wish to share with you their concerns about the approval, or possible approval, by your Directorate General and by the Standing Committeefor Food Chain and Animal Health (SCFCAH) of some active substances used in Europe for phytosanitary aims.

On July 7th 2006, Directive 2006/41/EC has indeed included clothianidin in Appendix I of Directive 91/414/EEC, allowing Member States to authorize products containing this active substance. Thiamethoxam has recently been approved by the Standing Committee and is now awaiting the final decision of the Commission. In addition, the documents related to inclusion of imidacloprid and fipronil to Appendix I are currently available through the EFSA website. It is thus possible to access the Draft Assessment Report (DRA) for both of these substances, and for one of them,fipronil, the conclusions of the Peer Review on the risk assessment.

Various reasons lead us to believe that Europe should abandon the inclusion of these substances in Appendix I. Having considered the particular nature of these substances, we have indeed some doubts on the conformity of their evaluation reports to the clauses of Directive 91/414/EEC and its appendix.

These compounds share some characteristics that, according to the clauses of the directive, fall under the following categories:

1. These substances are systemic.
Systemic treatments, which aim to address the entire plant, are liable to contaminate all its parts, including the flower. It is proven today, and nobody denies it, that the aforesaid active substances are present in the nectar and the pollen of plants coming from treated seeds. Besides, this fact is not ignored in the DRA of imidacloprid and fipronil. These substances are thus found in the food of bees and their brood.

2. These substances are neurotoxic.
The aforementioned substances are insecticides that have the effect of blocking some mechanisms of neurotransmission in the adult insect or in the larva. In very small doses (of about one part per billion -ppb) these compounds are able, without killing the insect, to cause behavioural disturbances (e.g. orientation errors) that could be deadly for the colony, whose survival relies on the integrity of the ability of its members.

3. These substances are persistent in the environment.
The documents appearing on the EFSA website state that worrying persistence occurs for imidacloprid and fipronil as well as for some of their metabolites. The same applies to clothianidin and thiamethoxam. This was somehow expected since the stability of these compounds is necessary for the systemic action supposed to last for the entire growing period of the plant, namely several months. As the pesticides are widely used and may be used on all cereals, maize, sugar beets, potatoes (as spray), as well as on beetroot, oilseed rapes or sunflower, for several consecutive years and in a systematic rotation, we believe it is necessary to study the behaviour of the substances in the soil after several successive years of treatment, and the possible contamination of untreated flowering crops that have been grown in a soil being treated for several consecutive years.

**4. These substances carry acute toxicity that
is extremely strong for bees.**
Directive 91/414/EEC foresees this situation. In fact, it requires that

Member States assess the hazard quotient (HQ) of phytosanitary compounds for bees before authorising them. The HQ is given by the dose of substance applied per hectare and the acute toxicity for bees due to oral intake or to contact. When the HQ is higher than 50, complementary tests have to be produced, in order to fully appreciate the effects (of the product) on honey bee larvae, on honey bee behaviour, colony survival and development after use of the plant protection product according to the proposed conditions of use.

The toxicity of these molecules for bees is significant ; in fact when the HQ is calculated, it reaches surprising figures: for example, for imidacloprid, HQ by oral acquisition reaches 40-540; while it gets to 1852 by contact. For clothianidin, HQ by oral intake scores more than 10,000. For fipronil, HQs have not been calculated because they are considered not relevant – we will come back to this issue later. However, it is easy to calculate these quotients on the basis of the elements provided by the documents and the values obtained through oral intake fall between 7,194 and 11,990 depending on the considered crop. The HQ figures that we could see for the compounds presented are of the same order of magnitude. Required tests on bee brood have not been carried out. Tests on the colony, considered as a system, are insufficient.

In the imidacloprid and fipronil files, it is stated that HQ would not be a relevant index for seed coatings. On this point, we have the following remarks :

- This index, whether it is relevant or not, is the only one that appears in Appendix VI of Directive 91/414/EEC which requires these tests when the coefficient is greater than 50. Neither EFSA, nor the Members States have the liberty to decide whether to eliminate the measures that they consider irrelevant.

- Several scientific publications propose another safety index 11 for the products used to treat the seeds. If it appears that this coefficient is more relevant that the HQ, it is up to the Council to modify Appendix VI of the directive, in accordance with the article 18 of the directive. As long as the directive is not modified, the current version of the legislation must apply.

- It would indeed be unacceptable that some measures concerning bee protection appearing in the legislation be merely swept away because the safety coefficient is not relevant for seed coatings. Indeed, as we have seen above, seed coatings have an impact on bees, as the products in the coatings, on one hand, contaminate the bees and the reserves of the colony, and on the other are liable to seriously disturb bees behaviour, and thus to put in peril the survival of the colony, even at low doses.

Reading the reports brings up more remarks. The reliability of some results is questionable. In addition, conflicting scientific studies are available but not at all represented in the report. Therefore, we consider the risk assessment of these active substances insufficient, whilst many phytosanitary products based on these active substances are on the market and are used widely across the Member States.

For all the above mentioned reasons we ask that no molecule showing high toxicity (HQ>50) towards bees, and in particular, fipronil and imidacloprid, is registered in Appendix I of Directive 91/414/EEC as long as independent and validated tests have not shown the innocuousness of the product for bees, their brood, and the functioning of the colony considered as a system.

The Clothianidin and Thiamethoxam cases
must be reassessed on this basis.
The registration of these molecules in Appendix I is unacceptable if the potential toxicity of the treatments by seed coating has not been accurately evaluated. Moreover, we note that Member States are currently not able to conform to the clauses of Appendix VI when authorising the products containing these active substances. Yet, it is up to the European authority to avoid any decision that would encourage Member States to act in violation of the rules that it has itself prescribed.

The European Commission has to earn more public credibility that it is committed to guarantee a high level of environmental protection to its citizens. Moreover, the future of our bees, valuable indicators of the state of the environment, fundamental components to our agriculture through their pollination services, and living organisms that we have the responsibility to protect, is extremely important.

We would greatly appreciate if you would meet with us in the near future to discuss these matters further.

We look forward to hearing from you soon.
Yours sincerely,

AAPI – Associzione Apicoltori Professionisti Italiani
Luca Bonizzoni, Président
Italia

Asociación Galega de Apicultura- AGA
Xesús Asorey Martínez
Secrétaire technique
Galica - España

Deutscher Berufs und Erwerbs Imker Bund
Manfred Hederer, Präsident
Deutschland

European Professional Beekeepers Association
Peter Bross, President
Hungary

Fédération Apicole Belge– Belgische Bijenteeltfederatie v.z.w.
Jean-Marie Bohet, président
Belgique

Friends of the Earth Europe
Fouad Hamdan
Belgique

Koninklijke Vlaamse Imkerbond
Chris Dauw, Voorzitter
Belgique

Lëtzebuerger Landesverband fir Beienzuucht
M. Robert Henckes
Luxembourg

Mitteldeutsche Imkerunion EV
Günther Jesse, Vorsitzender
Deutschland

Mouvement pour le droit et le respect des générations futures
François Veillerette, Président
France

Natagora
Harry Mardulyn
Belgique

Nature et Progrès Belgique
Marc Fichers
Secrétaire général
Belgique

Pesticide Action Network Europe
Sofia Parente,
PAN Europe Coordinator
Great-Britain

Syndicat national d'apiculture
Yves Védrenne, Président
France

Umweltbund
Dr. Friedhelm Berger
Präsident
Deutschland

Unione Nazionale Associazioni
Apicoltori Italiani
Francesco Panella, Président
Italia

Union nationale de l'apiculture
française
Henri Clément, Président
France

BBL – BRL – IEB – IEW
Jean-Yves SALIEZ
secrétaire général IEW,
Belgique

FIFRA Section 18 Exemptions for Imidacloprid (IMD)—EPA (Note: Last upated February 2008)

Chemical	Site	Pest	Applicant	Received Date	Response Date	Status	Tolerance Publication	Tolerance Expiration
Imidacloprid	Turnip, greens	Aphid	Arizona	1/12/01	1/26/01	Issued	-	-
Imidacloprid	Turnip, greens	Aphid	Arizona	2/7/00	3/10/00	Issued	-	-
Imidacloprid	Turnip, greens	Aphid	Arizona	1/27/00	1/27/00	Crisis approved	-	-
Imidacloprid	Vegetable, cucurbit, group 9	Whitefly	Arizona	3/17/99	5/7/99	Issued	-	-
Imidacloprid	Vegetable, cucurbit, group 9	Whitefly	Arizona	1/9/97	5/22/97	Issued	-	-
Imidacloprid	Vegetable, cucurbit, group 9	Whitefly	Arizona	2/26/98	5/19/98	Issued	-	-
Imidacloprid	Almond	Glassy winged sharpshooter	California	5/29/01	9/5/01	Issued	-	-
Imidacloprid	Almond	Glassy winged sharpshooter	California	6/3/02	6/13/02	Issued	-	-
Imidacloprid	Almond	Glassy winged sharpshooter	California	6/3/03	9/16/03	Issued	-	-
Imidacloprid	Beet, garden	Aphid	California	9/15/00	10/19/00	Issued	-	-
Imidacloprid	Beet, garden	Aphid	California	5/30/01	6/20/01	Issued	-	-
Imidacloprid	Beet, garden	Aphid	California	3/6/03	4/18/03	Issued	-	-

Chemical	Site	Pest	Applicant	Received Date	Response Date	Status	Tolerance Publication	Tolerance Expiration
Imidacloprid	Beet, garden	Green peach aphid	California	8/3/98	9/24/98	Issued	-	-
Imidacloprid	Beet, garden	Aphid	California	6/21/99	8/30/99	Issued	-	-
Imidacloprid	Beet, garden	Green peach aphid	California	7/8/97	8/11/97	Issued	-	-
Imidacloprid	Blackberry	Glassy winged sharpshooter	California	6/3/03	9/16/03	Issued		-
Imidacloprid	Blueberry	Glassy winged sharpshooter	California	6/3/02	6/13/02	Issued	-	-
Imidacloprid	Blueberry	Glassy winged sharps	California	5/29/01	9/5/01	Issued	-	-
Imidacloprid	Fruit, citrus, group 10	Scale	California	4/30/97	7/25/97	Issued	-	-
Imidacloprid	Fruit, citrus, group 10	Glassy winged sharpshooter	California	6/3/02	7/11/02	Issued	-	-
Imidacloprid	Fruit, citrus, group 10	Glassy winged sharpshooter	California	2/7/00	2/23/00	Issued	-	-
Imidacloprid	Fruit, citrus, group 10	Scale (red)	California	6/25/97	6/25/97	Crisis approved	-	-
Imidacloprid	Fruit, citrus, group 10	Glassy winged sharpshooter	California	2/1/01	2/9/01	Issued	-	-
Imidacloprid	Fruit, stone, group 12	Glassy winged sharpshooter	California	6/3/02	6/13/02	Issued	-	-

Chemical	Site	Pest	Applicant	Received Date	Response Date	Status	Tolerance Publication	Tolerance Expiration
Imidacloprid	Fruit, stone, group 12	Glassy winged sharpshooter	California	6/3/03	6/13/03	Withdrawn	-	-
Imidacloprid	Fruit, stone, group 12	Glassy winged sharpshooter	California	6/6/01	9/5/01	Issued	-	-
Imidacloprid	Fruit, stone, group 12	Glassy winged sharpshooter	California	5/29/01	9/5/01	Issued	-	-
Imidacloprid	Pomegranate	Whitefly	California	5/17/05	6/10/05	Issued	11/29/96	-
Imidacloprid	Pomegranate	Whitefly	California	2/8/05	6/10/05	Issued	11/29/96	-
Imidacloprid	Pomegranate	Whitefly	California	10/12/04	2/23/05	Withdrawn	11/29/96	-
Imidacloprid	Pomegranate	Silverleaf whitefly	California	2/24/06	3/20/06	Issued	11/29/96	-
Imidacloprid	Residential host crops	Glassy winged sharpshooter	California	6/3/03	8/11/03	Withdrawn		-
Imidacloprid	Strawberry	Silverleaf whitefly	California	8/29/01	9/5/01	Issued	-	-
Imidacloprid	Strawberry	Silverleaf whitefly	California	8/29/00	9/8/00	Issued	-	-
Imidacloprid	Strawberry	Silverleaf whitefly	California	11/24/98	11/24/98	Crisis approved	-	-
Imidacloprid	Strawberry	Silverleaf whitefly	California	10/7/98	12/24/98	Issued	-	-
Imidacloprid	Strawberry	Silverleaf whitefly	California	8/23/99	11/10/99	Issued	-	-

Chemical	Site	Pest	Applicant	Received Date	Response Date	Status	Tolerance Publication	Tolerance Expiration
Imidacloprid	Strawberry	Whitefly	California	8/27/02	11/1/02	Issued	-	-
Imidacloprid	Turnip	Aphid	California	9/15/00	10/19/00	Issued	-	-
Imidacloprid	Turnip, greens	Green peach aphid	California	8/3/98	9/24/98	Issued	-	-
Imidacloprid	Turnip, greens	Aphid	California	6/21/99	8/30/99	Issued	-	-
Imidacloprid	Turnip, greens	Green peach aphid	California	7/8/97	8/11/97	Issued	-	-
Imidacloprid	Vegetable, cucurbit, group 9	Whitefly	California	2/6/97	2/6/97	Crisis approved	-	-
Imidacloprid	Vegetable, cucurbit, group 9	Whitefly, aphid	California	1/23/98	3/3/98	Issued	-	-
Imidacloprid	Vegetable, cucurbit, group 9	Whitefly	California	3/10/99	3/10/99	Crisis approved	-	-
Imidacloprid	Vegetable, cucurbit, group 9	Whitefly	California	3/10/99	4/30/99	Issued	-	-
Imidacloprid	Vegetable, cucurbit, group 9	Whitefly	California	1/9/97	5/22/97	Issued	-	-
Imidacloprid	Corn, sweet	Flea beetle	Colorado	2/14/00	2/16/00	Issued	-	-
Imidacloprid	Corn, sweet	Corn flea beetle	Colorado	11/17/00	11/29/00	Issued	-	-

Chemical	Site	Pest	Applicant	Received Date	Response Date	Status	Tolerance Publication	Tolerance Expiration
Imidacloprid	Blueberry	Oriental beetle	Connecticut	3/12/02	5/8/02	Issued	-	-
Imidacloprid	Strawberry	Grub	Connecticut	6/24/03	6/25/03	Withdrawn	-	-
Imidacloprid	Strawberry	White grub	Connecticut	3/12/02	3/22/02	Issued	-	-
Imidacloprid	Strawberry	Root feeding beetle	Connecticut	3/19/01	5/21/01	Issued	-	-
Imidacloprid	Fruit, citrus, group 10	Aphid	Delaware	3/5/03	4/2/03	Issued	-	-
Imidacloprid	Fruit, stone, group 12	Aphid	Delaware	6/9/00	6/14/00	Issued	-	-
Imidacloprid	Fruit, stone, group 12	Aphid	Delaware	2/19/02	3/8/02	Issued	-	-
Imidacloprid	Fruit, stone, group 12	Aphid	Delaware	3/1/01	3/9/01	Issued	-	-
Imidacloprid	Fruit, citrus, group 10	Brown citrus aphid	Florida	3/18/97	6/3/97	Issued	-	-
Imidacloprid	Fruit, citrus, group 10	Brown citrus aphid	Florida	6/15/00	6/30/00	Issued	-	-
Imidacloprid	Fruit, citrus, group 10	Citrus leafminer	Florida	5/11/98	6/12/98	Issued	-	-
Imidacloprid	Fruit, citrus, group 10	Brown citrus aphid	Florida	5/11/98	6/12/98	Issued	-	-
Imidacloprid	Fruit, citrus, group 10	Citrus leafminer	Florida	6/15/00	6/30/00	Issued	-	-
Imidacloprid	Fruit, citrus, group 10	Citrus leafminer	Florida	3/18/97	6/3/97	Issued	-	-

Chemical	Site	Pest	Applicant	Received Date	Response Date	Status	Tolerance Publication	Tolerance Expiration
Imidacloprid	Fruit, citrus, group 10	Citrus leafminer	Florida	6/9/99	7/1/99	Issued	-	-
Imidacloprid	Fruit, citrus, group 10	Brown citrus aphid	Florida	6/9/99	7/1/99	Issued	-	-
Imidacloprid	Vegetable, legume, group 6	Silverleaf whitefly	Florida	7/19/99	9/27/99	Issued	-	-
Imidacloprid	Vegetable, legume, group 6	Silverleaf whitefly	Florida	11/2/00	11/17/00	Issued	-	-
Imidacloprid	Vegetable, legume, group 6	Silverleaf whitefly	Florida	9/9/98	11/13/98	Issued	-	-
Imidacloprid	Bean, succulent	Silverleaf whitefly	Georgia	6/15/00	8/2/00	Issued	-	-
Imidacloprid	Pecan	Yellow aphid	Georgia	9/5/97	4/20/98	Withdrawn	-	-
Imidacloprid	Pecan	Yellow aphid	Georgia	9/9/97	9/9/97	Crisis approved	-	-
Imidacloprid	Banana	Banana aphid	Hawaii	4/10/06	4/10/06	Crisis approved	-	-
Imidacloprid	Banana	Banana aphid	Hawaii	9/19/05	8/11/06	Withdrawn	-	-
Imidacloprid	Banana	Banana aphid	Hawaii	5/12/04	-	Withdrawn	-	-
Imidacloprid	Banana	Banana aphid	Hawaii	4/21/04	4/21/04	Crisis approved	-	-
Imidacloprid	Coffee	Green scale	Hawaii	10/21/05	8/11/06	Withdrawn	4/10/01	-
Imidacloprid	Coffee	Green scale	Hawaii	2/6/06	2/6/06	Crisis approved	4/10/01	-

Chemical	Site	Pest	Applicant	Received Date	Response Date	Status	Tolerance Publication	Tolerance Expiration
Imidacloprid	Vegetable, cucurbit, group 9	Silverleaf whitefly	Hawaii	2/3/99	2/22/99	Issued	-	-
Imidacloprid	Vegetable, cucurbit, group 9	Silverleaf whitefly	Hawaii	10/21/98	11/12/98	Issued		-
Imidacloprid	Watermelon	Silverleaf whitefly	Hawaii	2/12/98	3/30/98	Issued	-	-
Imidacloprid	Watermelon	Silverleaf whitefly	Hawaii	2/3/99	2/22/99	Issued	-	-
Imidacloprid	Watermelon	Silverleaf whitefly	Hawaii	4/8/97	4/8/97	Crisis approved	-	-
Imidacloprid	Watermelon	Silverleaf whitefly	Hawaii	3/17/97	3/23/98	Withdrawn		-
Imidacloprid	Corn, sweet	Corn flea beetle	Idaho	11/1/00	11/7/00	Issued	-	-
Imidacloprid	Corn, sweet	Flea beetle	Idaho	12/13/99	12/13/99	Crisis approved	-	-
Imidacloprid	Corn, sweet	Flea beetle	Idaho	12/8/99	2/4/00	Issued	-	-
Imidacloprid	Corn	Stewart's wilt	Illinois	4/17/98	4/17/98	Crisis approved	-	-
Imidacloprid	Corn, field	Corn flea beetle	Illinois	4/8/99	4/30/99	Withdrawn	-	-
Imidacloprid	Corn, field	Corn flea beetle	Indiana	4/5/99	4/8/99	Issued	-	-
Imidacloprid	Corn	Flea beetle	Iowa	4/20/98	4/20/98	Crisis approved	-	-

Chemical	Site	Pest	Applicant	Received Date	Response Date	Status	Tolerance Publication	Tolerance Expiration
Imidacloprid	Corn	Corn flea beetle	Iowa	3/25/99	4/2/99	Issued	-	-
Imidacloprid	Soybean	Bean leaf beetle	Iowa	4/16/01	4/16/01	Crisis approved	-	-
Imidacloprid	Soybean	Bean leaf beetle	Iowa	2/25/03	10/21/03	Withdrawn	-	-
Imidacloprid	Soybean	Bean leaf beetle	Iowa	2/2/04	2/6/04	Issued	-	-
Imidacloprid	Soybean	Bean leaf beetle	Iowa	4/3/03	4/3/03	Crisis approved	-	-
Imidacloprid	Soybean	Bean leaf beetle	Iowa	3/5/01	4/16/01	Withdrawn	-	-
Imidacloprid	Fruit, stone, group 12	Aphid	Maryland	3/21/01	3/30/01	Issued	-	-
Imidacloprid	Fruit, stone, group 12	Aphid	Maryland	4/24/00	5/2/00	Issued	-	-
Imidacloprid	Fruit, stone, group 12	Aphid	Maryland	2/25/02	3/8/02	Issued	-	-
Imidacloprid	Blueberry	White grubs	Massachusetts	4/2/02	6/24/02	Issued	-	-
Imidacloprid	Cranberry	Cranberry weevil	Massachusetts	7/2/01	9/18/01	Issued	-	-
Imidacloprid	Cranberry	Cranberry weevil	Massachusetts	7/9/01	7/9/01	Crisis approved	-	-
Imidacloprid	Strawberry	White grub	Massachusetts	4/2/02	6/26/02	Issued	-	-

Chemical	Site	Pest	Applicant	Received Date	Response Date	Status	Tolerance Publication	Tolerance Expiration
Imidacloprid	Blueberry	Japanese beetle	Michigan	4/17/02	6/11/02	Issued	-	-
Imidacloprid	Blueberry	Japanese beetle	Michigan	6/6/01	7/27/01	Issued	-	-
Imidacloprid	Blueberry	Japanese beetle	Michigan	2/9/04	5/17/04	Withdrawn	-	-
Imidacloprid	Blueberry	Japanese beetle	Michigan	7/20/01	7/20/01	Crisis approved	-	-
Imidacloprid	Blueberry	Japanese beetle	Michigan	5/9/03	5/16/03	Issued	-	-
Imidacloprid	Corn, sweet	Flea beetle	Minnesota	1/6/00	1/6/00	Crisis approved	-	-
Imidacloprid	Corn, sweet	Seed treatment	Minnesota	12/16/99	2/4/00	Issued	-	-
Imidacloprid	Corn, sweet	Flea beetle	Minnesota	11/13/00	11/29/00	Issued	-	-
Imidacloprid	Soybean	Soybean aphid	Minnesota	3/4/02	6/30/02	Withdrawn	-	-
Imidacloprid	Sunflower	Wireworm	Minnesota	5/11/04	5/11/04	Crisis approved	-	-
Imidacloprid	Sunflower	Wireworm	Nebraska	5/14/04	5/11/04	Crisis approved	-	-
Imidacloprid	Blueberry	Oriental beetle	New Jersey	2/4/04	5/17/04	Withdrawn	-	-
Imidacloprid	Blueberry	Beetle	New Jersey	3/6/03	3/13/03	Issued	-	-
Imidacloprid	Blueberry	Aphid	New Jersey	3/15/01	3/23/01	Issued	-	-

Chemical	Site	Pest	Applicant	Received Date	Response Date	Status	Tolerance Publication	Tolerance Expiration
Imidacloprid	Blueberry	Blueberry aphid	New Jersey	3/23/00	3/30/00	Issued	-	-
Imidacloprid	Blueberry	Blueberry aphid	New Jersey	3/31/99	5/14/99	Issued	-	-
Imidacloprid	Blueberry	Blueberry aphid	New Jersey	2/4/04	5/17/04	Withdrawn	-	-
Imidacloprid	Blueberry	Oriental beetle	New Jersey	3/23/00	3/30/00	Issued	-	-
Imidacloprid	Blueberry	Aphid	New Jersey	3/6/03	3/13/03	Issued	-	-
Imidacloprid	Blueberry	Blueberry aphid	New Jersey	3/27/02	5/7/02	Issued	-	-
Imidacloprid	Blueberry	Oriental beetle	New Jersey	3/27/02	5/7/02	Issued	-	-
Imidacloprid	Blueberry	Oriental beetle	New Jersey	3/15/01	3/23/01	Issued	-	-
Imidacloprid	Blueberry	Oriental beetle	New Jersey	3/31/99	5/14/99	Issued	-	-
Imidacloprid	Cranberry	Cranberry rootworm	New Jersey	3/19/99	5/14/99	Issued	-	-
Imidacloprid	Fruit, stone, group 12	Aphid	New Jersey	2/23/00	4/4/00	Issued	-	-
Imidacloprid	Fruit, stone, group 12	Aphid	New Jersey	3/12/02	3/14/02	Issued	-	-
Imidacloprid	Fruit, stone, group 12	Aphid	New Jersey	5/13/03	5/13/03	Crisis approved	-	-

Chemical	Site	Pest	Applicant	Received Date	Response Date	Status	Tolerance Publication	Tolerance Expiration
Imidacloprid	Fruit, stone, group 12	Aphid	New Jersey	5/13/03	6/18/03	Withdrawn	-	-
Imidacloprid	Fruit, stone, group 12	Aphid	New Jersey	4/4/01	4/20/01	Issued	-	-
Imidacloprid	Fruit, stone, group 12	Aphid	New York	3/28/01	4/20/01	Issued	-	
Imidacloprid	Fruit, stone, group 12	Aphid	New York	3/14/02	3/22/02	Issued	-	-
Imidacloprid	Fruit, stone, group 12	Aphid	New York	4/5/00	4/17/00	Issued	-	-
Imidacloprid	Sunflower	Wireworm	North Dakota	5/14/04	5/14/04	Crisis approved	-	-
Imidacloprid	Squash, winter	Green peach aphid	Oregon	2/27/97	5/2/97	Issued	-	-
Imidacloprid	Zucchini	Green peach aphid	Oregon	2/27/97	5/2/97	Issued	-	-
Imidacloprid	Fruit, stone, group 12	Green peach aphid	Pennsylvania	4/25/03	4/26/03	Issued	-	-
Imidacloprid	Fruit, stone, group 12	Aphid	Pennsylvania	3/12/01	3/23/01	Issued	-	-
Imidacloprid	Fruit, stone, group 12	Aphid	Pennsylvania	2/18/00	4/4/00	Issued	-	-
Imidacloprid	Fruit, stone, group 12	Aphid	Pennsylvania	3/12/02	3/22/02	Issued	-	-

Chemical	Site	Pest	Applicant	Received Date	Response Date	Status	Tolerance Publication	Tolerance Expiration
Imidacloprid	Vegetable, legume, group 6	Silverleaf whitefly	Tennessee	9/18/00	9/18/00	Crisis approved	-	-
Imidacloprid	Fruit, citrus, group 10	Citrus leafminer	Texas	3/23/99	5/5/99	Issued	-	-
Imidacloprid	Vegetable, cucurbit, group 9	Whitefly	Texas	1/28/97	1/28/97	Crisis approved	-	-
Imidacloprid	Vegetable, cucurbit, group 9	Sweetpotato whitefly	Texas	11/25/96	5/22/97	Issued	-	-
Imidacloprid	Vegetable, cucurbit, group 9	Sweetpotato whitefly	Texas	3/31/98	3/31/98	Crisis approved	-	-
Imidacloprid	Vegetable, cucurbit, group 9	Sweetpotato whitefly	Texas	3/25/98	6/26/98	Issued	-	-
Imidacloprid	Vegetable, cucurbit, group 9	Sweetpotato whitefly	Texas	6/28/99	8/2/99	Withdrawn	-	-
Imidacloprid	Fruit, stone, group 12	Aphid	Virginia	3/27/01	4/20/01	Issued	-	-
Imidacloprid	Fruit, stone, group 12	Aphid	Virginia	4/17/03	4/26/03	Issued	-	-
Imidacloprid	Fruit, stone, group 12	Aphid	Virginia	4/3/02	4/9/02	Issued	-	-

Chemical	Site	Pest	Applicant	Received Date	Response Date	Status	Tolerance Publication	Tolerance Expiration
Imidacloprid	Fruit, stone, group 12	Aphid	Virginia	5/25/00	6/1/00	Issued	-	-
Imidacloprid	Fruit, stone, group 12	Aphid	West Virginia	2/23/00	4/4/00	Issued	-	-
Imidacloprid	Nectarine	Aphid	West Virginia	3/14/01	3/20/01	Issued	-	-
Imidacloprid	Nectarine	Aphid	West Virginia	3/27/02	4/9/02	Issued	-	-
Imidacloprid	Nectarine	Aphid	West Virginia	3/26/03	4/2/03	Issued	-	-
Imidacloprid	Peach	Aphid	West Virginia	3/27/02	4/9/02	Issued	-	-
Imidacloprid	Peach	Aphid	West Virginia	3/26/03	4/2/03	Issued	-	-
Imidacloprid	Peach	Aphid	West Virginia	3/14/01	3/20/01	Issued	-	-
Imidacloprid	Soybean	Soybean aphid, blb	Wisconsin	1/31/02	6/30/02	Withdrawn		-
Imidacloprid	Soybean	Bean leaf beetle	Wisconsin	4/3/03	4/3/03	Crisis approved	-	-
Imidacloprid	Soybean	Bean leaf beetle	Wisconsin	3/13/03	10/21/03	Withdrawn	-	-

APPENDIX 4

Section 18 of Federal Insecticide, Fungicide, and Rodenticide Act (FIFRA)

Section 18 of Federal Insecticide, Fungicide, and Rodenticide Act (FIFRA) authorizes EPA to allow an unregistered use of a pesticide for a limited time if EPA determines that an emergency condition exists. The regulations governing Section 18 of FIFRA (found at Title 40 of the Code of Federal Regulations, part 166), define the term "Emergency Condition" as an urgent, non-routine situation that requires the use of a pesticide(s). Such uses are often referred to as "emergency exemptions," "Section 18s," or simply "exemptions."

Emergency exemptions may be requested by a state or federal agency. Most requests are made by state lead agricultural agencies. There are four types of emergency exemptions governing Section 18s of FIFRA:

1. Specific
2. Quarantine
3. Public Health
4. Crisis

Requests are made for pesticides needed for pest problems that impact production of agricultural goods when there are no alternatives for controlling the pest. Requests usually involve pesticides that have other approved uses, so EPA scientists have prior understanding of the requested chemical. State or federal agency submits request to EPA for situations that appear to meet criteria to be deemed an "emergency condition." Uses are requested for a limited period of time to address the emergency situation only.

1. Specific or public health exemptions: no longer than 1 year
2. Quarantine exemptions: no longer than 3 years.

EPA attempts to make decisions on the requests within a 50 day time frame from date of receipt, during which EPA performs a multi-disciplinary evaluation of the request, including the following:

1. Assessment of the validity of the emergency claim and economic loss.

2. Human dietary risk assessment.

3. Occupational risk assessment.

4. Ecological and environmental risk assessment.

5 Assessment of the progress toward registration for the use for specific or public health exemption requests.

If the emergency is determined to be valid and the risks are acceptable, EPA approves the emergency exemption request. EPA will deny an exemption request if the pesticide may not meet the Agency's safety standards, or if emergency criteria are not met.

If the exemption program involves the treatment of agricultural goods, EPA will establish formal tolerances (maximum allowable residue levels) to cover any pesticide residues in food that may result. As required by the Food Quality Protection Act of 1996 (FQPA), EPA must make the finding that there is "reasonable certainty that no harm" will result to human health from aggregate and cumulative exposure to the pesticide, before establishing a tolerance. Tolerances established for emergency exemption uses are time-limited, corresponding to the time that treated commodities might be found in channels of trade.

EPA rule giving IMD permanent approval on the following crops, later rulings approved most crops:

On June 13, 2003 the Agency issued a Final rule (68 FR 35303, FRL-7310-8) establishing tolerances for residues of imidacloprid in or on acerola; artichoke, globe; avocado; banana (import); canistel; corn, pop, grain; corn, pop, stover; cranberry; currant; elderberry; feijoa; fruit, stone, group 12; gooseberry; huckleberry; guava; jaboticaba; juneberry; lingonberry; longan; lychee; mango; mustard, seed; okra; papaya; passion fruit; persimmon; pulasan; rambutan; salal; sapodilla; sapote, black; sapote, mamey; Spanish lime; star apple; starfruit; strawberry; vegetable, leaves of root and tuber, group 2; vegetable, legume, group 6, except soybean; vegetable, root and tuber, group 1, except sugar beet; watercress; wax jambu. When the Agency conducted the risk assessments in support of this tolerance action it assumed that imidacloprid residues would be present on soybean, seed and soybean, meal as well as on all foods covered by the proposed and established tolerances. Residues on soybean, seeds and soybean, meal were included because there was a pending application under the Federal Insecticide, Fungicide, and

Rodenticide Act, 7 U.S.C. 136 et seq., to register imidacloprid on soybean, seed and soybean, meal.

It would really help if readers could contact the following officials at the EPA and politely request that they suspend IMD and neonicotinoid use until sublethal doses are shown to be safe for bees:

Registration Division Director, Office of Pesticide Programs, EPA
Section 18 Team Leader or Anthony Britten
USEPA Headquarters, Ariel Rios Building
1200 Pennsylvania Avenue, N. W. Mail Code: 7505P
Washington, DC 20460
(703) 308-8179
Britten.Anthony@epa.gov

Marcel Howard
USEPA Headquarters, Ariel Rios Building
1200 Pennsylvania Avenue, N. W. Mail Code: 7505P
Washington, DC 20460
(703) 305-6784
howard.marcel@epa.gov

APPENDIX 5

Colony Collapse Disorder in the United States

Sources: Apiary Inspectors of America Report, Phone Interviews with State Apiarists or equivalent,
USDA 2006 Agriculture Statistics

The Following States Do Not Report Colony Collapse Disorder:

State	Notes, Type Of Agriculture
Alabama	No CCD; only one smaller operation using migratory bees. State's agriculture consists of poultry, cattle, greenhouse production, eggs, and cotton. Cotton is self-pollinated. Indoor greenhouses use IMD (but indoor use not likely to harm bees).
Alaska	No CCD; no varroa mites. No fruit, nut, or vegetable crops (only two-tenths of a percent of land in state under cultivation).
Connecticut	No reported CCD. State's agriculture consists of greenhouse production, dairy, poultry, and aquaculture.
Delaware	No CCD. State's agriculture consists mostly of poultry, a little corn (wind-pollinated), greenhouse production, and soy.
Hawaii	No CCD; mites on Oahu only; just 500–1,000 hives on Oahu. State's agriculture consists of greenhouse production, pineapple (pollination avoided), sugar cane (asexual reproduction), macadamia nut (some self-pollination; other pollinators besides honey bee), and coffee (mostly self-pollinating).
Kansas	No CCD; even yards using migratory bees not reporting CCD. The corn crops use seeds painted with IMD but are said to lose neurotoxic potency in 28 days as pests return to older corn (KSU), so would not affect bees. State's agriculture also consists of greenhouse production.
Louisiana	No CCD; one operation using migratory bees. State's agriculture consists of cotton, sugar cane, rice, which do not need bees for pollination), and cattle.
Maine	No CCD ever seen, but hives not free from snow yet for 2008 check. Maine in 2008 is recommending IMD not be used on blueberries. State's agriculture also consists of potatoes (no nectar, so bees not attracted), dairy, eggs, and greenhouse production.
Maryland	No CCD; little to no use of IMD in minor fruit orchards. State's agriculture consists of poultry, greenhouse production, and dairy.
Nebraska	No CCD reported, but no inspections. Corn crops use seeds painted with IMD but said to lose neurotoxic potency in 28 days as pests return to older corn, as in Kansas (KSU)
Nevada	No CCD, according to Northern Nevada Association, but no inspections; no operations using migratory bees. State's agriculture consists of small-time hobbyists, desert, alfalfa, and (no IMD).
New Mexico	No CCD; no operations using migratory bees. State's agriculture consists of alfalfa (no IMD), and pecans, which is the only other main crop using IMD (pecans have no flowers for bees).
Rhode Island	No CCD; few yards using migratory bees. State's agriculture consists of small-time hobbyists, and greenhouse production.
Vermont	No CCD, according to the Vermont Beekeepers Association; no yards using migratory bees. State's agriculture consists of dairy, cattle, and greenhouse production. Apples not even 2% of production.
West Virginia	No CCD. Minor fruit orchards do not use IMD as the Assassin Beetle controls the aphids, so no need for IMD. State's agriculture consists of poultry, cattle, turkey, eggs, and dairy.

The rest of the states either do report CCD, or there have been news reports of CCD. However, Illinois, Indiana, Ohio and Kentucky do not seem to be experiencing Colony Collapse Disorder and bear further investigation. They could very well be gap states as well.

Appendix 6

Farmer Solutions

USDA National Organic Program
http://www.ams.usda.gov/nop/

Central Web site for the USDA NOP. Gives overview of certification and how it works. Other organizations below, especially The Rodale Institute, can help you sort through it all if you are interested. You can find links here on the NOP site for Certifying Agencies and consultants.

ATTRA
National Sustainable Agriculture Information Service
P.O. Box 3657
Fayetteville, AR 72702
Order publications: 800-346-9140 (English) 7a.m. to 7 p.m. Central Time
www.Attra.ncat.org
www.attra.ncat.org/attra-pub/gh-aphid.html (aphid control)
www.attra.ncat.org/attra-pub/nativebee.html (Alternative Pollinators: native bees)

Publications, information resources, information on sustainable agriculture, biological controls, native bees

The Rodale Institute
611 Siegfriedale Road
Kutztown, PA 19530
(610) 683-1400
Fax: 610-683-8548
info@rodaleinst.org
http://www.RodaleInstitute.org/
www.newfarm.org
www.kidsregen.org

Regenerative farming and science, organic gardening, advice on organic certification, educational training, International programs, organic transition plan, bookstore, online organic farming tools, newsletter, products, membership. Newfarm.org has the Organic Price Index,

261

OPX, which gives wholesale organic crop and livestock prices in different parts of the U.S. Kids Regen is for 9-12 year-olds to learn organic agriculture and living.

California Certified Organic Farmers (CCOF)
2155 Delaware Avenue, Suite 150
Santa Cruz, CA 95060
(831) 423-2263
ccof@ccof.org

CCOF promotes and supports organic food and agriculture through a premier organic certification program, trade support, producer and consumer education and political advocacy. From apples to zucchini, from almonds to wine, CCOF is involved in every facet of organics, with over 750 different organic crops and products, including livestock, processed products, and services.

CCOF provides certification services to all stages of the organic food chain from farms to processors, restaurants, and retailers. CCOF certifies to the USDA National Organic Program standards and CCOF international standards.

Hawaii Organic Farmers Association (HOFA)
P.O. Box 6863
Hilo, HI 96720
(808) 969-7789
hofa@hawaiiorganicfarmers.org

HOFA offers many publications and resources to assist producers and consumers with tropical organic agriculture. HOFA conducts workshops and conferences and participates in tradeshows. HOFA has a video, Growing toward the Light, which showcases Hawaii's organic farms.

Maine Organic Farmers and Gardeners Association (MOFGA)
P.O. Box 170
294 Crosby Brook Road
Unity, Maine 04988
(207) 568-4142

MOFGA has created a facility to support organic growers, and demonstrate the viability of organic agriculture. Located on 250+ acres of mixed farmland and forest in Unity, Maine, MOFGA's Common Ground Education Center provides ample space for the organization's renowned Fair while serving as an exciting venue for year-round educational programs, including gardening, farming and forestry management meetings, demonstrations, workshops, and courses.

Plan Bee Central
P. O. Box 45
Willow, NY 12495
www.PlanBeeCentral.com

"National Action Plan to Save the Bees," bee blog, activist campaigns, plant bee gardens and trees for bees, solutions for beekeepers, organic alternative solutions to toxic chemicals, regenerative agriculture, news, information, resources, guides, alternative products, bee products, and links.

Where to Buy: Organic Pest Control and Beneficial Insects

The Beneficial Insect Company
P.O. Box 119
Glendale Springs, NC 28629
(336) 973-8490
Jim Kluttz
bugfarm336@aol.com
http://www.thebeneficialinsectco.com/products.htm

Information, tips and guides. Available for purchase: Green lacewing larvae, fly predators, ladybugs, beneficial nematodes, and praying mantis.

Diatect International
875 S. Industrial Parkway
Heber City, UT 84032
Toll Free: 1-800-227-6616
(435) 654-4370
info@diatect.com

Diatect V Organic Insect Control, Certified Organic, for home gardens, lawns, greenhouses, orchards, and nurseries. Information, guides, FAQ, applicators. Outdoor and indoor organic pest control. Aphid killer.

DIRT WORKS
1195 Dog Team Road
New Haven, Vermont 05472
(802) 385-1064
www.dirtworks.net
John Meshna

Hot pepper wax for aphid, white fly, mites, thrip, mealy bugs, codling moth, leaf hoppers, scale, lace bug, and army worms.

ARBICO Organics
P.O. Box 8910
Tucson, AZ, 85738
1-800-827-2847
http://www.arbico-organics.com/organic-pest-control.html

Certified Organic pest controls, PyGanic insect knockdown and control, Arbico Pest Control Recipe, Beneficial Insects, and Bumblebee Hives.

APPENDIX 7

Organic Home and Lawn Solutions

NOFA, Northeast Organic Farming Association
Organic Land Care Program
P.O. Box 164
Stevenson CT 06491
Contact the Organic Land Care Program Manager or call
(203) 888-5146

Guides for homeowners and professionals, brochure, calendar, news, links, plus an accreditation program, find accredited professionals, Organic Land Care Course, NOFA Guide to Organic Land Care, NOFA Organic Lawn and Turf Handbook

Cornell University
Pesticide Management Education Program
Comprehensive information resources
http://pmep.cce.cornell.edu/index.html
http://pmep.cce.cornell.edu/facts-slides-self/index.html

Pesticide Safety Education Program at Cornell
Dr. Harvey Reissig, Director and Pesticide Coordinator
5123D Comstock Hall
Cornell University
Ithaca, NY 14853-0901
(607) 255-1866-3137
Fax: (607) 255-3075
whr1@cornell.edu

Comprehensive information resources, Pest Management Alternatives Program
Controversial Pesticide Issues:
http://pmep.cce.cornell.edu/issues/index.html
"Resource Guide for Organic Insect and Disease Management" resource guide
http://www.nysaes.cornell.edu/pp/resourceguide/

SafeLawns.org
Shepherd Ogden, Executive Director
60 Pineland Dr. Bldg 3, Suite 207
New Gloucester, ME 04260
Toll Free: 1-800-251-1784
(207) 688-8905

How-to videos on all aspects of organic lawn and gardens, creation and maintenance, news and events, resources, products, books, soil tests, initiatives, volunteer resources, Speakers Network and general membership, and blogs.

National Coalition Against the Misuse of Pesticides
BeyondPesticides.org
701 E Street SE #200
Washington, DC 20003
(202) 543-5450
info@beyondpesticides.org

National pesticide forum, information services, alerts and actions, news blog, online store, free memberships, activist tools, resources and campaigns.

Pesticide Action Network North America
Panna.org
panna@panna.org
(415) 981-1771

Local, national, international campaigns, membership, information resources, news, action plans. Information on health threats, schools, exposed farmers, children, women and elderly, ecosystem disruption, and chemical companies control of food production.

RefuseToUseChemLawn.org
 Toxics Action Center
44 Winter Street
Boston, MA 02108
(617) 292-4821
info@toxicsaction.org

Information resources and reports, Report your stories: children, workers, pet exposures.

Health threats, water supply, birds, fish and other wildlife.

See also: PesticideWatch.org

Sierra Club
National Headquarters
85 Second Street, 2nd Floor
San Francisco, CA 94105
(415) 977-5500
Fax: (415) 977-5799
information@sierraclub.org

Alternative Lawns
http://www.sierraclub.org/e-files/alternative_lawns.asp

Informational resources, activism, newsletter, outings, blogs, magazine, and membership information.

NRDC
National Resources Defense Council
40 West 20th Street
New York, NY 10011
(212) 727-2700
nrdcinfo@nrdc.org
"Native Lawns," native plant alternatives to mowed lawns www.nrdc.org/onearth/02spr/livgreen.asp
Review: "America Green: The Obsessive Quest for the Perfect Lawn" by Ted Steinberg
www.nrdc.org/onearth/06spr/reviews3.asp

Living green, how-to articles, politics, subscriptions, podcasts, reviews, and links.

Capital District Community Gardens
40 River Street
Troy, NY 12180
(518) 274-8685
Fax: (518) 272-2744
e-mail: info@cdcg.org

How to grow organic gardens, control recipe, beneficial insects and bumblebee hives.

APPENDIX 8

Beekeeper Solutions for Mites and Bee Health

NOD Apiary Products Ltd.
P.O. Box 117
2325 Frankford Road
Frankford, Ontario K0K 2C0
Toll Free: 1-866-483-2929
(613) 398-8422
Fax: (613) 398-0495
www.Mite Away.com
info@Mite Away.com

MiteAway formic treatments for Varroa, other products that make bee-keeping easier! Under the direction of beekeeper and CEO David Van-derDussen.

HONEY-B-HEALTHY Inc.
108 Blackiston Ave.
Cumberland, MD 21502
Toll Free: 866-542-0879
(703) 880-6670
Fax: 703-880-5115
www.honey-b-healthy.com
sales@honeybhealthy.com

Honey-b-Healthy essential oil concentrate feeding stimulant. Under the direction of Dr. James Amrine.

The Following Bee Supply Companies all Sell Honey-B-Healthy:

BeeBox Honey & Supplies
Hammar Dr.
P.O. Box 74
Aurora, WV 26705
(304) 735-6051

BeeCARE
P.O. Box 1070
Leander, TX 78646
(512) 259-4156
Fax: (512) 682-9065
www.beecare.com

Bee-commerce.com
WoodsEnd, Inc.
11 Lilac Lane
Weston, CT 06883
Toll Free: 1-800-784-1911
(203) 222 2268
http://www.bee-commerce.com/
info@beecommerce.com

Betterbee
8 Meader Road
Greenwich, NY 12834
1-800-632-3379
www.betterbee.com

Blossonland Supply
999 W. Front Street
Buchanan, MI 49107
(269) 695-2310
Fax: (269) 695-2510
http://www.blossomland.com

Bottazzo Apiaries
525 California Ave.
San Martin, CA 95046
(408) 683-2324

Cedar Glen Bees
15507 72nd Dr. NW
Stanwood, WA 98292
(360) 652-8967
www.cedarglenbees.com

Draper's Super Bee
914 S Street
Auburn, NE 68305
(402) 274-3725

GloryBeeFoods Inc.
120 N. Seneca
P.O. Box 2744
Eugene, OR 97402
1-800-456-7923
www.glorybee.com/

Golden Bee
1-888-465-3231
http://www.golden-bee.com

Honey-B-Products
George Kahl
7641 W. Hickory Creek Dr
Frankfort, Illinois 60423
(815) 469-1036

Honey-B-Products
John Kahl
12513 Evitts Drive
Cumberland, Md 21502
(301) 724-3529

Lapps Bee Supply
P.O Box 278
500 South Main Street
Reeseville, WI 53579

Miller Bee Supply
496 Yellow Banks Rd.
North Wilkesboro, NC 28659
1-888-848-5184
http://www.millerbeesupply.com/

PermComb Systems
John Seets, National/Internation-
al Distributor
2203 Belleview Rd.
Catonsville, MD 21228
(410) 471-4335

Queen Right Colonies
43655 SR 162
Denzil/Sheila St. Clair
Spencer OH, 44275
(440) 647.2602

Sacramento Beekeeping
Supplies
2110 X Street
Sacramento, CA 95818
(916) 451-2337

Simpsons Bee Supply
15642 Tiger Valley Rd.
Danville, OH 43041
(740) 599-7914
(740) 393-2111
www.simpsonsbeesupply.com/

Research On Formic Acid and Wintergreen Oil to Control Mites

Info only on formic acid fumigator and wintergreen grease patties from Dr. Amrine at WVU, beekeepers use at their own risk: www.wvu.edu/~agexten/varroa06.htm

Web Resource: www.BeeSource.com

Book: *Natural Beekeeping: Organic Approaches to Modern Apiculture*, Ross Conrad
Chelsea Green Publishing (2007)

APPENDIX 9

List of Foods Pollinated By Bees

Alfalfa
Allspice
Almonds
Alsike clover
Apples
Artichoke
Asparagus
Avocado
Berseem
Blackberries
Blueberries
Broccoli
Brussels sprouts
Buckwheat
Cabbage
Cacao
Cantaloupe
Carambolo
Caraway
Cardamom
Carrots
Casaba
Cashew
Cauliflower
Celeriac
Celery
Chayote
Cherries
Chicory
Chinese gooseberry
or kiwi
Chives
Cicer milkvetch
Cinnamon
Citron
Citrus

Clovers, minor
Cole crops
Collards
Coriander
Cranberries
Crenshaw
Crimson clover
Crownvetch
Cucumbers
Currants
Cut flower seeds
Dewberry
Dill
Drug plants
Eggplants
Fennel
Garlic
Gooseberries
Honeyball
Honeydew
Huckleberry
Jujube
Kale
Kenaf
Kohlrabi
Kola nut
Lavender
Leek
Litchi
Longan
Lotus
Macadamia
Mango
Muskmelons
Mustard
Niger

Nutmeg
Onion
Parsley
Parsnip
Passion fruit
Peaches & nectarines
Pears
Persian melon
Persimmon
Pimenta
Plums & prunes
Pummelo
Pumpkin & squash
Quinine
Radish
Rape
Raspberries
Red clover
Rutabagas
Sainfoin
Sapote
Sunflower
Sweetclovers
Sweetvetch
Tangelo
Tangerine
Tea
Tendergreens
Trefoils
Tung
Turnips
Vetch (hairy)
Watermelon
Welsh onion
White clover

Excerpted from Beekeeper's Handbook, *Sammataro/Avitabile* ©1998 page 7-8

INDEX

Index

Index

repeal anti-beekeeping
ordinances, 211–13
scientific adaptation to
environment, 143
worldview paradigm shifts,
145–46
Song Be Golf Resort, 187
spearmint oil, 198–201
*Standards for Organic Land Care:
Practices for Design and
Maintenance of Ecological
Landscapes* (NOFA), 181
Stasny, Terry, 197–98
Stein, Jill, 172
Stihler, Craig, 22
stinging wasps, 162
stress, environmental stress, 21–22,
42–43
stress disorders, 40–41
*The Structure of Scientific
Revolutions* (Kuhn), 88–90
"Study of Pesticides and Children
Stirs Protests," 121
Sundberg, Lance, 24
sunflowers, 54–63, 70
Sunspray Horticulture Oil, 162
"A Survey of Pesticide Residues
in Pollen Loads" (Agence
Française de Sécurité Sanitaire
des Aliments), 62
synergistic effects of chemicals,
116, 130, 131, 133, 151, 193

taste genes of bees, 7
television programs, 90–91, 97,
132–33
Temporary Sales and Marketing
Authorizations, 71–72
termites, 54, 169
Terramycin, 36
Thailand, and golf course
development, 186
thiamethoxam, 80, 81

thiophanate, 116
Thorp, Robbin, 159–60
thyme, oil of, 196
Thymol, 196
thyroid glands, 119
tobacco smoke, 200
tomatoes, 12, 163
top-bar hives, 46
"Toxic Fairways: Risking
Groundwater Contamination
from Pesticides on Long Island
Golf Courses," 183
toxicology, 148–49. *See also*
chemical testing
Toxics Action Center, 168
trees, bee-attracting, 207, 208
Triple Stack Corn, 151
TruGreen ChemLawn, 179
turf. *See* golf courses; lawns
"Turf Wars" (*The Wall Street
Journal*), 174
2,4-D, 170, 173, 183

UNAF (Union Nationale de
l'Apiculture Française)
CCD/IMD conclusions, 57–59, 62
on chemical company denials, 82
Clément-Bayer lawsuit, 73
IMD suspension and bee return,
68, 70, 77–78, 80
protests lead by, 67
urban beekeeping, 213
United Kingdom, 83
United States. *See also* EPA
(Environmental Protection
Agency); USDA (United
States Department of
Agriculture)
Bush Administration, 94, 117,
120, 122, 123
CCD in
destruction and cost statistics,
16, 17–18, 24, 93–94